PROJECTS IN
MACHINE
INTELLIGENCE
FOR YOUR
HOME
COMPUTER

Other TAB books by the author:

No. 1391
$17.95

PROJECTS IN
MACHINE
INTELLIGENCE
FOR YOUR
HOME
COMPUTER

BY DAVID L. HEISERMAN

TAB BOOKS Inc.
BLUE RIDGE SUMMIT, PA. 17214

FIRST EDITION

FIRST PRINTING

Copyright © 1982 by TAB BOOKS Inc.

Printed in the United States of America

Library of Congress Cataloging in Publication Data

Heiserman, David L. 1940-
    Projects in machine intelligence for your home computer.

    Includes index.
    1. Microcomputers. 2. Artificial intelligence.
I. Title.
QA76.5.H4463   001.64′2   81-18233
ISBN 0-8306-0057-4   AACR2
ISBN 0-8306-1391-9 (pbk.)

2191515

Contents

Introduction

This is a book of ideas. It is a book that shows how home computer systems can be applied to carrying out scientific projects and demonstrations that are otherwise terribly expensive, time consuming and, in a few instances, virtually impossible.

The theme is machine intelligence and the way it can express itself. The unique feature is that there is no attempt to impose some preconceived theories about animal intelligence onto an electronic system. Rather, the system is allowed to express forms of intelligent behavior in its own right. Thus, you will not find a lot of lengthy and complicated discussions about the theories of animal physiology and neural activity, and there are virtually no references to the principles and language of modern artificial intelligence. Instead of all that, the simulated creatures are treated as behavioral mechanisms in their own right—mechanisms that can be viewed as the proper objects of psychological observation.

The programs are written for two different kinds of home computer systems: Model I TRS-80 with Level II BASIC and 16k of RAM, and Apple II equipped with ROM-based Applesoft and 16k of RAM. With a bit of minor tinkering, the TRS-80 programs can be adapted to the Model III system, and the Applesoft programs at the beginning of the book can be translated to Integer BASIC (although the programs using multi-dimensioned arrays do not convert to Integer BASIC very well).

Chapter 1
About This Book

You can read, or experience, this book on any one of four different levels: philosophical, scientific, technical, or on a simple game playing level. All four elements are woven into the projects, demonstrations and discussions, and you are invited to choose the perspective that best suits your mood.

Unfortunately a number of practical considerations makes it virtually impossible to balance all four viewpoints evenly throughout the work. To do that would call for a terribly large book.

The emphasis, in terms of volume, is clearly on the technical side of the matter—what the programs do, how to use them, and how they work. The rest would be meaningless without them; or at best, the rest would be no more credible than a discussion around a few drinks on a Saturday night.

The scientific perspectives appear from time to time in the earlier chapters but become quite obvious through the work suggested in the last few chapters. While none of the programs are really designed to be a game, suggested modifications to the demonstration programs provide enough insight to make it possible to transform them into some rather unusual and compelling games.

The philosophical issues underlie just about every discussion, but they aren't always obvious. Those views are described in an overt fashion in this opening chapter, but they will have to suffice as a springboard for further consideration on your part.

HOW THIS BOOK AND ITS IDEAS EVOLVED

I have done a lot of work with robotics since 1974. My first working robot is described in my book, *Build Your Own Working*

Robot (Tab Books #841). That book describes how to build one particular little machine I named Buster. When I began the project, I had nothing more sophisticated or meaningful in mind than simply satisfying a long-standing urge to build a little machine that could blunder around a room and feed itself when the batteries ran low. Buster was built around rather ordinary TTL technology (no microprocessors), and it worked according to well established conventions for simple control systems. Once Buster was nearly completed—completed at least to the point where he could roam around the room—he began taking on a personality of sorts. Buster seemed to be quite helpless, or vulnerable, in many ways, yet he seemed to possess an admirably high level of determination. Some accounts of his experiences are described in the book.

While putting the finishing touches on the manuscript for the book, my first-hand experiences with Buster began teaching me something about robots, what they are and what they ought to be. These matters were not altogether clear at that time, but in retrospect I can see how they fit into a larger pattern.

For one thing, I realized that it is more important for some of us to build the kinds of robots that can be built with present technology, and not, like so many, waste years waiting for new scientific studies and technological developments to provide the foundations for one's ideal conception of a robot machine. Buster is certainly not very sophisticated in a technological sense, but narrowing our consideration to purely technical evaluations eliminates the possibility of learning things of a broader and even more productive nature.

Things started to get exciting when I began regarding Buster as a pet rather than a terribly disappointing and crude copy of one of the robots from the film *Star Wars*. Buster was not and, given the state of technology, could not be like one of those incredible machines. But a pet is something to be regarded and enjoyed on its own terms. Buster fit the bill quite nicely.

I was never completely satisfied with what was accomplished with Buster, though. I had at least a vague notion that more could be done with the critter's intellectual side. It was then that I became convinced that it is more important to deal with machine intelligence than the hardware it supports. Hence Rodney began to take shape on the drawing board.

Rodney is the subject of *How to Build Your Own Self-Programming Robot* (Tab Books #1241). The earlier robot, Buster, knew what to do under a given set of circumstances because I

2

programmed him to respond a certain way under those conditions. I had to consider all logical circumstances and hardwire the system to respond in a way that let Buster cope with them successfully. Rodney was cut from a different cloth.

Rather than preprogramming Rodney to respond a certain way under every conceivable set of conditions, I worked it out so that Rodney could figure out the responses himself. Rodney does not have to be told what to do. He begins with a blank memory, works out solutions to problems on his own, and remembers them for future reference. The programming is passed to the machine—and out of the hands of human companions.

The basic idea was to fire up little Rodney, put him into a room, close the door, and walk away for a few days. I will never forget listening to Rodney blundering around in that room through the wee hours of the night, working a couple hours at a time to perfect his own perception of the environment and ways for dealing with it.

It should be clear from the Rodney project that a substantial portion of a robot's programming ought to be generated by the machine, itself. Doing so, the human programmer is relieved of the tremendous tasks of anticipating every possible event in the robot's life, working out the appropriate responses in a step-by-step fashion, and entering all that data into the machine's memory. It isn't unreasonable to expect many man-years of programming would be necessary before the machine could become fully operational. Self-programming robots, such as Rodney, require a minimal amount of preprogramming before it is turned loose on the world. The robot then writes its programs as they are needed, possibly using some techniques to anticipate proper responses to situations that have not yet occurred.

That is the technology lesson from the Rodney machine. It expresses *how* a certain problem ought to be solved. At that time, I had a hunch there was more to Rodney than a technical demonstration of the feasibility of self-programming robots.

Self-programming machines behave in ways that are rather unique. During the earlier phases of their learning activities, they behave in a seemingly random way; but given time and further experiences, each Rodney machine took on a sort of personality of its own. I'm not speaking of the sort of personality one might impose on another sort of machine such as a boat, bike or car; but rather a set of mannerisms that appear whenever the machine encounters certain kinds of situations. No two Rodney machines ever perform in exactly the same way. Some tend to be more aggressive than others, and some seem to take longer to learn their way around than others do.

It is difficult to go through studies of the machines' behavior patterns for a couple of reasons. First, they run around the floor rather slowly, and a human investigator can spend endless hours attempting to compile data regarding the machine's patterns of behavior. Second, the batteries hold up for only a couple of hours at a time, and then the machine has to go to its battery-charger "nest" for eight or ten hours.

It occurred to me that it would be far more efficient to study the principles of self-programming machine intelligence on a home computer system, rather than by watching a piece of hardware blundering around the room. The same mechanisms of machine intelligence could be programmed into the home computer and the physical environment, including the robot, could be simulated on the crt. Things would run a lot faster and the projects could run on an unlimited time schedule. As a bonus, using the computer makes it possible to compile a lot of data about the performance and personality characteristics of the simulated robots.

The first result of that idea is *Robot Intelligence— with experiments* (Tab Books # 1191). That book deals mainly with three distinct classes of machine intelligence, showing BASIC program listings for demonstrating their essential features. Again, the emphasis is really on *how* a job can be done (and it is certainly a lot easier to do it on a home computer system than with a homemade robot machine).

The book you are now reading is a natural sequel to the previous ones. Here, the nature of the self-programming mechanisms are taken for granted. The emphasis is on acquiring a better understanding of those forms of machine intelligence. It is no longer a matter of trying to justify the procedure, but rather to see what the procedure means in the broadest sense. The simulated creatures are treated as creatures in their own right. The objective is to study their behavior as though we had only the foggiest idea about how they work. *How* they work isn't nearly as important a matter as *what* they can do.

TWO LEVELS OF ADAPTIVE MACHINE INTELLIGENCE

While the emphasis of this book is on what the simulated creatures do and how they behave, it is necessary to explain a bit about how they work. This is especially important to convince you there are no special tricks built into the programs.

4

You will find that a very small portion of each program is actually devoted to the creatures' mechanisms of intelligence. Most of the programming has to do with the schemes for simulating the creature and its environment on the crt screen.

Alpha-Class Intelligence

The first series of demonstration programs work with a simple creature intelligence I have called Alpha-Class intelligence. The basic function is blocked out for you in the flowchart in Fig. 1-1. If the scheme seems difficult, perhaps it is only because you are expecting it to be that way—it isn't.

The Alpha creature begins its life by selecting a random response. If the creature happens to have 24 different response modes available to it, it will select one (or a combination of more than one) at random. Certainly that means that there is no telling what the creature will do when you first energize it. It is programmed to do something, but the exact nature of that response is left to chance.

So the creature begins its life by doing something. It then checks its immediate environment through one or more of its available sensory mechanisms to see whether or not the response works. Now, what is meant by *works?* That can be defined a number of different ways, but in the context of the current projects, a

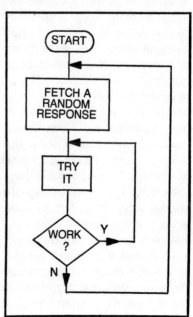

Fig. 1-1. General flowchart for Alpha-Class behavior.

response that works is one that doesn't get the creature into some sort of trouble—trouble such as running into an obstacle.

If the response works, the flowchart shows that the creature simply does the same thing again. Why mess around with a good thing? If it works, keep on doing it. That's simple; in fact it is so simple that it is often overlooked as a viable mechanism for machine behavior.

When the response does not work, the system simply loops back up to the point where it picks another random response. The creature tries that response, and if it works, the creature uses that response over and over again, at least until that one no longer works. If the creature happens to come up with a response that doesn't work the first time, there is no harm done. It simply loops back to pick yet another random response. Quite often the creature gets itself tangled up in some complicated situations and ends up picking and trying any number of responses until it finds one that works.

An Alpha-Class creature is always doing one of two things at any given moment. It is either trying a workable response or it is picking and trying a random response. In a manner of speaking, an Alpha-Class exhibits the qualities of purely reflex behavior. It responds to a negative situation without "thinking" about anything; it simply responds to a randomly selected response code.

The basic Alpha-Class elements of behavior can be embodied in less than a dozen lines of BASIC programming. The rest of the programming is used for manipulating the creature's environment and operating its sensory and response systems. And it isn't only simple; it is also workable. Try it, and you will see how simple and workable the Alpha scheme is.

That is not to say it is a trivial scheme. As you progress through the series of Alpha-Class demonstration programs, you will see some modes of behavior that appear to have undertones of rationality. An Alpha creature cannot be rational. It cannot possibly think about anything because it has no memory of past responses to draw upon. The creature exists in the moment with no awareness of its past experiences nor any notion of future consequences of its actions. It is a purely responsive creature, and its responses are randomly selected in every case. But as the complexity of the environment is increased, and as the number of available response modes and sensory mechanisms are increased, you will clearly see forms of behavior that might be considered rational—rational, at least, if you didn't know better.

How much of what we normally consider rational animal behavior is really irrational, or reflex, behavior exhibiting itself in a complex environment? What role does the nature of a creature's environment play in our interpretation of its intelligence? Those are, I think, some very penetrating questions. The answers (and the nature of the questions themselves) border on some of the most recent views of nature as expressed in theoretical physics—quantum mechanics, for instance. Those notions are so new and obtuse that they rarely reach the general scientific and technical community.

So the principles of Alpha-Class behavior are exceedingly simple, but the implications of the demonstrations and experiments aren't necessarily easy to follow. They aren't difficult to follow because they are inherently complicated, but because they fly in the face of traditional ways of regarding creature behavior.

Beta-Class Intelligence

A Beta creature is little more than a simple Alpha creature that has a memory of past encounters with its environment. An elementary Beta-Class flowchart is shown in Fig. 1-2.

Notice that the creature begins its life by selecting a random response, trying it, and noting whether or not it works. If it does work the creature continues doing whatever that initial random response dictates. That part of the flowchart is virtually identical to that of an Alpha creature. The big difference lies in the way the creature deals with a response that no longer works.

Whenever the prevailing response ceases to work, the Beta creature refers to its memory. It turns to its memory of past situations to see what might have been done under a similar set of circumstances in the past.

Now, it is important to realize that a Beta creature begins its life with a blank memory. You can bet that the first time the creature refers to its memory, it is going to come up dry. It will most certainly come up with a response that will not work. Nevertheless, the creature will refer to its memory and check out the response contained therein. If it doesn't work (which it won't if the creature hasn't encountered the circumstance before), it fetches a random response; it tries something—anything. Then that response is tried, and another is picked at random if that one doesn't work.

The creature continues picking random responses, behaving as a simpler Alpha creature, until it comes across one that resolves the problem at hand. At that time, the workable response is placed into

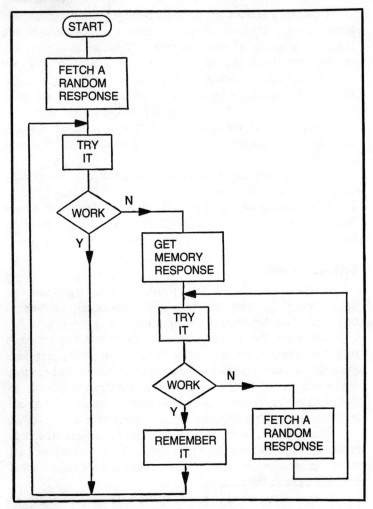

Fig. 1-2. General flowchart for Beta-Class behavior.

the creature's memory, and the system loops back to the place in the
flowchart where it continues performing the response until it no
longer works.

Every time the system leaves the Beta memory portion of the
flowchart, a workable response to the situation at hand is deposited
in the memory system. When the creature encounters that situation
again at some time in the future, that workable response is available
for immediate implementation—implementation without any reference to picking a random response.

When a Beta creature is first energized, its memory is blank, so it makes a relatively large number of references to randomly selected responses. As its experience grows, it begins making more references to remembered responses. Ideally, the creature eventually experiences about everything it can experience in its environment, and it makes first-time good responses to any conflict situation that arises.

The ability to stack its own memory with workable responses is the self-programming feature of Beta-Class creatures. There is no need for a human programmer to tell a Beta creature what it is supposed to do under every conceivable situation. The creature will eventually discover the situations on its own and devise its own ways for dealing with them.

The Beta memory is not only self-programming, but also self-correcting. Notice that the flowchart is designed so that even workable remembered responses are *re-remembered* at the end of the Beta memory cycle. Sometimes, responses that work one time will not work at another. How can this be? Well, the creature's mechanisms of perception are not perfect, and a conflict situation that might appear to be identical to one encountered in the past can, in reality, have some subtle differences that render the remembered response unworkable. As a result, the creature will be forced to select a new random response; and when it finds one that works, it remembers that one, replacing the one that worked under simpler conditions before. The creature certainly isn't aware of any reason why a remembered response doesn't work; it is only concerned with remembering responses that work under the widest possible spectrum of environmental conditions.

HOW TO USE THIS BOOK

It is important that you work your way through this book one step at a time. Much of the meaning is lost if you simply pick and choose the projects at random. What I am attempting to share with you cannot be gotten from any one of the projects.

You should also save the programs on tape or disk as you go along. This will serve two purposes. First, you will be able to use some of the programming from an earlier project as a starting point for entering the programming for a later one. Then, too, it is sometimes helpful to review the workings of an earlier project without having to type in the whole thing from scratch.

So begin your work by studying Chapter 2 carefully. Then study the introductory comments for Chapter 3, type in the suggested programming, observe the results, and attempt to relate it with the theory of operation. Finally, save the program on tape or disk, and go on to Chapter 4. One step at a time—that's important.

This is not a book of collected facts, theories, and procedures. Those elements are present, but the main idea is to convey a whole new way of thinking about machines and computers in particular. You will miss the point if you aren't working systematically and thinking and imagining as you go along.

Chapter 2
How the Creatures
Move and Search Ahead

The primary mode of response for the creatures described in this book is that of moving from one place to another on the crt screen. Alternate responses are introduced as necessary, but they play a secondary role to the simple motion of moving around in the simulated environments.

The primary sensory mode is that of sensing contact with another object on the screen. Again, some alternate sensory mechanisms will be used from time to time, but they enhance, rather than replace, the contact-sensing scheme.

This chapter describes the motion-producing and contact-sensing routines in some detail. You will soon discover that these routines, or slight variations of them, are used in all subsequent program listings. That fact, alone, justifies some special consideration of the ideas here in the early part of the project.

MOTION CODES

All the creatures described in this book move from one place to another in short, discrete steps. As illustrated in Fig. 2-1, a single step can carry the creature from an initial place on the screen to any one of 24 surrounding locations.

Creating the effect of motion is a matter of taking a series of such discrete steps in fairly rapid succession.

Each step is built up from two main motion components; a horizontal, and a vertical, motion component. In keeping with the crt screen formats for both the TRS-80 and Apple systems:
- A positive horizontal component displaces the creature to the right

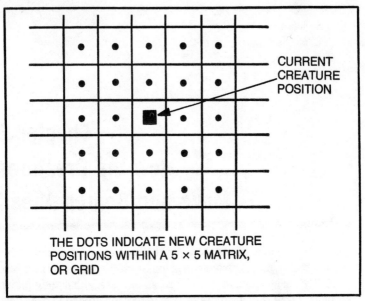

Fig. 2-1. Possible next-step destinations for the moving creature.

● A negative horizontal component displaces the creature to the left

● A positive vertical component displaces the creature downward

● A negative vertical component displaces the creature upward

For our purposes here, a *motion code* is a set of one horizontal and one vertical component of motion that displaces the creature from its current position to any one of 24 surrounding character spaces. Combining a horizontal and vertical component, the motion codes can be related to screen displacements in this way:

● If the horizontal and vertical components are both positive, the displacement is downward and to the right

● If the horizontal component is positive and the vertical is negative, the displacement is upward and to the right

● If the horizontal component is negative and the vertical component is positive, the displacement is downward and to the left

● If the horizontal and vertical components are both negative, the displacement is upward and to the left

There has to be more to a motion code than the signs of the horizontal and vertical components. A complete vector representation of motion requires a magnitude as well as a sign. The allowable absolute-value magnitudes for all the experiments in this book are integer values 0, 1 and 2.

Thus a complete horizontal vector such as −2 will contribute a displacement of 2 character spaces to the left of the original position. A vertical component of +1, on the other hand, contributes a displacement of 1 character space downward. Combining those two particular vector components yields one complete motion code −2,1. Throughout this book, motion codes are shown as two numbers separated by a comma. The first number is the horizontal component of motion and the second is the vertical component.

When that particular motion code is executed, the creature will jump from its original position to a new one that is 2 spaces to the left and 1 below.

If either vector component of a motion code is zero, motion in that direction is inhibited altogether. Thus a motion code such as 1, 0 displaces the creature 1 character space to the right. There is no vertical displacement in that instance.

Setting both components of the motion code to zero stops the creature. For reasons that will become apparent later on, a 0, 0 motion code is usually avoided by the system programming.

The full range of vectors for horizontal displacement is −2, −1, 0, 1, and 2. The same series of vector values is available for vertical displacement as well. Given these five signed magnitudes and two axes of motion, it figures that there are 25 possible combinations of motion codes. The creature can thus be displaced into any one of 24 character locations surrounding it. The 25th motion code is 0, 0 which causes no displacement at all.

Table 2-1 summarizes all 25 possible motion codes and offers a brief verbal description of each.

Perhaps the terms *fast* and *slow* used in that table require some explanation. The motion codes create the visual impression of constant motion across the screen by applying them in rapid succession. Generally speaking, the system programming first deletes the image of the creature from the screen, uses the motion code to determine its new position, and then draws the creature in that new position.

The rate of execution of those operations is fairly constant during a given experiment. That being the case, running with motion codes having 2s in them create the impression that the creature is moving about twice as fast as when the motion codes are made up of 1s. That justifies the use of terms slow and fast in Table 2-1.

Table 2-1. Complete Listing of Motion Codes and Their Literal Meanings.

Variable I is the horizontal component of motion
Variable J is the vertical component of motion

Motion Code		General Description
I	**J**	
−2	−2	Left fast, upward fast
−2	−1	Left fast, upward slow
−2	0	Left fast
−2	1	Left fast, downward slow
−2	2	Left fast, downward fast
−1	−2	Left slow, upward fast
−1	−1	Left slow, upward slow
−1	0	Left slow
−1	1	Left slow, downward slow
−1	2	Left slow, downward fast
0	−2	Upward fast
0	−1	Upward slow
0	0	Stop
0	1	Downward slow
0	2	Downward fast
1	−2	Right slow, upward fast
1	−1	Right slow, upward slow
1	0	Right slow
1	1	Right slow, downward slow
1	2	Right slow, downward fast
2	−2	Right fast, upward fast
2	−1	Right fast, upward slow
2	0	Right fast
2	1	Right fast, downward slow
2	2	Right fast, downward fast

Figure 2-2 illustrates all possible discrete steps a creature can make. Starting from its original position in the middle of the character-space array, the creature can skip to any one of the surrounding 24 character locations. The motion codes required for reaching each character space are shown in those spaces.

The drawings are different for the TRS-80 and Apple systems for the simple reason that the TRS-80 uses character spaces that are about 3 units taller than wide. The Apple's character spaces, on the other hand, are virtually square.

In either case, it is possible to find a motion code, or a series of motion codes, that will move the creature from any given place on the screen to any other place. The geometry of the TRS-80 screen

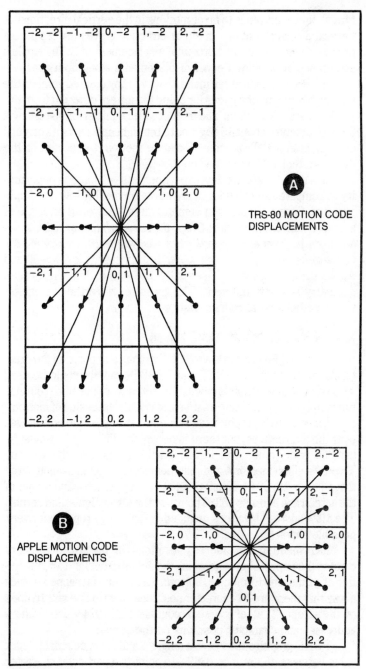

Fig. 2-2. Motion code displacements. (A) TRS-80. (B) Apple.

format, however, tends to favor motions in the vertical directions. A vertical displacement of 1 in either direction moves the creature a greater distance than any horizontal displacement of 1. The Apple's screen geometry shows equal displacements along both axes.

A TRS-80 creature can make its way to any desired point on the screen, but the motion codes for doing the job are different from the Apple creature's version. The motion code required for displacing a TRS-80 creature about 45 degrees to the right and above its original position is 2, −1. That same 45-degree motion is executed on the Apple system with motion code 2, −2.

It is unfortunate that few experimenters will have an opportunity to compare the behavior of creatures on the TRS-80 and Apple systems. Such a comparison demonstrates a powerful principle of adaptive machine behavior: *Given the same behavioral tools, creatures can perform equally well when vastly different environmental frameworks are imposed upon them.* In this case, the TRS-80 and Apple programming is essentially the same, but the screen geometry is vastly different. The creatures nevertheless exhibit the same behavioral characteristics.

Fundamentals of TRS-80 BASIC Motion

The TRS-80 system uses POKE graphics to position the creature's image on the crt. SET and RESET graphics could be used with somewhat greater simplicity, but it turns out that such routines run far too slowly to create a satisfying visual impression of motion.

Using POKE graphics offers a number of positive advantages over the alternatives, but there is one minor difficulty that must be handled with some care. POKE graphics deal directly with the TRS-80's video memory, and that memory is mapped in such a way that address 15360 (decimal) points to the upper left-hand corner of the screen and address 16383 points to the lower right-hand corner. The 1024 address locations included in that range represent every possible character space.

Incrementing the address locations in the video memory creates the impression of scanning the screen from left to right, one line at a time, and from top to bottom. The screen is mapped in such a way that there are 64 character positions on each line and 16 lines on the screen. That, of course, accounts for all 1024 video memory addresses and character positions on the screen.

POKE graphics thus uses a single number—a decimal integer value between 15360 and 16383—to point to a particular character position on the screen. Motion codes for moving the creatures, however, are 2-valued terms. Getting the creature to move from one spot to the next is a matter of translating the 2-valued motion code into a single-valued POKE address.

The translation is straightforward in the case of horizontal motion. If variable CP is taken as the current video address of the creature (its current position on the screen), and CI is taken as the horizontal component of its motion, the following BASIC sequence will move the creature to its new position:

```
POKE CP, 32
CP=CP+CI
POKE CP,42
```

The first statement clears the creature's image from its current position on the screen. The second operation determines the new creature position by simply summing the old video memory address with the horizontal component of the motion code. The last operation plots the creature, an asterisk in this case, at its new position on the screen.

Looping through that sequence a number of times in succession creates the impression of an asterisk figure moving left or right across the screen. The direction and apparent speed of that motion depends on the value of the CI vector (an integer value between -2 and 2).

Move the creature in a vertical direction is a matter of applying the fact that there are 64 character spaces on each line. Thus, adding 64 to the current creature address will drop its image down one line. Adding 128 will make the creature's image skip down two lines.

A BASIC routine for moving the creature in a vertical direction thus takes this general form:

```
POKE CP, 32
CP=CP+64*CJ
POKE CP,42
```

where CJ is the vertical component of the motion code vector.

Combining the two sequences just described, the overall motion-producing routine for the TRS-80 looks something like this:

```
POKE CP,32
CP=CP+CI+64*CJ
POKE CP,42
```

That is how a 2-valued motion code vector is reconciled with a single-valued video memory address.

It is important to realize, however, that these routines merely demonstrate the essential idea of creature motion on the screen— creature motion as it relates to its current single-valued position,

CP, and its current motion code vector, CI and CJ. The programs used for the actual projects accomplish the same effect is a somewhat more roundabout fashion. See the section in this chapter dealing with the search-ahead routine.

Fundamentals of Apple BASIC Motion

The Apple system uses PLOT graphics to position the creature's image on the screen. The creature's position can thus be represented by two variables CX and CY. CX is the horizontal position, and it takes the form of positive integer values between 0 and 39. CY is the vertical component of the creature's position, and it takes on integer values between 0 and 36 (leaving 3 lines at the bottom of the screen for the text window).

A creature is set to a new position on the screen by adding the horizontal component of the motion code to CX, and summing the vertical component of the motion code with CY. If CI and CJ are taken as the horizontal and vertical components of the motion code, respectively, the following BASIC routine creates the visual impression of creature motion:

```
COLOR 0:PLOT CX,CY
CX=CX+CI:CY=CY+CJ
COLOR 9:PLOT CX,CY
```

The first statement clears the creature's image from its current position on the screen by plotting black, color 0, in its place. The next line sets up the new creature position, and the last line plots an orange square (color 9) at the new creature position.

Looping through that BASIC sequence a number of times in fairly rapid succession creates the visual effect of a little orange creature moving about. The direction and speed of the motion will change only as the values of CI and CJ change.

The sample motion-generating routine merely illustrates the principles of motion. The actual programming through this book uses a somewhat more involved technique for doing essentially the same thing. That is explained in the following section of this chapter.

THE SEARCH AHEAD ROUTINE

The search ahead routine appears in all program listings in this book; and, indeed, it is one of the most vital elements of the entire project. From a scientific perspective, the search ahead routine satisfies one important requirement; it allows a creature to deal with the geometry of its environment without having to know its true position with respect to a fixed framework.

The creature does not have to know where the fixed boundaries of its environment are located. That being the case, it need not know where it is situated with respect to those boundaries. The creature is only concerned with its immediate environment—where it is going with respect to its current position.

A less abstract consequence of this relativistic view of the creature's positional geometry is that the dimensions and shape of its boundaries are not directly relevant to its basic modes of behavior. As demonstrated in a later experiment, the boundaries and content of the environment can be altered without upsetting the basic nature of the creature's responses to it.

The basic idea behind the search ahead mechanism follows this general pattern:

1. Save the current creature position.
2. Generate a new creature position based on the current motion code.
3. Look at the screen at the new creature position and generate a contact code that represents the characteristics of that new position.

In a manner of speaking, search ahead answers this question: *What is the nature of the path between my current position and the next one?*

Search ahead is essentially a sensory mechanism, and as such, it makes no decisions regarding how to deal with the objects it senses. The routine cannot *do* anything in itself. Rather, it provides the system with information needed to make a decision and take appropriate action.

Suppose a creature is moving along a blank area of the screen at a constant speed and fixed direction. This is possible by repeating the motion generating routine with a fixed motion code. Prior to making each move, the system calls the search ahead routine. The result—if the path ahead is clear—is a set of search ahead values that reflect the fact that there are no sensible obstacles in the way.

As the creature approaches an obstacle, the motion that would normally move the creature across or into the obstacle is checked by information returning from the previous search ahead routine. The move does not take place, and the system calls upon a different mechanism for determining what to do about the situation.

Figure 2-3 is a simplified flowchart of a creature-moving routine. Assuming the creature already possesses a well-defined current position and motion code, the scheme calls the search ahead routine. If the nature of the next position shows the path ahead is clear, the creature is moved to that new position, and the

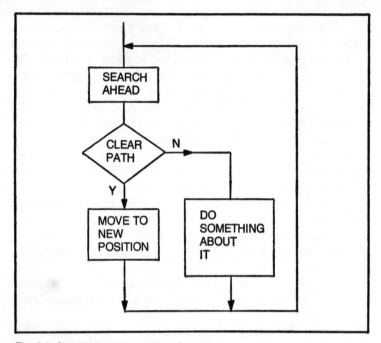

Fig. 2-3. Simplified creature motion flowchart.

search ahead routine is called to check on the next move. Whenever the system finds the path ahead is not clear, it takes some appropriate action and eventually loops back to start the search ahead routine again.

If the creature could only move one step at a time straight up, down, to the left or right, the search ahead routine could be a very simple one. That is not the case, however. The creature is able to move at angles from the horizontal and vertical axes and, indeed, move in such a way that it effectively skips over some character-space locations. This wide range of possible motions, especially those having the space-skipping character, complicates the search ahead routine.

So the search ahead routine must do more than simply check the content of the character space where the creature will ultimately reside if the step is taken. The routine also has to check every character space between the current position and the next one determined by the motion code.

Figure 2-4 is an overall flowchart for the search ahead routine. It is applicable to both the TRS-80 and Apple versions used through this book.

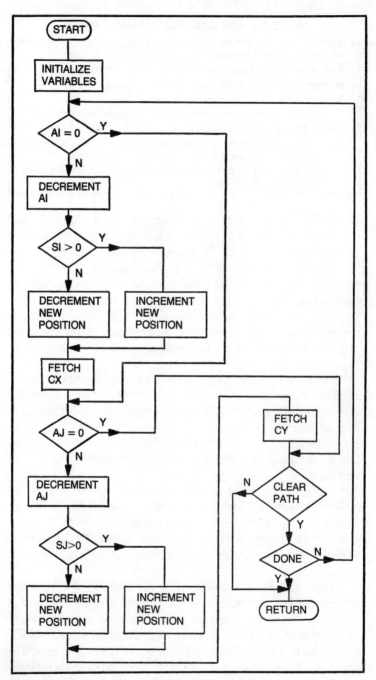

Fig. 2-4. General flowchart for the SEARCH AHEAD routine.

Table 2-2. Variable List for the SEARCH AHEAD Routine.

AI—Absolute value of the horizontal component of the motion code

AJ—Absolute value of the vertical component of the motion code

SI—Sign of the horizontal component of the motion code

SJ—Sign of the vertical component of the motion code

X POSITION—Horizontal component of a new trial position on the screen

Y POSITION—Vertical component of a new trial position on the screen

CX—A value representing the nature of a character space found by the preceding X-POSITION operation

CY—A value representing the nature of a character space found by the preceding Y-POSITION operation

A number of different variables are cited on the flowchart, and they ought to be defined before trying to analyze how the scheme works. See a summary of the variables in Table 2-2.

The search ahead routine begins by initializing some relevant variables. The exact nature of the variables and the ways they are initiated depend on the programming format being used.

The next step, a conditional operation, determines whether or not AI is equal to zero. Have all the required steps in the horizontal direction been taken? If so, the program jumps to a similar conditional operation, AJ=0.

But if it turns out that AI is greater than zero, the next step is to decrement that value by 1. If AI was 2 at the outset (the largest possible value it can have in a BASIC routine), it is decremented to 1. If AI was 1 at the outset, it is decremented to 0. AI is never decremented below zero because the preceding conditional operation prevents the decrementing step from occurring if AI is 0 at the outset.

After decrementing AI, the system checks the sign of the horizontal component of the motion code is checked. If SI is greater than zero (positive) the current, tentative X POSITION is incremented by 1. Otherwise, it is decremented by 1. Thus, the trial X POSITION variable is incremented or decremented just 1 space at a time.

After making that adjustment in the trial X POSITION, the system checks the character in the current trial position on the screen. If there is a character residing at that place (normally interpreted as an obstacle of some sort), the program sets the CX variable to that value. And whether or not an obstacle is sensed at this point, the program goes to the AJ=0 conditional operation.

Notice that all of those horizontal incrementing, decrementing and character-testing operations are bypassed whenever AI is equal to 0—when there are no more horizontal steps to test.

The vertical components of motion are treated in the same manner by the second major phase of the search ahead routine. If, for instance, AJ is equal to 0, there is no need for making any further vertical-motion tests. That being the case, the system jumps down to the ANY CONTACT conditional operation. But as long as there is at least one more vertical step to test, the current AJ value is decremented, the tentative new Y POSITION variable is incremented or decremented according to the sign of SJ, and the CY variable is set to whatever character code comes from testing the new tentative space on the screen.

Once both major phases of the routine have been run, the ANY CONTACT conditional looks at the CX and CY contact variables. If either, or both, have a contact-related code number in them, the system immediately leaves the search ahead routine, carrying those contact codes with it. Those codes, in a manner of speaking, allow the creature to recognize the nature of the obstacle of object in its immediate path.

But if no contact is sensed after the first pass through the routine, the next conditional deals with the matter of finding out whether or not the stepping process is done. If AI and AJ have both been decremented to zero, it means the search ahead operation is completely done. Otherwise, the program loops back to run the whole routine, excluding the initialization phase, all over again.

Basically, the search ahead routine begins with variables representing the creature's current position on the screen and its current motion code. The routine concludes with two variables that indicate the nature of the path ahead, and, if the path is clear, it also carries out the next character position.

PROGRAM LISTINGS FOR SEARCH AHEAD

The following listings are offered here only to illustrate how the search ahead flowchart in Fig. 2-4 is implemented on the computer systems used in these projects. As you progress through future projects, you will probably find you want to refer back to this section for an explanation, or at least a review, of how the search ahead routine works.

TRS-80 Version

The TRS-80 version of the search ahead routine is shown in Listing 2-1. Most of the variables match those already defined in

Table 2-2. The additional variables relate to earlier discussions of creature motion.

NP—Tenative new position for the creature; a value representing an address in video memory.

CP—The creature's current position on the screen.

Listing 2-1. TRS-80 Version of the SEARCH AHEAD Routine.

```
2000 REM ** SEARCH AHEAD, V.1—TRS-80 BASIC **
2005 NP=CP:CX=32:CY=32
2010 SI=SGN(CI):SJ=SGN(CJ):AI=ABS(CI):AJ=ABS(CJ)
2015 IF AI=0 THEN 2030 ELSE AI=AI−1
2020 IF SI>0 THEN NP=NP+1 ELSE NP=NP−1
2025 CX=PEEK(NP)
2030 IF AJ=0 THEN 2045 ELSE AJ=AJ−1
2035 IF SJ>0 THEN NP=NP+64 ELSE NP=NP−64
2040 CY=PEEK(NP)
2045 IF NOT(CX=32 AND CY= 32) THEN RETURN
2050 IF AI=0 AND AJ=0 THEN RETURN ELSE GOTO 2015
```

The lines of instructions can be compared with the search ahead flowchart in this manner:

Line 2005—INITIALIZE SEARCH VARIABLES. The tenative new creature position, NP, is set equal to the actual current position, CP. Contact codes CX and CY are both set to 32 (the "all clear" character code).

Line 2010—More initialization. The values of SI and SJ are fixed, and the initial values of AI and AJ are set. All of these variables are related to the current motion code vectors, CI and CJ.

Line 2015—Test the current value of AI. Decrement if it is greater than zero.

Line 2020—Test the value of SI. If positive, increment the current X POSITION, otherwise decrement it.

Line 2025—Set CX equal to the character value found at the current new tenative position.

Line 2030—If AJ is not zero, decrement it. If AJ is zero, jump to ANY CONTACT test.

Line 2035—Test the value of SI. If positive, set the value of NP down one line on the screen; otherwise set NP up one line.

Line 2040—Set CY equal to the character value found at the adjusted tenative position.

Line 2045—If ANY CONTACT then return.

Line 2050— If AI and AJ are both zero, then return; otherwise jump back to line 2015.

Applesoft Version

The Applesoft version of the search ahead routine is shown in Listing 2-2. Most of the variables serve the purposes already defined for the flowchart in Table 2-2. The additional variable names relate to earlier discussions as follows:

NX—Horizontal component of the creature's new position

NY—Vertical component of the creature's new position

PX—Horizontal component of the creature's current position

PY—Vertical component of the creature's current position

Listing 2-2. Applesoft Version of the SEARCH AHEAD Routine.

```
2000 REM ** SEARCH AHEAD, V.1 — APPLESOFT BASIC **
2005 NX=PX:NY=PY:CX=0:CY=0
2010 SI=SGN(CI):SJ=SGN(CJ):AI=ABS(CI):AJ=ABS(CJ)
2015 IF AI=0 THEN 2045
2020 AI=AI−1
2025 IF SI>0 THEN NX=NX+1:GOTO 2035
2030 NX=NX−1
2035 CX=SCRN(NX,NY)
2040 IF AJ=0 THEN 2065
2045 AJ=AJ−1
2050 IF SJ>0 THEN NY=NY+1:GOTO 2060
2055 NY=NY−1
2060 CY=SCRN(NX,NY)
2065 IF NOT(CX=0 AND CY=0) THEN RETURN
2070 IF AI=0 AND AJ=0 THEN RETURN
2075 GOTO 2015
```

Lines 2005,2010—INITIALIZE SEARCH VARIABLES; set the new tenative screen position variables, NX and NY, equal to the creature's current screen position, PX and PY; set the screen "contact" color codes, CX and CY, to zero (black screen); and derive the signs of the current motion code vector, SI and SJ, and the absolute values, AI and AJ.

Lines 2015, 2020—If AI is zero, jump to check the vertical search parameters; otherwise DECREMENT AI.

Lines 2025, 2030—If the sign of CI is positive, INCREMENT X POSITION, NX; otherwise DECREMENT X POSITION, NX.

Line 2035—Get the current contact color code, and save it as CX.

Lines 2040,2045—If AJ is zero, jump to check the contact status; otherwise DECREMENT AJ.

Lines 2050, 2055—If the sign of CJ is positive, INCREMENT Y POSITION, NY; otherwise DECREMENT Y POSITION, NY.

Line 2060—Get the current contact color code, and save it as CY.

Line 2065—If contact code CX or CY have a value other than zero (black screen), return to the mainline program.

Line 2070—If AI and AJ have both been decremented to zero, return to the mainline program.

Line 2075—If the screen contact colors are both black and there are more AI and AJ moves to test, jump back to test the value of AI again.

Variables carried into this subroutine are the creature's current position on the screen, PX and PY, and the current motion code vectors, CI and CJ. It returns to the mainline with a new tentative screen position, NX and NY, and the contact codes CX and CY.

Chapter 3
Fundamental
Alpha Demonstration

It is finally time to get one of the little creatures running around on the screen of your own computer system. The program offered in this chapter is a rather simple one; at least it is a bare-bones version of an Alpha program.

Entering and running the program will give you a firsthand look at an Alpha creature at work. Then, too, it represents your first opportunity to begin building a file of commonly used subroutines that can be saved on cassette tape or disk for use in more complicated programs.

Figure 3-1 is the general flowchart for the FUNDAMENTAL ALPHA DEMO program. It is a simple variation of the basic Alpha flowchart described in Chapter 1. The only real difference is the initial instructions for getting the program set up for your own computer system.

The program clears the screen and draws a rectangular border figure. That rectangle represents the creature's constraints—it cannot move through or over it. It is free to roam the space within the border figure at will, however.

You will see the creature moving around within its environment, moving at a fixed speed and direction until it blunders into a section of the border figure. When the creature makes contact with the border figure, it selects randomly generated motion codes until it finds one that carries it away from the border. Then, it moves at that speed and direction until it runs into the border figure again.

The program, as listed here, runs indefinitely. The only way to terminate the action is by doing the appropriate type of program-interrupt operation.

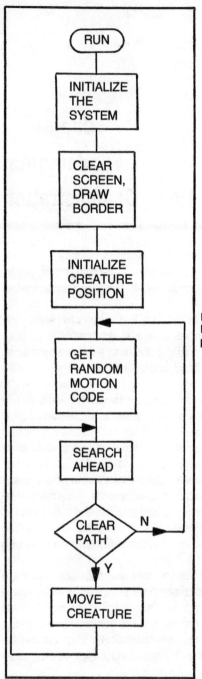

Fig. 3-1. General flowchart for the FUNDAMENTAL ALPHA DEMO program.

After watching this Alpha creature for a while, you are invited to experiment with several minor modifications. You can, for instance, change the general appearance of the creature, or you can make it leave behind a trail of footprints wherever it goes on the screen.

There are two variations of the trail-drawing modification. In one case, the creature's own trail becomes an impenetrable barrier (just as the border figure always is). The second variation lets the creature pass through previously drawn segments of the trail with no trouble at all.

The creature's behavior while working with the impenetrable trail is especially meaningful in the context of machine psychology. Unlike the spartan environment offered by the basic program listing, using the impenetrable trail modification presents the Alpha creature with a highly dynamic and ever-worsening environment. Ultimately, the creature becomes hopelessly trapped between segments of its own trail and, perhaps, a portion of the border figure. But until that happens, the creature often exhibits some rather surprising modes of behavior.

Unless the creature is completely surrounded with sections of its own trail or border figure, it seems to have a remarkable capacity for getting itself out of tight situations. It can find its way free as long as the barest path is still available to it.

If you didn't know better—if you didn't know for sure that the Alpha creature is making purely random, reflex-like responses—you might be lead to believe it is programmed to search out and use a path it can find out of a tight corner.

After observing this simple Alpha creature dealing with its impenetrable trail, one begins wondering how much so-called intelligent behavior that is commonly attributed to some of the lower animals is really a case of a simple, reflex-oriented creature functioning in a complex and dynamic environment. What role does the environment play in our judgments about creature intelligence? The question has some powerful implications for both animal and machine psychology.

The program offered in this chapter lets the Alpha creature move freely only as long as the path ahead of it is a black section of screen. Any graphic (other than a blank space) is interpreted and treated as an obstacle to be avoided. The second trail-drawing modification, however, extends the creature's sensory discrimination. Its own trail is treated as a blank section of screen; so the creature moves through it without stopping.

While there are no obvious points of special interest in this case, you can at least see how well your Alpha creature can cover all sections of the environment.

All three modifications are incorporated into a single program in the next chapter.

TRS-80 VERSION

The TRS-80 version of FUNDAMENTAL ALPHA DEMO is shown here as Listing 3-1. Since it is the first full program offered in the project, it will have to be loaded in its entirety from the keyboard. Save a copy on tape or disk, however, so that you won't have to load the subroutines again from the keyboard.

Listing 3-1. FUNDAMENTAL ALPHA DEMO—TRS-80 Version.

```
  10 REM   FUNDAMENTAL ALPHA DEMO
  15 REM        TRS-80
  20 REM
  25 REM
 100 REM ** ALPHA MAINLINE, V.1—TRS-80 **
 110 CLS:GOSUB 1000:PRINT @ 912,"FUNDAMENTAL
     ALPHA DEMO"
 115 CP=15776+RND(5)-3+64*(RND(5)-3)
 120 CI=RND(5)-3:CJ=RND(5)-3:IF CI=0 AND CJ=0
     THEN 120
 125 GOSUB 2000
 130 IF CX=32 AND CY=32 THEN 140
 135 GOTO 120
 140 POKE CP,32
 145 CP=NP:POKE CP,42
 150 GOTO 125
 155 REM
 160 REM
1000 REM ** BORDER, V.1—TRS-80 **
1005 F0=15360:F1=15432:F2=16128:F3=16191
1010 FOR N=F0 TO F1:POKE N,176:NEXT N
1015 FOR N=F2 TO F3:POKE N,131:NEXT N
1020 FOR N=F0 TO F2 STEP 64:POKE N,170:NEXT
1025 FOR N=F1 TO F3 STEP 64:POKE N,149:NEXT
1030 POKE F0, 160:POKE F1,144:POKE F2,130:POKE
     F3,129
1035 RETURN
1040 REM
```

30

Listing 3-1 continued from page 30.

```
1045 REM
2000 REM ** SEARCH AHEAD, V.1—TRS-80 **
2005 NP=CP:CX=32:CY=32
2010 SI=SGN(CI):SJ=SGN(CJ): AI=ABS(CI):AJ=ABS(CJ)
2015 IF AI=0 THEN 2030 ELSE AI=AI−1
2020 IF SI>0 THEN NP=NP+1 ELSE NP=NP−1
2025 CX=PEEK(NP)
2030 IF AJ=0 THEN 2045 ELSE AJ=AJ−1
2035 IF SJ>0 THEN NP=NP+64 ELSE NP=NP−64
2040 CY=PEEK(NP)
2045 IF NOT(CX=32 AND CY=32) THEN RETURN
2050 IF AI=0 AND AJ=0 THEN RETURN ELSE GOTO 2015
2055 REM
2060 REM
```

Theory of Operation

The variables are defined for you in Table 3-1. You will need them, plus the general flowchart in Fig. 3-1, in order to understand the expanded commentary that follows.

Line 110—Clear the screen, draw the border figure, and print the project title.

Line 115—Initialize the creature position near the center of the screen, using a small, random offset.

Line 120—Select a random motion code; if it is the stop code, select another one.

Line 125—Do the search-ahead routine.

Line 130—If the path ahead is clear, go to the creature-moving routine; otherwise, . . .

Line 135—. . . go back to select a new motion code to get into the clear again.

Line 140—Erase the creature's image from its current position on the screen.

Line 145—Get the new creature position and draw it on the screen (as an asterisk figure).

Line 150—Loop back to the search-ahead routine for the next step.

Lines 1000-1035—Border drawing subroutine.

Lines 2000-2050—Search ahead subroutine (see the explanation in Chapter 2).

Table 3-1. Variable List for FUNDAMENTAL ALPHA DEMO—TRS-80 Version.

CP	Current creature position
NP	New creature position
CI	Horizontal component of current motion code
CJ	Vertical component of current motion code
CX	Horizontal component of contact code
CY	Vertical component of contact code
SI	Sign value of CI
SJ	Sign value of CJ
AI	Absolute value of CI
AJ	Absolute value of CJ
F0	Upper-left corner of the border figure
F1	Upper-right corner of the border figure
F2	Lower-left corner of the border figure
F3	Lower-right corner of the border figure

Running the Program

The program is always started by doing a RUN command. Since it can loop indefinitely, it can be interrupted by striking the BREAK key.

Suggested Modifications

Here is how to implement the modifications suggested in the opening section of this chapter.

To change the appearance of the creature, alter the graphic code number that is POKEd in line 145. It is shown as an ASCII 42 (an asterisk) in the program listing, but you can use any of the alphanumeric or graphic codes listed in the user's manual.

To create the effect of an impenetrable creature trail, alter the graphic code number that is POKEd in line 140. You can use any valid alphanumeric or graphic code number, but 191 (a full character space of light) is quite nice; that is, make line 140 look like this:

140 POKE CP, 191

To let the creature leave a trail it can pass through, modify line 130 to look like this:

130 IF (CX=32 or CX=191) AND (CY= 32 OR CY= 191) THEN 140 and in addition, change line 140 to read:

140 POKE CP,191

Using these suggested modifications for lines 130 and 140 will yield a penetrable trail made up of large rectangles of light. You can change the appearance of the trail by substituting some other graphic code for the 191s shown here. *Do not, however, use any of the graphic codes included in the BORDER, V.1 subroutine*—do that, and your creature will pass through the border figure and blow up the whole program.

APPLESOFT VERSION

The Applesoft version of FUNDAMENTAL ALPHA DEMO is shown in Listing 3-2. The entire program must be loaded from the keyboard this time, but if you save it on tape or disk, you can load the subroutines much easier later on in the project.

Listing 3-2. FUNDAMENTAL ALPHA DEMO—Applesoft Version.

```
 10 REM   FUNDAMENTAL ALPHA DEMO
 15 REM       APPLESOFT
 20 REM
 25 REM
100 REM ** MAINLINE, V.1—APPLESOFT **
105 DEF FN R(R) = INT (5 * RND (1)) – 2
110 HOME : GR : GOSUB 1000
115 PRINT TAB(10);"FUNDAMENTAL ALPHA DEMO"
120 PX = 20 + FN R(0):PY = 20 + FN R(0)
125 CI = FN R(0):CJ = FN R(0): IF CI = 0 AND CJ = 0 THEN
    125
130 GOSUB 2000
135 IF NOT (CX = 0 AND CY = 0) THEN 125
140 COLOR=0: PLOT PX,PY
145 PX = NX:PY = NY
150 COLOR=9: PLOT PX,PY
155 GOTO 130
160 REM
165 REM
1000 REM ** BORDER,V.1—APPLESOFT **
1005 COLOR=15
1010 HLIN 0,39 AT 0: HLIN 0,39 AT 36
1015 VLIN 0,36 AT 0: VLIN 0,36 AT 39
1020 RETURN
1025 REM
1030 REM
2000 REM ** SEARCH AHEAD, V.1—APPLESOFT **
2005 NX = PX:NY = PY:CX = 0:CY = 0
2010 SI = SGN (CI):SJ = SGN (CJ):AI = ABS (CI):AJ = ABS
     (CJ)
2015 IF AI = 0 THEN 2040
2020 AI = AI – 1
2025 IF SI > 0 THEN NX = NX + 1: GOTO 2035
2030 NX = NX – 1
2035 CX = SCRN (NX,NY)
```

Listing 3-2 continued from page 33.

```
2040  IF AJ = 0 THEN 2065
2045  AJ = AJ - 1
2050  IF SJ > 0 THEN NY = NY + 1: GOTO 2060
2055  NY = NY - 1
2060  CY = SCRN (NX,NY)
2065  IF NOT (CX = 0 AND CY = 0) THEN RETURN
2070  IF AI = 0 AND AJ = 0 THEN RETURN
2075  GOTO 2015
2080  REM
2085  REM
```

Theory of Operation

The variables for this program are defined in Table 3-2. Use them in conjunction with the general flowchart in Fig. 3-1 while studying the following commentary.

Line 105—Define the motion code random generator function.

Line 110—Clear the screen, set the graphic mode, and draw the rectangular border figure.

Line 115—Print the project title.

Line 120—Initialize the creature's position on the screen, using a small, random offset.

Line 125—Select a random motion code. If it is the stop code, select another one.

Line 130—Do the search-ahead routine.

Line 135—If the path ahead is not clear, go back to get a new motion code.

Line 140—Clear the creature's image from its current position on the screen.

Line 145—Get the new creature position.

Line 150—Plot the creature's image in its new position (as an orange rectangle).

Line 155—Loop back to search the path ahead.

Lines 1000-1020—Rectangular border drawing subroutine.

Lines 2000-2075—Search ahead subroutine.

Running the Program

The program is always started by doing a RUN command from the keyboard. It runs in an endless loop, but it can be stopped by doing a CTRL C operation at the keyboard.

FN R(0)	Function for generating a motion code parameter (between −2 and 2)
PX	Horizontal component of current creature position
PY	Vertical component of current creature position
NX	Horizontal component of new creature position
NY	Vertical component of new creature position
CI	Horizontal component of motion code
CJ	Vertical component of motion code
CX	Horizontal component of contact code
CY	Vertical component of contact code
SI	Sign value of CI
SJ	Sign value of CJ
AI	Absolute value of CI
AJ	Absolute value of CJ

Suggested Modifications

The modifications suggested in the opening section of this chapter can be implemented as follows:

●To change the creature color, alter the color value in line 150. It is shown in the listing as a 9 (orange), but you can substitute any other number between 0 and 15. (Using a 0 color might be confusing because it won't allow you to see the creature at work.)

●To make the creature leave behind an impenetrable trail, change the color code specified in line 140 to something other than 0.

●Two lines have to be changed in order to create the effect of a penetrable trail. For instance:

135 IF NOT(CX=0 OR CX=13) AND (CY=0 OR CY=13) THEN 125

140 COLOR 13:PLOT PX,PY

The 13s in those two lines yield a penetrable yellow trail. You can substitute any other color code for the 13s in the example *but do not use 15.* If you use 15 for a penetrable trail color, the creature will be able to pass through the white border figure and terminate the program with a function code error.

Chapter 4
Fundamental Alpha
with Selectable Options

The program featured in this chapter is, in principle, a simple extension of the fundamental Alpha demonstration program in Chapter 3. Here, you can select the appearances of both the creature and its trail without having to modify the program listing. What's more, you can erase the current pattern of footprints without interrupting the program.

The whole purpose of the program is to give you a bit more flexibility in experimenting with the creature's responses to a changing environment—an environment that changes continuously as the creature moves around.

The program begins by requesting an appropriate creature code number. Your reply to that request determines the appearance of the creature. If you happen to select a creature code that produces an invisible creature, the program will ask whether or not you are sure you want to do that. An invisible creature that leaves a visible trail can be interesting, but I seriously question the value of doing that. It can be done, however, with this program.

After entering a valid creature-type code number, the programs ask for a trail code number. This one determines the appearance of the creature's footprints. If the trail code represents a visible trail character or color, it will be an impenetrable trail (you might want to review the significance of using impenetrable trails in the opening sections of Chapter 3). But if you select an invisible trail code number, the program asks whether or not you are sure you want to do that. If you do want an invisible trail, the creature will behave as though it is leaving no trail at all. (TRS-80 users have an interesting variation of the invisible trail option available to them—see the specific operating instructions.)

Once you have selected both a valid creature and trail code, the program reviews your selections and asks whether or not you are really satisfied with them. If not, the program begins all over, giving you an opportunity to change your selection. Otherwise, the actual Alpha routine begins.

Once the Alpha routine starts, you can erase all the previously drawn trails by simply striking any key on the keyboard. This is especially handy when the creature becomes hopelessly trapped by its own trail. Striking any key clears the trail and releases the creature to go about its business.

The general flowchart for this program is shown in Fig. 4-1. The first major part of the flowchart deals with the matter of selecting the creature and trail codes. The actual Alpha part of the program begins at the first CLEAR SCREEN, DRAW BORDER operation.

The Alpha section of the flowchart generally follows the fundamental version in Fig. 3-1. The only significant difference is the inclusion of the FRESH TRAIL conditional and a second CLEAR SCREEN, DRAW BORDER operation. After every SEARCH AHEAD routine, the system scans the keyboard. If a key depression has occurred, the FRESH TRAIL condition is satisfied and the system does the extra CLEAR SCREEN, DRAW BORDER. The creature is not affected, however. It will hold the same position and motion code it had prior to clearing the screen and redrawing the border figure.

If no key depression is found after SEARCH AHEAD, the Alpha program proceeds in its usual fashion.

The discussions dealing with specific programs for the TRS-80 and Apple systems include some minor modifications you might find fun or interesting.

TRS-80 VERSION

The complete listing for the TRS-80 version of FUNDAMENTAL ALPHA DEMO WITH SELECTABLE OPTIONS is shown in Listing 4-1. To save yourself some programming time, load Listing 3-1 into your system first; that will get the two major subroutines, BORDER and SEARCH AHEAD, into the system for you. Then delete the old MAINLINE listing and type in MAINLINE, V.2 as shown here (lines 10 through 260).

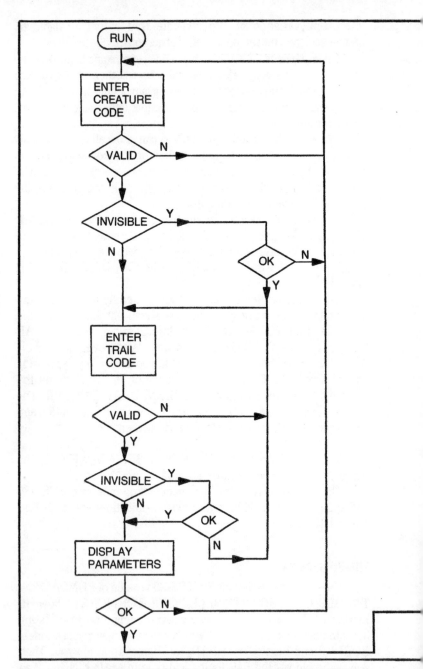

Fig. 4-1. General flowchart for FUNDAMENTAL ALPHA DEMO WITH SELECT-ABLE OPTIONS.

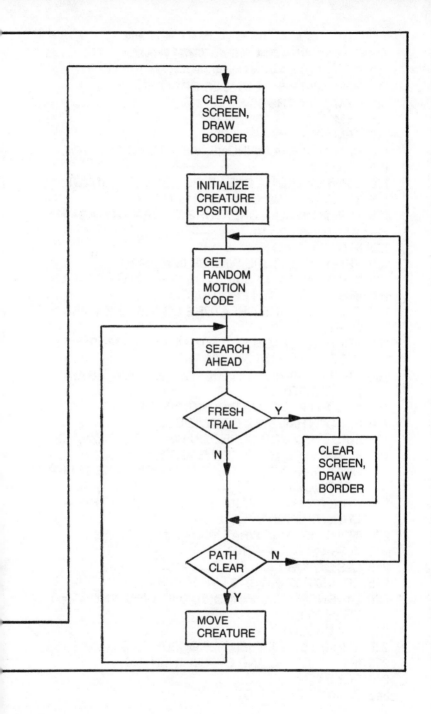

Listing 4-1. TRS-80 Version of FUNDAMENTAL
ALPHA DEMO WITH SELECTABLE OPTIONS.

```
10 REM    FUNDAMENTAL ALPHA DEMO
15 REM    WITH SELECTABLE OPTIONS
20 REM      ** TRS-80 **
25 REM
30 REM
100 REM ** ALPHA MAINLINE, V.2—TRS-80 **
105 CLS:PRINT
110 INPUT"SELECT A CREATURE CODE (33-191)";CT
115 IF CT>=33 AND CT<=191 THEN 125
120 PRINT "INVALID CREATURE CODE—TRY AGAIN"
    :PRINT:GOTO 110
125 IF CT<>128 THEN 145
130 PRINT "CREATURE WILL BE INVISIBLE . . . "
135 INPUT "ARE YOU SURE YOU WANT THAT (Y/N)";S$
140 IF S$<>"Y" THEN PRINT:GOTO 110
145 CLS:PRINT "THE CREATURE LOOKS LIKE THIS—";
    CHR$(CT)
150 PRINT:INPUT "SELECT A TRAIL CODE (32-191)";TT
155 IF TT>=32 AND TT<=191 THEN 165
160 PRINT "INVALID TRAIL CODE—TRY AGAIN":
    PRINT:GOTO 150
165 IF NOT(TT=32 OR TT=128) THEN 185
170 PRINT "TRAIL WILL BE INVISIBLE . . ."
175 INPUT"ARE YOU SURE YOU WANT THAT (Y/N)";S$
180 IF S$<>"Y" THEN PRINT:GOTO 145
185 CLS:PRINT "YOUR CREATURE LOOKS LIKE THIS—
    ";CHR$(CT)
190 PRINT "ITS  TRAIL  LOOKS  LIKE  THIS—";
    CHR$(TT):PRINT
200 INPUT "IS THAT WHAT YOU WANT (Y/N)";S$
205 IF S$<>"Y" THEN 100
210 CLS:GOSUB 1000
215 CP=15776+RND(5)-3+64*(RND(5)-3)
220 CI=RND(5)-3:CJ=RND(5)-3:IF CI=0 AND CJ=0
    THEN 220
225 GOSUB 2000
230 IF INKEY$<>"" THEN CLS:GOSUB 1000
235 IF NOT (CX=32 AND CY=32) THEN 220
240 POKE CP,TT
245 CP=NP:POKE CP,CT
```

```
250  GOTO 225
255  REM
260  REM
1000 REM ** BORDER, V.1—TRS-80 **
1005 F0=15360:F1=15423:F2=16128:F3=16191
1010 FOR N=F0 TO F1:POKE N,176:NEXT N
1015 FOR N=F2 TO F3:POKE N,131:NEXT N
1020 FOR N=F0 TO F2 STEP 64:POKE N,170:NEXT
1025 FOR N=F1 TO F3 STEP 64:POKE N,149:NEXT
1030 POKE F0,160:POKE F1,144:POKE F2,130:POKE
     F3,129
1035 RETURN
1040 REM
1045 REM
2000 REM ** SEARCH AHEAD, V.1—TRS-80 **
2005 NP=CP:CX=32:CY=32
2010 SI=SGN(CI):SJ=SGN(CJ):AI=ABS(CI):AJ=ABS(CJ)
2015 IF AI=0 THEN 2030 ELSE AI=AI−1
2020 IF SI>0 THEN NP=NP+1 ELSE NP=NP−1
2025 CX=PEEK(NP)
2030 IF AJ=0 THEN 2045 ELSE AJ=AJ−1
2035 IF SJ> 0 THEN NP=NP+64 ELSE NP=NP−64
2040 CY=PEEK(NP)
2045 IF NOT(CX=32 AND CY=32) THEN RETURN
2050 IF AI= 0 AND AJ=0 THEN RETURN ELSE GOTO 2015
2055 REM
2060 REM
```

Theory of Operation

The variable list for this program is shown in Table 4-1. Use it in conjunction with the general flowchart in Fig. 4-1 while going through this analysis.

Lines 105-140—Select a valid creature code between 33 and 191. If outside that range, select again. If it is 128 (a graphic space), inform the user that the creature will be invisible. If that is OK, go on to the next phase of the job; otherwise, go back to select another code.

Lines 145-180—Select a valid trail code between 32 and 191. If outside that range, select again. If it is 32 or 128 (spaces), inform the user that the trail will be invisible. If that is OK, then go on to the next phase; otherwise, go back to select another trail code.

Table 4-1. Variable List for TRS-80 Version.

CT	Creature character code (33-191)
TT	Trail character code (32-191)
S$	General-purpose string variable
FN	R(0) Function for generation motion code parameters
CP	Current creature position
NP	New creature position
CI	Horizontal component of current motion code
CJ	Vertical component of current motion code
CX	Horizontal component of contact code
CY	Vertical component of contact code
SI	Sign value of CI
SJ	Sign value of CJ
AI	Absolute value of CI
AJ	Absolute value of CJ
F0	Upper-left corner of border figure
F1	Upper-right corner of border figure
F2	Lower-left corner of border figure
F3	Lower-right corner of border figure
N	General-purpose numerical variable

Lines 185-205—Doublecheck the selections for creature and trail codes. Show them on the screen and ask if they are OK. If so, go on to the Alpha phase of the job; otherwise, go all the way back to the beginning to select new codes.

Lines 210-215—Clear the screen, draw the border figure, and initialize the creature position.

Line 220—Get a random motion code. If it is a stop code, get another one.

Line 225—Do the search ahead routine.

Line 230—If any key is depressed, clear the screen and redraw the border figure (clear the old trail without disturbing the creature's current position and motion code).

Line 235—If the path ahead is not clear, go back to get a new motion code.

Lines 240-250—Move the creature figure and leave behind a trail; use the specified creature and trail codes. Return to search the path ahead for the next move on the screen.

Lines 1000-1035—Border drawing subroutine.

Lines 2000-2050—Search ahead subroutine.

Some Operating Hints

The program runs indefinitely. To terminate it, strike the BREAK key.

If you select both visible creature and trail codes, the creature will ultimately work its way into a trapped situation. To clear the trail and free and creature (without having to restart the program), simply strike any key on the keyboard—the ENTER key works nicely.

The goof-proofing in the program does not allow you to select an invisible creature code, 32. You can, however, select code 128 to make an invisible creature.

There are two codes that will create invisible trails—32 and 128. If you select 32 as a trail code, that is tantamount to having no trail at all; the creature runs freely for an indefinite period of time. But if you select trail code 128, the trail will be invisible to you, but the creature will be able to sense it and respond as though it is an impenetrable barrier.

Suggested Modifications

If you would like to see a special signal whenever the creature selects a new motion code, add this line to the program:

    222 PRINT@ 896,"#":PRINT@ 896,CHR$(32);

The pound-sign character will now flash near the lower left-hand corner of the screen whenever the creature blunders into an obstacle and is subsequently forced to select a new motion code. It might be interesting to note how many motion codes the creature must select to get out of a contact situation.

If you would like to keep an actual running tally of the number of blunders the creature makes, add these lines to the basic listing:

    207 BC=0
    223 BC=BC+1:PRINT@ 897,STRING$(32,32);
    224 PRINT@ 900,BC;

and edit line 230 to read:

    230 IF INKEY$<> " " THEN CLS:GOSUB 1000:BC=0

Now a running count of the number of times the creature must select a new motion code appears near the bottom of the border figure. The count is cleared to zero whenever you exercise the trail-erasing option—striking a key during the execution of the program.

More extensive event-counting operations are incorporated into programs suggested later in this book.

APPLESOFT VERSION

The Apple listing for FUNDAMENTAL ALPHA DEMO WITH SELECTABLE OPTIONS is shown as Listing 4-2. You can save yourself some programming time by first loading the listing from Listing 3-1 (assuming you have saved it or tape of disk); that will load the necessary subroutines, BORDER and SEARCH AHEAD for you. Then all you do is delete the old MAINLINE and substitute the MAINLINE, V.2 shown here.

Listing 4-2. Applesoft Version of FUNDA-MENTAL ALPHA DEMO WITH SELECTABLE OPTIONS.

```
10 REM   FUNDAMENTAL ALPHA DEMO
15 REM   WITH SELECTABLE OPTIONS
20 REM      ** APPLESOFT **
25 REM
30 REM
100 REM ** MAINLINE,V.2—APPLESOFT **
105 HOME : PRINT
110 PRINT "SELECT A CREATURE COLOR (0-15)": PRINT
    : INPUT CT
115 IF CT > = 0 AND CT < = 15 THEN 125
120 PRINT "INVALID CREATURE COLOR—TRY AGAIN":
    PRINT: GOTO 110
125 IF CT < > 0 THEN 145
130 PRINT "CREATURE WILL BE INVISIBLE . . ."
135 INPUT "ARE YOU SURE YOU WANT THAT (Y/N)?";S$
140 IF S$ < > "Y" THEN PRINT : GOTO 110
145 HOME : PRINT : PRINT "YOUR CREATURE COLOR
    CODE IS";CT
150 PRINT : PRINT "SELECT A TRAIL COLOR (0-15)":
    INPUT TT
155 IF TT > = 0 AND TT < = 15 THEN 165
160 PRINT "INVALID TRAIL CODE—TRY AGAIN": PRINT :
    GOTO 150
165 IF TT < > 0 THEN 185
170 PRINT : PRINT "TRAIL WILL BE INVISIBLE . . ."
175 INPUT "ARE YOU SURE YOU WANT THAT (Y/N)?";S$
180 IF S$ < > "Y" THEN PRINT : GOTO 145
185 HOME : PRINT : PRINT "CREATURE COLOR IS ";CT
190 PRINT "TRAIL COLOR IS ";TT
195 PRINT
200 INPUT "IS THAT WHAT YOU WANT (Y/N)?";S$
205 IF S$ < > "Y" THEN 100
210 DEF FN R(R) = INT (5 * RND (1)) − 2
```

```
215 HOME : GR : GOSUB 1000
220 PX = 20 + FN R(0):PY = 20 + FN R(0)
225 CI = FN R(0):CJ = FN R(0): IF CI = 0 AND CJ = 0 THEN
    225
230 GOSUB 2000
235 IF PEEK ( − 16384) > 127 THEN TEXT : HOME : GR :
    GOSUB 1000
240 POKE − 16368,0: IF NOT (CX = 0 AND CY = 0) THEN
    225
245 COLOR = TT: PLOT PX,PY
250 PX = NX:PY = NY
255 COLOR= CT: PLOT PX,PY
260 GOTO 230
265 REM
270 REM
1000 REM ** BORDER,V.1—APPLESOFT **
1005 COLOR=15
1010 HLIN 0,39 AT 0: HLIN 0,39 AT 36
1015 VLIN 0,36 AT 0: VLIN 0,36 AT 39
1020 RETURN
1025 REM
1030 REM
2000 REM ** SEARCH AHEAD, V.1—APPLESOFT **
2005 NX = PX:NY = PY:CX = 0: CY = 0
2010 SI = SGN (CI):SJ = SGN (CJ):AI = ABS (CI):AJ = ABS
     (CJ)
2015 IF AI = 0 THEN 2040
2020 AI = AI − 1
2025 IF SI > 0 THEN NX = NX + 1: GOTO 2035
2030 NX = NX − 1
2035 CX = SCRN(NX,NY)
2040 IF AJ = 0 THEN 2065
2045 AJ = AJ − 1
2050 IF SJ > 0 THEN NY = NY + 1: GOTO 2060
2055 NY = NY − 1
2060 CY = SCRN(NX,NY)
2065 IF NOT (CX = 0 AND CY = 0) THEN RETURN
2070 IF AI = 0 AND AJ = 0 THEN RETURN
2075 GOTO 2015
2080 REM
2085 REM
```

Table 4-2. Variable List for Applesoft Version.

CT	Selected creature color (0-15)
TT	Selected trail color (0-15)
S$	General-purpose string variable
FN R(0)	Function for generation motion code parameters
PX	Horizontal component of current creature position
PY	Vertical component of current creature postion
NX	Horizontal component of new creature position
NY	Vertical component of current creature position
CI	Horizontal component of motion code
CJ	Vertical component of motion code
CX	Horizontal component of contact code
CY	Vertical component of contact code
SI	Sign value of CI
SJ	Sign value of CJ
AI	Absolute value of CI
AJ	Absolute value of CJ

Theory of Operation

The variable list for the program is shown in Table 4-2. Use it, along with the general flowchart in Fig. 4-1, as a guide for following the program's line-by-line analysis.

Lines 105-140—Select a valid creature color code between 0 and 15. If outside this range, select again. Then if it is 0 (black), inform the user that the creature will be invisible. If that is OK, then go to the next phase of the program; otherwise, go back to select another creature color code number.

Lines 145-180—Select a valid trail code number between 0 and 15. If outside that range, select again. If it is black, inform the user that the trail will be invisible and insensible to the creature. If that is OK, go to the next step; otherwise, go back to select another trail color code.

Lines 185-205—Doublecheck the color selections for the creature and trail. Show the color code numbers on the screen and ask if they are OK. If so, go on to the Alpha part of the program; otherwise loop back to pick new creature and trail color code numbers.

Lines 210-220—Define the random motion code function, clear the screen set up the graphics mode, and draw the border figure.

Line 225—Pick a random motion code. If it is the stop code, pick another one.

Line 230—Do the search ahead routine.

Line 235—Scan the keyboard. If a key is depressed, clear the screen and re-draw the border figure (start a new trail).

Line 240—Reset the keyboard scan. If the path ahead is not clear, loop back to pick up a new random motion code.

Lines 245-260—Plot the trail, move the creature, and loop back to search the path ahead for the next step on the screen.

Lines 1000-1020—Border drawing subroutine.

Lines 2000-2075—Search ahead subroutine (see Chapter 2).

Some Operating Hints

The program will run indefinitely. To terminate it, do a CTRL C operation from the keyboard.

If you select both visible creature and trail colors, the creature will ultimately work its way into a trapped situation. To clear the trail and free the creature (without having to start the program all over again), simply strike a character key—the RETURN key works nicely, too.

It is possible to select an invisible creature (code 0). If you select a visible creature, but call for an invisible trail color code (code 0), the creature will run freely all the time.

Suggested Modifications

The following additions to the main listing will add some acoustical effects that are both interesting and enlightening:

226 CALL 198
256 POKE-16336,0

The first one inserts a clincking sound with every creature move, and the second addition creates a beep every time the creature is forced to select a new motion code. The latter modification gives you a good idea how hard the creature must work in order to get away from an obstacle. The beeping, of course, becomes continuous when the creature becomes inexorably trapped by its own trail.

If you want to keep an actual running tally of the number of times the creature is forced to select a new motion code, add these lines to the existing listing:

222 BC=0
227 BC=BC+1: HOME: PRINT BC

and extend line 235 to read:

235 IF PEEK (−16384)> 127 THEN TEXT: HOME: GR:GOSUB 1000:BC=0

With those modifications, a running count of the number of times the creature must select a new motion code appears just below the lower left-hand corner of the border figure. The count is cleared to zero whenever you exercise the trail-erasing option—striking a key during the execution of the Alpha portion of the program.

More extensive event-counting operations of this type are incorporated into programs suggested later in this book.

Chapter 5
Killer Alpha Demonstration

In terms of animal psychology, the Alpha responses used in all of the previous experiments and demonstrations have the nature of *flight responses*. That is to say, the creature deals with an obstruction in its path by running away from it and setting off on another path.

There can be no doubt that flight responses can play vital roles in the survival and adaptability of animal and machine creatures. A rabbit coming face-to-face with a hungry fox has a decent chance of survival if it abandons its present form of activity and flees the predator. And under certain circumstances, a human creature comes out of a situation better by running away from it; or at least changing the present course of action to work around the problem.

It is possible, however, to greatly enrich a creature's spectrum of effective responses by offering a *fight response* option. Rather than working around the problem, a fight response calls for dealing with the problem in a more direct fashion.

The Alpha creature introduced in this chapter possesses both flight and fight responses. And upon encountering an obstacle in its path, there is a 50-50 chance it will deal with that obstacle by killing it. If the reflex response does not call for killing the obstacle, it will flee from it.

Upon running the program as it is listed here, you will see the system draw the usual rectangular border figure. But then the program scatters 64 randomly distributed "things" around within the border. Those things represent killable obstacles. The border, itself, is considered not killable.

So as the Alpha creature begins moving around in this thing-cluttered environment, it soon encounters one of the killable things or a segment of the border figure. If the obstacle is one of the killable things, the creature randomly selects one of two possible reflex responses—either a new motion code that carries it away from the obstacle (a flight response) or a kill code that deletes the obstacle from the screen (a fight response) and lets the creature continue its present course of action.

If the obstacle happens to be a segment of the border figure, the creature likewise makes either a flight or fight response. In the case of the border obstacle, however, it cannot be killed or deleted. It can be damaged, but never broken open so that the creature can escape from the screen environment.

The fact that the things scattered around in the environment can be killed and segments of the border figure cannot is imposed by the programming that is external to the Alpha routines. In a manner of speaking, the creature does not know whether an obstacle can be killed or not. The creature is only concerned with the matter of maintaining a clear path ahead of it; and in an attempt to do so, it might take a shot at killing anything in its way. If that obstacle happens to be a section of the border figure, the kill will not be wholly successful, and the creature responds by either trying to kill it again or by selecting a motion code that makes it flee the situation.

The creature in this chapter has no more intelligence than any presented in earlier chapters; only the family of random, reflex-like responses has been extended. Observing this killer creature in action, however, one might get the impression that it does possess some elements of rational behavior—especially when the listing is modified so that the creature leaves behind an impenetrable trail.

Earlier experiments with the impenetrable trail showed that an Alpha creature having only flight responses inevitably becomes hopelessly trapped by elements of its own trail or sections of the border figure and trail. The Alpha creature having a fight-response option can become trapped by its own trail, but it can fight its way out.

In terms of animal psychology, this ability to fight out of a trapped situation reminds one of a creature that is predictably nasty only when it is backed into a corner. But wait. How can we say that an Alpha creature—one functioning only by random reflex responses—is predictable? There seems to be a contradiction of terms. Random behavior is not supposed to be predictable.

It is time to overhaul a lot of old notions about randomness and predictability. In this sort of situation at least, analyzing behavior into its most elementary components causes more confusion than enlightenment.

Indeed, at any given moment, the Alpha creature's response to an obstacle is random and, thus, unpredictable. But back that killer Alpha into a corner, and it will eventually come up with a successful kill response—a response that will delete one of the killable sections of its path from the screen, leaving an open space for escape. Yes, a single response at a given instant is unpredictable; but given enough time to deal with the matter, you can bet good money that the Alpha will fight its way out of a trapped situation. The response, overall, is 100-percent predictable.

Traditional scientific thinking demands that a mechanism can be understood only by breaking it down into its most elementary components. While such thinking has unquestionably lead to a great deal of sound and useful knowledge, it has also created some tough intellectual dilemmas. There is good reason to hope that we are on the threshold of a new age of scientific thinking, however. Many scientists and philosophers are fed up with being straight-jacketed by nearly 400 years of purely mechanistic thinking, and they are trying out some "heretical" synthetic approaches to generating theories about nature.

The theory of knowledge offered here is not one that is generally known to the current generation of computer scientists and technicians. Having created the entire science from scratch ourselves, we have the distinct impression that we can know all there is to know about every working detail. But many of us are losing sight of the broader picture. We are so interested in counting pebbles we aren't aware that we are standing on a beach that offers even greater opportunities for excitement and enjoyment.

THE FLOWCHART FOR KILLER ALPHA

The flowchart for the KILLER ALPHA DEMO program is shown in Fig. 5-1. A cursory inspection will show that it is divided into three main parts.

The first main section of the flowchart simply sets up the system for the project. It calls for drawing the border figure on the screen, initializing and drawing the creature figure, and then drawing the killable things at random places on the screen.

The second major portion of the flowchart is the basic Alpha scheme. That section begins by selecting a random motion code and doing a search ahead routine. If the path ahead is clear, the creature is moved to its next position on the screen and operations loop back to check the path ahead again.

The third phase of the operation is called only the path ahead is found to be obstructed—when the answer to the CLEAR PATH conditional is NO. When that happens, the creature responds with a kill or no-kill reflex. If the kill code dictates a no-kill response, the KILL conditional is not satisfied and the program loops back into the mainstream of Alpha activity—it fetches a flight-type random motion code.

Now, if that flight response works, everything remains in the main Alpha loop. But if it doesn't work, the creature chooses between kill and no-kill again. Remember the kill or no-kill response is a 50-50 matter; and the creature gets out of the contact situation (eventually) by responding to a no-kill decision with a random motion code that works.

But suppose the creature picks up a kill response from GET RANDOM KILL CODE. In that case, the KILL conditional is satisfied, and the system encounters the KILLABLE conditional.

Whether or not the obstacle is killable is imposed by the nature of the environment. The Alpha creature cannot make that selection on its own. Obstacles that are not killable in this program are elements of the border figure. If the obstacle is not killable, the flowchart shows that the creature will TRY TO KILL the obstacle; by the nature of the programming imposed upon the system, however, that sort of obstacle can be altered, but not deleted from the screen. The significance is that the creature will attempt to kill a section of the border figure that is in its way. Eliminating that possibility—as ridiculous as it might seem to be to us—would destroy the essentail nature of the demonstration. *An Alpha creature must not be given the ability to exclude unproductive responses.* All we can do as investigators is make certain that such responses will be unproductive.

Returning to the KILLABLE conditional on the flowchart, suppose the obstacle is defined as killable. In that case the creature is endowed with the capacity for deleting the obstacle from the screen at the KILL THE THING operation.

After attempting to kill an obstacle, whether that obstacle is really killable or not, the next step is to SEARCH AHEAD; to search the path to see if the kill response did indeed clear the path ahead. If the kill response clears the path ahead (as determined by the result of the SEARCH AHEAD operation), the creature moves on through the "corpse" to continue its former direction and speed of motion.

If the kill response does not work—if the creature attempts to

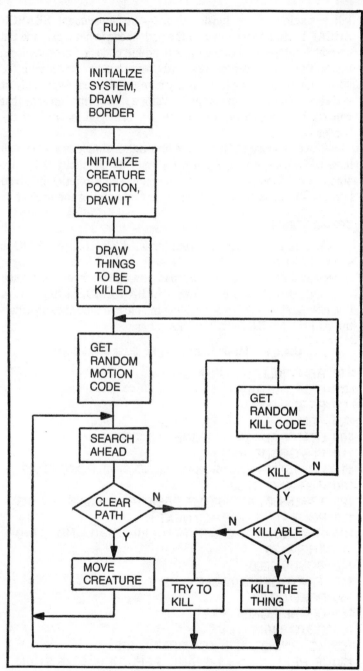

Fig. 5-1. General flowchart for KILLER ALPHA DEMO.

kill a section of the border figure—the subsequent SEARCH AHEAD routine will show that the path ahead is not clear, and the creature will select the random kill/no-kill code and proceed from there. Thus, the creature frequently responds to contact with the border figure by trying to kill it any number of times. Eventually, it will select a no-kill response and look for a random motion code that will carry it away from the intact, but damaged, section of the border.

The flowchart might seem to be a rather simple one when you have had a chance to study it for a time. Its simplicity belies its significance, though. There are some powerful subtleties involved here, and to miss them is to miss the real point of the project.

TRS-80 VERSION

The TRS-80 program listing for KILLER ALPHA DEMO is shown in Listing 5-1. It is fairly easy to load into the system, especially if you can load the two main subroutines from tape or disk as saved from FUNDAMENTAL ALPHA DEMO, Listing 3-1. In that case, all you have to do is delete the old mainline and substitute the ALPHA MAINLINE, V.3 shown here.

Listing 5-1. TRS-80 Programming for KILLER ALPHA DEMO.

```
 10 REM   KILLER ALPHA DEMO
 15 REM      TRS-80
 20 REM
 25 REM
100 REM ** ALPHA MAINLINE, V.3—TRS-80 **
110 CLS:GOSUB 1000
115 CP=15776+RND(5)−3+64*(RND(5)−3):POKE CP,42
120 FOR N=0 TO 63
125 TP=15360+RND(831):IF PEEK(TP)< > 32 THEN 125
130 POKE TP,RND(32)+33:NEXT N
135 CI=RND(5)−3:CJ=RND(5)−3:IF  CI=0  AND  CJ=0
    THEN 135
140 GOSUB 2000
145 IF NOT(CX=32 AND CY=32) THEN 165
150 POKE CP,32
155 CP=NP:POKE CP,42
160 GOTO 140
165 KC=RND(2)−1: IF KC= 0 THEN 135
170 IF PEEK(NP)>=129 AND PEEK(NP)<=176 THEN
    POKE NP,153:GOTO 140
```

```
 175  POKE NP,32:GOTO 140
1000  REM ** BORDER, V.1—TRS-80 **
1005  F0=15360:F1=15423:F2=16128:F3=16191
1010  FOR N=F0 TO F1:POKE N,176:NEXT N
1015  FOR N=F2 TO F3:POKE N,131:NEXT N
1020  FOR N=F0 TO F2 STEP 64:POKE N,170:NEXT
1025  FOR N=F1 TO F3 STEP 64:POKE N,149:NEXT
1030  POKE F0,160:POKE F1,144:POKE F2,130:POKE
      F3,129
1035  RETURN
1040  REM
1045  REM
2000  REM ** SEARCH AHEAD, V.1—TRS-80 **
2005  NP=CP:CX=32:CY=32
2010  SI=SGN(CI):SJ=SGN(CJ):AI=ABS(CI):AJ=ABS(CJ)
2015  IF AI=0 THEN 2030 ELSE AI=AI−1
2020  IF SI>0 THEN NP=NP+1 ELSE NP=NP−1
2025  CX=PEEK(NP)
2030  IF AJ=0 THEN 2045 ELSE AJ=AJ−1
2035  IF SJ>0 THEN NP=NP+64 ELSE NP=NP−64
2040  CY=PEEK(NP)
2045  IF NOT(CX=32 AND CY=32) THEN RETURN
2050  IF AI=0 AND AJ=0 THEN RETURN ELSE GOTO 2015
2055  REM
2060  REM
```

Theory of Operation

Use the variable list in Table 5-1 and the flowchart in Fig. 5-1 to help you work through this analysis of the program.

Line 110—Clear the screen and draw the border figure.

Line 115—Initialize the creature and plot its figure.

Lines 120-130—Draw the 64 killable things on the screen. Select a random position, then check to see whether or not any other character is plotted there. If so, select another random position; otherwise plot the thing. Continue until all 64 are in place. The things, themselves, are randomly selected from character codes 34 through 76 (messy, perhaps, but interesting).

Line 135—Select a random motion code for the creature. If it is the stop code, select another one.

Line 140—Search the path ahead.

CP	Current creature position on the screen
NP	New, or next, creature position on the screen
N	General-purpose numerical variable
TP	Position of "things" to be killed
CI	Horizontal component of the current motion code
CJ	Vertical component of the current motion code
CX	Horizontal component of the current contact code
CY	Vertical component of the current contact code
KC	Kill code; 0 is "don't kill," 1 is "kill"
F0	Upper-left corner of the border figure
F1	Upper-right corner of the border figure
F2	Lower-left corner of the border figure
F3	Lower-right corner of the border figure
SI	Sign value of CI
SJ	Sign value of CJ
AI	Absolute value of CI
AJ	Absolute value of CJ

Lines 145-160—If the path is not clear, go to the KILL routine beginning at line 165; otherwise move the creature figure to its new place on the screen and loop back to search the path ahead again.

Line 165—Select a random kill code, 0 or 1. If 0 (no kill), loop back to pick a new random motion code (make the flight response). Otherwise, jump to line 170.

Line 170—Check to see whether or not the obstacle is killable. Codes between 129 and 176 are considered non-killable, and include the graphic elements of the border figure. If the obstacle is non-killable, replace it with "damage" code number 153 and loop back to search ahead—to see whether or not that fight response worked (which it won't in the case of encounters with the border figure).

Line 175—Kill the obstacle by deleting it from the screen, and loop back to the search ahead routine to see whether or not the kill response worked.

Lines 1000-1035—Border drawing subroutine.

Lines 2000-2050—Search ahead subroutine.

Running the Program

Initiate the program by doing a RUN command. Note that the creature often bounces away from the killable obstacles scattered randomly about the screen. Just as often, however, the creature will kill the obstacle and move on with the motion code it had prior to the encounter.

Attempts to kill an element of the border figure produce a clearly discernable graphic 153.

Let the program run long enough, and you will see the Alpha doing away with all of the killable things and putting a lot of "dents" into the border figure.

Suggested Modification

While the essence of the killable Alpha creature is fully exhibited by the listing shown in Listing 5-1, the matter is more clearly illustrated when using an impenetrable barrier option. The program demonstrates the notion that it is dangerous to back a killer Alpha into a corner. Review the discussion of this matter in the opening section of this chapter.

To create the trail effect, simply modify line 150 to read:

150 POKE CP, 191

Doing that, the creature will leave behind a trail of 191 graphic characters. It will respond to them as it does any of the other killable creatures on the screen—sometimes bouncing away from it with a newly generated random motion code, and sometimes responding by biting its way through it. That latter response is especially significant when the Alpha finds itself trapped.

How is this killing effect making the Alpha better suited for adapting to a changing environment than the impenetrable trail option offered in Chapter 3 and 4?

APPLESOFT VERSION

The Applesoft program for KILLER ALPHA DEMO is shown in Listing 5-2. You can save yourself some programming time by first loading FUNDAMENTAL ALPHA DEMO, Listing 3-1, into the system from tape or disk. After doing that, delete the old mainline and replace it with ALPHA MAINLINE, V.3 shown here.

Listing 5-2. Applesoft Programming for KILLER ALPHA DEMO.

```
 10 REM    KILLER ALPHA DEMO
 15 REM       APPLESOFT
 20 REM
 25 REM
 30 REM
100 REM ** ALPHA MAINLINE, V.3—APPLESOFT **
105 DEF FN R(R) = INT (5 * RND (1)) – 2
110 HOME : GR : GOSUB 1000
115 PX = 20 + FN R(0):PY = 20 + FN R(0): COLOR= 9:
    PLOT PX,PY
```

```
120 FOR N = 0 TO 63
125 TX = INT (38 * RND (1)) + 1:TY = INT (35 * RND (1)) + 1
130 IF SCRN(TX,TY) < > 0 THEN 125
135 COLOR= INT (12 * RND (1)) + 1: PLOT TX,TY
140 NEXT N
145 CI = FN R(0):CJ = FN R(0): IF CI = 0 AND CJ = 0 THEN
    145
150 GOSUB 2000
155 IF NOT (CX = 0 AND CY = 0) THEN 175
160 COLOR= 0: PLOT PX,PY
165 PX = NX:PY = NY
170 COLOR= 9: PLOT PX,PY: GOTO 150
175 KC = INT (RND (1) + .5): IF KC = 0 THEN 145
180 IF SCRN (NX,NY) < 14 THEN 190
185 COLOR= 14: PLOT NX,NY: GOTO 150
190 COLOR= 0: PLOT NX,NY: GOTO 150
1000 REM ** BORDER,V.1—APPLESOFT **
1005 COLOR= 15
1010 HLIN 0,39 AT 0: HLIN 0,39 AT 36
1015 VLIN 0,36 AT 0: VLIN 0,36 AT 39
1020 RETURN
1025 REM
1030 REM
2000 REM ** SEARCH AHEAD, V.1—APPLESOFT **
2005 NX = PX:NY = PY:CX = 0:CY = 0
2010 SI = SGN (CI):SJ = SGN (CJ):AI = ABS (CI):AJ = ABS
     (CJ)
2015 IF AI = 0 THEN 2040
2020 AI = AI − 1
2025 IF SI > 0 THEN NX = NX + 1: GOTO 2035
2030 NX = NX − 1
2035 CX = SCRN(NX,NY)
2040 IF AJ = 0 THEN 2065
2045 AJ = AJ − 1
2050 IF SJ > 0 THEN NY = NY + 1: GOTO 2060
2055 NY = NY − 1
2060 CY = SCRN(NX,NY)
2065 IF NOT (CX = 0 AND CY = 0) THEN RETURN
2070 IF AI = 0 AND AJ = 0 THEN RETURN
2075 GOTO 2015
2080 REM
2085 REM
```

Theory of Operation

Use the variable list in Table 3-2 and the general flowchart in Fig. 3-1 as guides for working through this line-by-line analysis of the program.

Lines 105-110—Define the motion code function, clear the screen, set up the graphic mode and draw the usual border figure on the screen.

Line 115—Initialize the creature position and plot it as an orange spot.

Lines 120-140—Plot the randomly distributed killable things. Do 64 of them, using color codes 1 through 13. Check the screen before plotting each one of them, making sure it isn't plotted over anything but a blank section of screen; if something is already plotted there, pick another random place for the particular thing.

Line 145—Pick a random motion code for the creature. If it is the stop code, pick another one.

Line 150—Search the path ahead.

Lines 155-170—If the screen is not clear, jump down to the kill routine in line 175; otherwise, move the creature to its next position on the screen.

Line 175—Select a random kill code, 0 or 1. If 0 (no kill), loop back to pick a new random motion code (make the flight response). Otherwise jump to line 180 to set up the fight response.

Line 180—See whether or not the obstacle is a killable one. If the screen code is 14 or 15, it is not killable.

Table 5-2. Applesoft Variable List for KILLER ALPHA DEMO.

FN R(R)	Random motion code function
PX	Horizontal component of current creature position
PY	Vertical component of current creature position
NX	Horizontal component of new, or next, creature position
NY	Vertical component of new, or next, creature position
TX	Horizontal component of "thing" position
TY	Vertical component of "thing" position
N	Number of "things" plotted
CI	Horizontal component of the current motion code
CJ	Vertical component of the current motion code
KC	Kill code; 0 is "don't kill," 1 is "kill"
SI	Sign value of CI
SJ	Sign value of CJ
AI	Absolute value of CI
AJ	Absolute value of CJ

Line 185—The obstacle is not killable. Respond by replacing it with color code 14; then go back to search the path ahead.

Line 190—The obstacle is killable. Respond by deleting it from the screen and looping back to search the path ahead.

Lines 1000-1020—Border drawing subroutine.

Lines 2000-2075—Search ahead subroutine.

Running the Program

Initiate the program by doing a RUN command. Note that the creature often bounces away from the killable obstacles. Just as often, however, it will kill them and move through the spot with the motion code it possessed prior to the encounter.

Attempts to kill segments of the border figure will always fail, but they are noted by changing the color of that portion of the border figure from white (color 15) to green (color 14).

Let the program run long enough, and you will see the killer Alpha doing away with most of the killable things and putting a lot of "dents" into the border figure.

Conclude the program by doing a CTRL C from the keyboard.

Suggested Modification

The listing as shown in Listing 5-2 is adequate for demonstrating the essence of a killer Alpha creature, but the matter is more clearly illustrated by modifying the program so that the creature leaves behind a killable trail of footprints. Recall the notion that it is dangerous to back a killer Alpha into a corner; review the opening section of this chapter if you aren't clear on this particular point.

To create the trail effect, simply modify line 160 to read:

160 COLOR 13:PLOT PX,PY

Now, the creature will leave behind a trail of yellow light. It will respond to that trail as though it is a killable thing—sometimes bouncing away from it with a newly generated motion code, and sometimes responding by biting its way through it. The latter response is especially meaningful when the Alpha gets trapped into a tight spot.

How is this killing effect making the Alpha more suited for adapting to a changing environment than the impenetrable trail option offered in Chapters 3 and 4?

Chapter 6
Multiple Alpha Demonstration

If you think your little Alpha creatures have been lonely during their solo performances on your crt screen, here is your chance to offer some companionship. The companion in this case is another Alpha.

You will find, however, that these two Alphas seem to prefer being alone—they respond to each other as obstacles to be avoided. Technically speaking, they cannot distinguish one another from the border figure. (But as you might imagine, that will be remedied later.)

The program in this chapter is an important one in two respects. First, it represents the first opportunity to get more than a single creature onto the screen at the same time. And second, it sets the stage for experiments that are aimed at observing the social behavior of two or more machine creatures.

Later experiments will deal with the sociology in greater depth. Here, the social interaction of the two Alpha creatures is simple; almost to the point of being trivial.

The following discussions emphasize a programming technique that is essential for running experiments with more than one creature. The technique is not an especially difficult one, but a cursory glance at the program listings show that it is, indeed, far more abstract than the listings for single-creature experiments and demonstrations.

The technique is known as *asynchronous multitasking,* and it is described in some detail in the following section. It will be used in all later experiments calling for running more than one creature at a time, but this discussion will be adequate for all of those future programs.

ASYNCHRONOUS MULTITASKING

Asynchronous multitasking isn't an expression that is normally bantered about in home computer circles. It is a term from the world of sophisticated process control and big mainframe computer systems. Simply, it means fooling a computer into giving the impression that it is doing a number of different, independent tasks at the same time.

A microprocessor chip—the heart and brain of your home computer—can do just one elementary operation at a time. Its ability to carry out relatively complex operations rests on the fact that it can do a whole lot of simple, one-at-a-time tasks in a very short period of time.

Under the control of a program, your computer can accept numbers from the keyboard, process them and display the results on the crt. The task is carried out in a systematic fashion, one step at a time. And, usually, one part of the task is completed before the program moves to the next part. Learning elementary computer programming calls for disciplining yourself to think in terms of a long series of small steps.

The notion of staying with a single task until it is completed is inadequate for some computer applications, however. It is sometimes necessary to use a computer in such a way that it behaves as though it is several computers doing several different tasks at the same time. That is multitasking—doing multiple tasks, apparently at the same time.

The impression is only apparent, however, because as mentioned a moment ago, a processor can do just one thing at a time. The trick is to prepare programs that let the processor work out one little bit of one program task, set aside the results, and then move to another task. The individual tasks are thus carried out in a piecemeal fashion, with some of them eventually coming to a conclusion while others are still being worked through the system.

A common example of multitasking is the situation where more than one computer user sits at individual terminals connected to a central computer system. Each user gets the impression that he or she is the only one using the computer; but in reality, all the users are sharing the main computer. The main computer services each user one at a time and in a piecemeal way. The computer executes one user's program, saves the results, and then goes on to serve another user. Used in that way, multitasking is sometimes called time sharing. Each user gets a small share of computer time. There is just one computer doing one operation at a time, but the overall impression is that of many computers doing different tasks.

It is possible to multitask, time share, or multiplex (they all mean about the same thing in our present context) a single Alpha program sequence for any number of creatures. The idea would be to write one complete Alpha program, such as the one featured in Chapter 3, and then surround it with a programming scheme that selects one creature at a time to be serviced.

Suppose such a program is set up for three Alpha creatures that are to be serviced in rotation. The multitasking portion of the program would keep track of each creature's current position on the screen and motion code. To service creature number 1, the program would fetch its screen position and motion code, and then call the main Alpha sequence. That sequence would run until the creature found a legitimate move on the screen. And if the search-ahead portion of the Alpha sequence sensed impending contact with an obstacle, that creature would dominate the computer time until it found a new motion code that carried it away from the obstacle. Only then would the new position and motion code be saved for a time when that particular creature is to be serviced again.

After dealing with creature number 1, the multitasking portion of the program would call up the variables for creature number 2. That creature would then dominate the computer time until it found a legitimate move in the framework of the fundamental Alpha sequence.

Then creature number 3 gets its turn; then creature number 1, then 2, then back to 3, and so on. The multitasking part of the program cycles through the three creatures' parameters, executing a complete Alpha sequence for each in turn. The scheme can run indefinitely, obstensibly giving the impression that each creature has access to its own microprocessor and Alpha program.

Unfortunately, that particular multitasking example is not fully adequate for the proper study of our machine creatures. The main problem is that one Alpha creature is permitted to dominate the entire system through the sometimes lengthy process of finding a random motion code that gets it away from an obstacle. Through that interval, the other Alpha creatures are frozen on the screen, unable to do anything at all while the one creature is struggling with an obstacle. That feature all but destroys the possiblity of building meaningful studies of creature interactions.

The way around the problem is to slice up the fundamental Alpha sequence into smaller phases. One creature can be serviced with one phase of the sequence, its parameters saved, and then the system can go on to another creature. The creatures are still serviced in turn, but it is quite possible that each can be serviced with a different phase of the sliced-up Alpha routine.

This technique allows the individual creatures to be running different phases of the Alpha routine when their turn comes around. They can run completely out of phase with one another; and while one is stuck trying to get away from an obstacle, the others get their time to work at their particular operating phase. The creatures are no longer synchronized to a particular Alpha sequence. The scheme is technically called asynchronous multitasking. It is asynchronous because the creature being serviced can be executing a section of the Alpha routine that is entirely different from the section to be executed by the others. It is a multitasking operation in the sense that each creature is treated as one having its own programming.

THE GENERAL FLOWCHART

The general flowchart for the MULTIPLE ALPHA DEMO is shown here as Fig. 6-1. It is a fundamental Alpha flowchart that is expanded to incorporate asynchronous multitasking for two Alpha creatures.

The scheme calls for assigning a value of 1 or 2 to a creature-number variable, CN. Whenever CN is set to 1, the system services creature number 1; and setting CN to 2 causes the system to service creature number 2.

The fundamental Alpha sequence is divided into two phases, phase 1 and phase 2. When a creature is to execute phase 1, the system fetches a new random motion code for it, and sets it up for running phase 2.

Phase 2 does the search ahead routine. If the path ahead is clear, the creature is moved to its new position and its phase is set to phase 2 again. But if the path ahead is obstructed, the creature is set up to execute phase 1 when its turn comes around again.

Now, the flowchart begins with the usual initialization routines, doing things such as initializing the positions of the creatures, drawing the border figure, and generally getting things ready for running the system.

The final initialization step sets both creatures for doing a phase-1 routine and establishes the fact that creature number 1 is the first to be serviced.

According to the flowchart, phase-1 is executed for that creature as long as its own phase variable is equal to 1. That means FETCH NEW MOTION CODE FOR CN (the creature being ser-

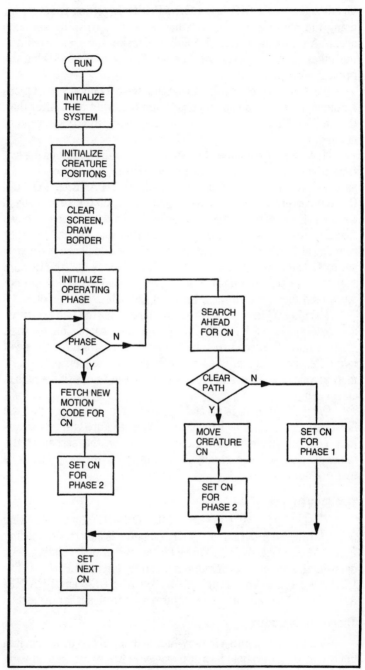

Fig. 6-1. General flowchart for MULTIPLE ALPHA DEMO.

viced) and doing a SET CN FOR PHASE 2 (getting it set up for doing the phase-2 operations when it is its turn to be serviced again.) After doing that, SET NEXT CN makes the system point to the other creature—creature number 2, if you are following the present example.

If creature number 2 is still set for phase-1 operations, it picks a random motion code and its phase number is set to 2. After that, the SET NEXT CN operation sets up the system to service creature number 1.

Now, creature number 1 was set for phase-2 operations the last time it was serviced. That means the PHASE 1 conditional is not satisfied, and the system branches to SEARCH AHEAD FOR CN (let the current creature, creature number 1, do the search ahead routine). If the path for that creature is clear, the flowchart shows that the creature is moved to its next position and its phase number remains at 2. But if it encounters an obstacle, its phase number is set to 1. The implication of the latter operation is that the random motion code selected during an earlier phase-1 operation did not work, and the creature must be set up to select another one.

The general idea is that the system services the two creatures alternately. The SET NEXT CN operation is responsible for that. Furthermore, the creature being serviced can work through one of two different phases of the fundamental Alpha sequence; the new motion code sequence, and the search ahead and move (if the path is clear) sequence.

Once the system is up and running, there is no way that the flowchart can tell you which phase a given creature will be executing. That all depends on what it is doing on the screen at the moment. You will see, though, that the computer keeps track of matters quite nicely.

TRS-80 VERSION

The listing for MULTIPLE ALPHA DEMO is shown as Listing 6-1. Getting the program into your computer is a matter of loading FUNDAMENTAL ALPHA DEMO from tape or disk (Listing 3-1), deleting the mainline programming, and typing in ALPHA MAIN-LINE, V.4 (lines 10 through 210). The BORDER and SEARCH AHEAD routines are identical to those used in all earlier projects.

Theory of Operation

Before getting into a line-by-line analysis of this program, it is important to understand how it uses some newly introduced variables, including a 2-dimensional array.

Listing 6-1. TRS-80 Listing for MULTIPLE ALPHA DEMO.

```
10 REM   MULTIPLE ALPHA DEMO
15 REM      TRS-80
20 REM
25 REM
100 REM ** ALPHA MAINLINE, V.4—TRS-80 **
105 DIM AC(2,8)
110 AC(1,8)=42:AC(2,8)=37
115 CLS:GOSUB 1000
120 FOR  CN=1 TO 2:AC(CN,2)=15576+RND(5)−3+64
    *(RND(5)−3):NEXT
125 IF AC(1,2)=AC(2,2) THEN 120
130 AC(1,1)=1:AC(2,1)=1:CN=1
135 ON AC(CN,1) GOTO 150,165
140 IF CN=1 THEN CN=2 ELSE CN=1
145 GOTO 135
150 FOR    N=4    TO    5:AC(CN,N)=RND(5)−
    3:NEXT N
155 IF AC(CN,4)=0 AND AC(CN,5)=0 THEN 150
160 AC(CN,1)=2:GOTO 140
165 CI=AC(CN,4):CJ=AC(CN,5):CP=AC(CN,2)
170 GOSUB 2000
175 IF NOT(CX=32 AND CY=32) THEN AC(CN,1)=1:GOTO
    195
180 POKE CP, 32
185 CP=NP:POKE CP,AC(CN,8)
190 AC(CN,1)=2
195 AC(CN,2)=CP:AC(CN,4)=CI:AC(CN,5)=CJ
200 GOTO 140
205 REM
210 REM
1000 REM ** BORDER, V.1—TRS-80 **
1005 F0=15360:F1=15423:F2=16128:F3=16191
1010 FOR N=F0 TO F1:POKE N,176:NEXT N
1015 FOR N=F2 TO F3:POKE N,131:NEXT N
1020 FOR N=F0 TO F2 STEP 64:POKE N,170:NEXT
1025 FOR N=F1 TO F3 STEP 64:POKE N,149:NEXT
1030 POKE F0,160:POKE F1,144:POKE F2,130:POKE
    F3,129
1035 RETURN
1040 REM
1045 REM
```

```
2000 REM ** SEARCH AHEAD, V.1—TRS-80 **
2005 NP=CP:CX=32:CY=32
2010 SI=SGN(CI):SJ=SGN(CJ):AI=ABS(CI):AJ=ABS(CJ)
2015 IF AI=0 THEN 2030 ELSE AI=AI−1
2020 IF SI>0 THEN NP=NP+1 ELSE NP=NP−1
2025 CX=PEEK(NP)
2030 IF AJ=0 THEN 2045 ELSE AJ=AJ−1
2035 IF SJ> 0 THEN NP = NP+64 ELSE NP=NP−64
2040 CY=PEEK(NP)
2045 IF NOT(CX=32 AND CY=32) THEN RETURN
2050 IF AI=0 AND AJ=0 THEN RETURN ELSE GOTO 2015
2055 REM
2060 REM
```

According to the variable list in Table 6-1, variable CN indicates the current creature number, 1 or 2. Whenever CN is set to 1, the system services creature number 1; and when CN is set to 2, the system works with creature number 2. Notice that CN always appears as the first element in a 2 dimensional array, AC.

The 2 dimensional array carries integer values 1 through 8, each value pointing to a particular Alpha variable. When CN is equal

Table 6-1. TRS-80 Variable List for MULTIPLE ALPHA DEMO.

CN	Current creature number (1 or 2)
AC(CN,1)	Alpha phase number for creature CN
AC(CN,2)	CP value for creature CN
AC(CN,3)	NP value for creature CN
AC(CN,4)	CI value for creature CN
AC(CN,5)	CJ value for creature CN
AC(CN,6)	CX value for creature CN
AC(CN,7)	CY value for creature CN
AC(CN,8)	Graphic code number for creature CN
CP	Current creature position on the screen
NP	Next creature position
CI	Horizontal component of the motion code
CJ	Vertical component of the motion code
CX	Horizontal component of the contact code
CY	Vertical component of the contact code
SI	Sign value of CI
SJ	Sign value of CJ
AI	Absolute value of CI
AJ	Absolute value of CJ
N	General purpose numerical value
F0	Upper-left corner of the border figure
F1	Upper-right corner of the border figure
F2	Lower-left corner of the border figure
F3	Lower-right corner of the border figure

to 1, the array points to the variables for creature number 1; and when CN is 2, the same array applies to the variables for creature number 2.

For example, AC (1,1) points to the phase number for creature number 1, while AC(2,1) points to the phase number for creature number 2. By the same token, AC(1,5) is the current CJ motion code term for creature 1, and AC(2,8) is the graphic code number for setting the appearance of creature number 2. The second elements in the array are defined for your in the variable listing.

It must be pointed out that the use of a 2 dimensional array is not dictated by the nature of the asynchronous multitasking operations. The array simply makes it easier to make up variable names and, in later experiments, expand the program to deal with any number of creatures without having to make any serious changes in the program listing shown here.

With that bit of introductory information, you are in a better position to study the following line-by-line analysis.

Line 105—Dimension the array.

Line 110—Set the creature graphic codes; an asterisk for creature number 1, and a percent sign for creature number 2.

Line 115—Clear the screen and draw the border figure.

Lines 120-125—Select initial screen positions for both creatures. If they come up the same, do it again.

Line 130—Initialize the creatures for phase-1 operations and for servicing creature number 1 first.

Line 135—Go to the phase to be executed.

Lines 140-145—Switch to service the other creature, and go back to the phase-selection line.

Lines 150 through 160 are phase-1 operations

Lines 150-155—Select a random motion code. If it is the stop code, select again.

Line 160—Set the creature for phase-2 operations, then return to service the other creature.

Lines 165 through 200 are phase-2 operations

Line 165—Get the variables required for running the search ahead subroutine.

Line 170—Call the search ahead subroutine.

Line 175—If there is a contact situation, set the creature for phase-1 operations, and jump to lines 195 and 200.

Lines 180-190—Move the creature and set it for phase-2 operations.

Lines 195-200—Reset the variables for the current creature, and return to service the other creature.

The remaining lines are devoted to the two Alpha subroutines

Lines 1000-1035—Border drawing subroutine.

Lines 2000-2050—Search ahead subroutine.

Running the Program

Upon running this program, you should see two Alpha creatures, an asterisk and a pound-sign figure, at work. They move alternately, and one should be allowed to move while the other is apparently tied up in a contact situation at the border figure.

The routine runs indefinitely. Do a BREAK to end it.

Suggested Modification

The two creatures can be made to leave impenetrable trails by altering line 180 to read:

180 POKE CP,191

You can make a little game of it; betting on which creature will remain free to move for a longer period of time. The first to become trapped, in other words, is the loser.

Refinements of this game will appear in later programs.

APPLESOFT VERSION

The program for MULTIPLE ALPHA DEMO is shown in Listing 6-2. You can get the two main Alpha subroutines into the system by loading FUNDAMENTAL ALPHA DEMO (Listing 3-2) from tape or disk. Delete the mainline portion of that old program, and type in ALPHA MAINLINE, V.4 (lines 10 through 225).

Listing 6-2. Applesoft Listing for MULTIPLE ALPHA DEMO.

```
10 REM   MULTIPLE ALPHA DEMO
15 REM      APPLESOFT
20 REM
25 REM
30 REM
100 REM ** ALPHA MAINLINE, V.4—APPLESOFT **
105 DIM AC(2,10)
110 DEF FN R(R) = INT (5 * RND (1)) - 2
115 AC(1,10) = 9:AC(2,10) = 7
120 FOR CN = 1 TO 2: FOR N = 2 TO 3
125 AC(CN,N) = 20 + FN R(0): NEXT N,CN
130 IF AC(1,2) = AC(2,2) AND AC(1,3) = AC(2,3) THEN 120
```

```
135  HOME : GR : GOSUB 1000
140  AC(1,1) = 1:AC(2,1) = 1:CN = 1
145  ON AC(CN,1) GOTO 160,175
150  IF CN = 1 THEN CN = 2: GOTO 145
155  CN = 1: GOTO 145
160  FOR N = 6 TO 7:AC(CN,N) = FN R(0): NEXT N
165  IF AC(CN,6) = 0 AND AC(CN,7) = 0 THEN 160
170  AC(CN,1) = 2: GOTO 150
175  PX = AC(CN,2):PY = AC(CN,3):CI = AC(CN,6):CJ =
     AC(CN,7)
180  GOSUB 2000
185  IF NOT (CX = 0 AND CY = 0) THEN AC(CN,1) = 1:
     GOTO 210
190  COLOR =0: PLOT PX,PY
195  PX = NX:PY = NY
200  COLOR= AC(CN,10): PLOT PX,PY
205  AC(CN,1) = 2
210  AC(CN,2)  =  PX:AC(CN,3)  =  PY:AC(CN,6)  =
     CI:AC(CN,7) = CJ
215  GOTO 150
220  REM
225  REM
1000 REM ** BORDER,V.1—APPLESOFT **
1005 COLOR= 15
1010 HLIN 0,39 AT 0: HLIN 0,39 AT 36
1015 VLIN 0,36 AT 0: VLIN 0,36 AT 39
1020 RETURN
1025 REM
1030 REM
2000 REM ** SEARCH AHEAD, V.1—APPLESOFT **
2005 NX = PX:NY = PY:CX = 0:CY = 0
2010 SI = SGN (CI):SJ = SGN (CJ):AI = ABS (CI):AJ = ABS
     (CJ)
2015 IF AI = 0 THEN 2040
2020 AI = AI − 1
2025 IF SI > 0 THEN NX = NX + 1: GOTO 2035
2030 NX = NX − 1
2035 CX = SCRN(NX,NY)
2040 IF AJ = 0 THEN 2065
2045 AJ = AJ − 1
2050 IF SJ > 0 THEN NY = NY + 1: GOTO 2060
2055 NY = NY − 1
```

```
2060  CY = SCRN(NX,NY)
2065  IF NOT (CX = 0 AND CY = 0) THEN RETURN
2070  IF AI = 0 AND AJ = 0 THEN RETURN
2075  GOTO 2015
2080  REM
2085  REM
```

Theory of Operation

Before getting into a line-by-line analysis of this program, it is important to understand how it uses some newly introduced variables, including a 2 dimensional array.

According to the variable list in Table 6-2, variable CN indicates the current creature number, 1 or 2. Whenever CN is at 1, the system is servicing creature number 1; and when it is set to 2, the system services creature number 2. The main task of the multitasking part of the program is to alternate the value of CN between 1 and 2.

Notice that the value of CN always appears as the first element in the 2 dimensional array, AC. That array points to all the main Alpha variables for an Alpha creature—the first element points to

Table 6-2. Applesoft Variable List for **MULTIPLE ALPHA DEMO**.

FN R(R)	Random motion code function
CN	Current creature number (1 or 2)
AC(CN,1)	Operating phase number for creature CN
AC(CN,2)	PX value for creature CN
AC(CN,3)	PY value for creature CN
AC(CN,4)	NX value for creature CN
AC(CN,5)	NY value for creature CN
AC(CN,6)	CI value for creature CN
AC(CN,7)	CJ value for creature CN
AC(CN,8)	CX value for creature CN
AC(CN,9)	CY value for creature CN
AC(CN,10)	Color code number for creature CN
PX	Horizontal component of current screen position
PY	Vertical component of current screen position
NX	Horizontal component of next screen position
NY	Vertical component of next screen position
CI	Horizontal component of motion code
CJ	Vertical component of motion code
CX	Horizontal component of contact code
CY	Vertical component of contact code
SI	Sign value of CI
SJ	Sign value of CJ
AI	Absolute value of CI
AJ	Absolute value of CJ
N	General-purpose numerical variable

the creature number, and the second element designates the Alpha variable.

So whenever CN is equal to 1, the array is dealing with variables for creature number 1. AC(1,2), for example, carries the current PX value for creature 1, while AC(2,2) carries PX for creature number 2.

The phase number, 1 or 2, is carried by AC(CN,1). If creature number 1 is running phase 2 of the program, you will find AC(1,1) equal to 2. If creature number 2 is running phase 1 of the project, AC(2,1) will be equal to 1.

It must be pointed out that the use of a 2 dimensional array in this program is not dictated by the nature of the asynchronous multitasking feature. The array simply makes it easier to compose variable names for more than one creature and, in later experiments, modify the scheme to include any number of creatures without having to make any major changes in the programming.

With that bit of introductory information at hand, you are in a better position to study the following line-by-line analysis.

Lines 105-110—Dimension the array and define the motion
code function.

Line 115—Set creature 1 color to orange, creature 2 to dark
blue.

Lines 120-130—Initialize screen positions for both creatures.
If they happen to be the same, do it again.

Line 135—Clear the screen, set the graphics mode, and draw
the border figure.

Line 140—Set both creatures for running phase-1 operations,
and begin by dealing with creature number 1.

Line 145—Do the indicated operating phase.

Lines 150-155—Switch to service the other creature, then go
back to do the indicated operating phase.

Lines 160 through 170 are for phase-1 operations

Lines 160-165—Get a random motion code. If it is the stop
code, get another one.

Line 170—Set the current creature for phase-2 operations, and
go back to work with the next creature.

Lines 175 through 215 are for phase-2 operations

Line 175—Get the variables for doing the search-ahead
routine.

Line 180—Do the search-ahead routine.

Line 185—If there is a contact situation, set for phase-1 operations and jump to line 210 to get out of phase 2 with the

variables intact.

Lines 190-205—Move the creature and set for phase-2 operations.

Lines 210-215—Save the phase-2 variables, and jump back to service the next creature.

The remaining lines are devoted to the Alpha subroutines

Lines 1000-1020—Border drawing subroutine.

Lines 2000-2075—Search ahead subroutine.

Running the Program

Upon running this program, you should see two creatures, one orange and one blue, at work in an Alpha-like fashion. They move alternately, but one should be allowed to move freely while the other is occupied with the task of getting away from a tough contact situation.

The program runs indefinitely. Terminate it by doing a CTRL C from the keyboard.

Suggested Modification

The two creatures can be made to leave impenetrable trails by modifying line 190 to read:

190 COLOR=13:PLOT PX,PY

That will cause both creatures to leave yellow footprints wherever they go.

You can make a little game of it; betting on which creature will remain free to move for a longer period of time. The first to become trapped, in other words, is the loser.

Refinements of this game idea will appear in later programs.

Chapter 7
A Simple Alpha Community

If two simple Alphas seem to get along together rather nicely, how about making a whole little community of them? The basic ideas from the 2 Alpha project in the previous chapter are extended here to let you select up to 10 Alphas. Having to share computer time with so many creatures slows down the action a bit, but you can still appreciate the random hustle and bustle of an Alpha community.

You can also scatter up to 63 randomly positioned obstacles around the screen, giving the Alphas something besides each other to bounce against.

The flowcharts for the current program, SIMPLE ALPHA COMMUNITY, are shown in Fig. 7-1. Most of the mainline programming is concerned with letting you specify a valid number of Alpha creatures and obstacles. Once that is done, the system begins multitasking the creatures.

The creatures are serviced one at a time and in a rotational sequence. If the current creature is to perform the phase-1 operations (fetch a new motion code), it will do that before letting the system cycle to the next creature. The phase-2 operations do the search ahead routine and move the current creature if the path ahead is clear. If that path isn't clear, the creature is set up to do phase-1 operations when its turn comes around again.

The program runs indefinitely, giving you a chance to observe the hustle and bustle of an Alpha community as long as it interests you.

TRS-80 VERSION

The TRS-80 version of SIMPLE ALPHA COMMUNITY is shown in Listing 7-1. You can load an earlier program, such as

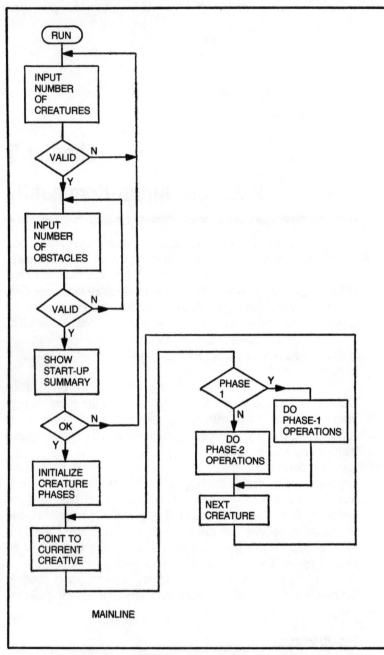

Fig. 7-1. Flowcharts for the SIMPLE ALPHA COMMUNITY: Mainline, Phase-1 operations, and Phase-2 operations.

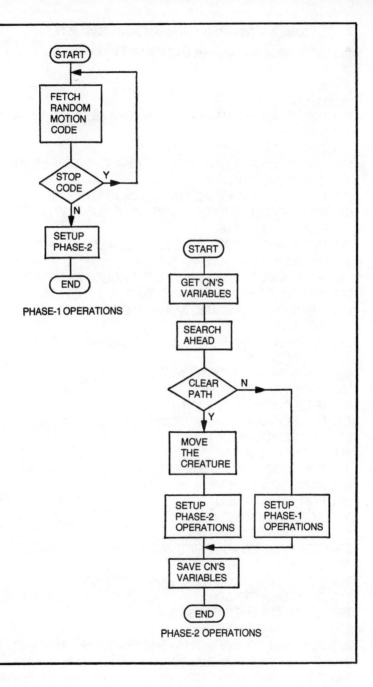

PHASE-1 OPERATIONS

PHASE-2 OPERATIONS

Listing 7-1. TRS-80 Listing for SIMPLE ALPHA COMMUNITY.

```
10 REM    SIMPLE ALPHA COMMUNITY
15 REM        TRS-80
20 REM
25 REM
100 REM ** ALPHA MAINLINE, V.5—TRS-80 **
105 REM
110 CLS
115 PRINT:INPUT "HOW MANY ALPHA CREATURES IN
    THE COMMUNITY (1-10)";CQ
120 CQ=INT(CQ):IF CQ>0 AND CQ<=10 THEN 130
125 PRINT:PRINT "INVALID NUMBER OF ALPHAS . . . TRY
    AGAIN":GOTO 115
130 CLS:PRINT "THERE WILL BE "CQ" ALPHAS IN THE
    COMMUNITY"
135 PRINT:INPUT "HOW MANY OBSTACLES (0-63)";TQ
140 TQ=INT(TQ):IF TQ>=0 AND TQ<= 63 THEN 150
145 PRINT:PRINT "INVALID NUMBER OF OBSTACLES . . .
    TRY AGAIN":GOTO 115
150 CLS:PRINT "THERE WILL BE "CQ" ALPHAS AND "TQ"
    OBSTACLES"
155 PRINT "IN THE COMMUNITY."
160 PRINT:INPUT "OK (Y/N)";S$
165 IF S$< > "Y" THEN 110
170 DIM AC(CQ,8)
175 CLS:GOSUB 1000
180 FOR N=1 TO TQ
185 TP=15360+RND(831):IF PEEK(TP)< >32 THEN 185
190 POKE TP,191:NEXT N
195 FOR CN=1 TO CQ
200 AC(CN,2)=15360+RND(831):IF PEEK(AC(CN,2))<
    >32 THEN 200
205 AC(CN,8)=CN+64:POKE  AC(CN,2),AC(CN,8):NEXT
    CN
210 FOR CN=1 TO CQ:AC(CN,1)=1:NEXT CN
215 FOR CN=1 TO CQ
220 ON AC(CN,1) GOTO 235,250
230 NEXT CN:GOTO 215
235 FOR N=4 TO 5:AC(CN,N)=RND(5)−3:NEXT N
240 IF AC(CN,4)=0 AND AC(CN,5)=0 THEN 235
245 AC(CN,1)=2:GOTO 230
250 CP=AC(CN,2):CI=AC(CN,4):CJ=AC(CN,5)
```

```
255 GOSUB 2000
260 IF NOT (CX=32 AND CY=32) THEN AC(CN,1)=1:
    GOTO 275
265 POKE CP,32
270 CP=NP:POKE CP,AC(CN,8):AC(CN,1)=2
275 AC(CN,2)=CP:AC(CN,4)=CI:AC(CN,5)=CJ
280 GOTO 230
285 REM
290 REM
1000 REM ** BORDER, V.1—TRS-80 **
1005 F0=15360:F1=15423:F2=16128:F3=16191
1010 FOR N=F0 TO F1:POKE N,176:NEXT N
1015 FOR N=F2 TO F3:POKE N,131:NEXT N
1020 FOR N=F0 TO F2 STEP 64:POKE N,170:NEXT
1025 FOR N=F1 TO F3 STEP 64:POKE N,149:NEXT
1030 POKE F0,160:POKE F1,144:POKE F2,130:POKE
     F3,129
1035 RETURN
1040 REM
1045 REM
2000 REM ** SEARCH AHEAD, V.1–TRS-80 **
2005 NP=CP:CX=32:CY=32
2010 SI=SGN(CI):SJ=SGN(CJ):AI=ABS(CI):AJ=ABS(CJ)
2015 IF AI=0 THEN 2030 ELSE AI=AI−1
2020 IF SI> 0 THEN NP=NP+1 ELSE NP=NP−1
2025 CX=PEEK(NP)
2030 IF AJ=0 THEN 2045 ELSE AJ=AJ−1
2035 IF SJ>0 THEN NP=NP+64 ELSE NP=NP−64
2040 CY=PEEK(NP)
2045 IF NOT(CX=32 AND CY=32) THEN RETURN
2050 IF AI=0 AND AJ=0 THEN RETURN ELSE GOTO 2015
2055 REM
2060 REM
```

FUNDAMENTAL ALPHA DEMO (Listing 3-1) from tape or disk, delete the old mainline and replace it with ALPHA MAINLINE, V.5. See lines 10 through 290.

When you RUN the program, appropriate messages will prompt you to enter the number of Alpha creatures and obstacles. If you want to see a lot of Alphas at work without complicating matters with the obstacles, simply respond to the HOW MANY OBSTACLES (0-63)? message with a xero.

The creatures appear as alphabetical characters. Creature number 1 is an *A*, number 2 is a *B*, creature 3 is a *C*, and so on. As the system rotates its service to each of the creatures, you will see them responding in alphabetical order.

Incidentally, don't be overly concerned when you find a creature remaining motionless in a corner of the border figure. It might take 10 or 12 tries at random motion codes to get one that works, and that means 10 or 12 cycles through all the creatures before that one begins to move again. Have patience; they will all have their turn at moving when the conditions are right.

Theory of Operation

The variable list for the program is shown in Table 7-1. Use the table in conjunction with the program listing and flowchart while studying the following analysis of the system.

Table 7-1. TRS-80 Variable List for SIMPLE ALPHA COMMUNITY.

CQ	Selected number of Alpha creatures (1-10)
TQ	Selected number of fixed obstacles (0-63)
N	General-purpose numerical variable
S$	General-purpose string variable
TP	Tenative screen position of a fixed obstacle
CN	Current creature number (1 to CQ)
AC(CN,1)	Current operating phase for creature CN
AC(CN,2)	CP for creature CN
AC(CN,3)	NP for creature CN
AC(CN,4)	CI for creature CN
AC(CN,5)	CJ for creature CN
AC(CN,6)	CX for creature CN
AC(CN,7)	CY for creature CN
AC(CN,8)	Graphic character code for creature CN
CP	Current creature position on the screen
NP	Next position for the current creature
CI	Horizontal component of the motion code
CJ	Vertical component of the motion code
CX	Horizontal component of the contact code
CY	Vertical component of the contact code
SI	Sign value of CI
SJ	Sign value of CJ
AI	Absolute value of CI
AJ	Absolute value of CJ
F0	Upper-left corner of border figure
F1	Upper-right corner of border figure
F2	Lower-left corner of border figure
F3	Lower-right corner of border figure

Lines 110-125—User input the number of Alpha creatures to reside in the community. Make sure it is an integer value between 1 and 10. If not, go back to request the input again.

Lines 130-145—User input the number of obstacles to be randomly distributed through the community. Make sure it is an integer value between 0 and 63; if not, go back to try again.

Lines 150-165—Summarize the user's specifications for number of Alphas and obstacles. If that isn't satisfactory, start all over again. But if it's OK, begin the activity.

Lines 170-175—Dimension the creature variables, clear the screen, and draw the border figure.

Lines 180-190—Draw the specified number of obstacles (graphic 191) at random positions. If the screen is not clear at a random point, select another place.

Lines 195-210—Initialize all creature positions at random, unused places on the screen. Set their character codes as alphabetical characters, and initialize all creatures for phase-1 operations.

Lines 215-230—Cycle the creature numbers and jump to the appropriate operating phases for each one.

Lines 235-245—Phase-1 operations (select a valid random motion code).

Lines 250-280—Get the creature's variables and do the search ahead routine. If the path ahead is not clear, leave with the creature setup to do Phase-1 operations. Otherwise, move the creature to its next position and return with the creature set for Phase-2 operations again.

Lines 1000-1035—Border drawing subroutine.

Lines 2000-2050—Search ahead subroutine.

Suggested Modifications

Modify line 265 to read:

265 POKE CP,191.

Then specify 10 Alpha creatures and no obstacles. What do you suppose will happen? If you aren't sure, try it for yourself.

APPLESOFT VERSION

The Applesoft version of SIMPLE ALPHA COMMUNITY is shown here as Listing 7-2. You can load an earlier program, such as

FUNDAMENTAL ALPHA DEMO (Listing 3-2) from tape or disk, delete the old mainline, and replace it with ALPHA MAINLINE, V.5, as shown here. See lines 10 through 355.

Listing 7-2. Applesoft Listing for SIMPLE ALPHA COMMUNITY.

```
10 REM   SIMPLE ALPHA COMMUNITY
20 REM      APPLESOFT
25 REM
30 REM
100 REM ** ALPHA MAINLINE, V.5—APPLESOFT **
105 TEXT : HOME
110 PRINT : PRINT "HOW MANY ALPHA CREATURES"
115 INPUT "IN THE COMMUNITY (1-10)?";CQ
120 CQ = INT (CQ): IF CQ > 0 AND CQ > = 10 THEN 135
125 PRINT: PRINT "INVALID NUMBER OF CREA-
    TURES. . ."
130 PRINT TAB(5);"TRY AGAIN.": GOTO 110
135 HOME : PRINT "THERE WILL BE ";CQ
140 PRINT "CREATURES IN THE COMMUNITY."
145 PRINT : INPUT "HOW MANY OBSTACLES (0-63)?";TQ
150 TQ = INT (TQ):IF TQ > = 0 AND TQ < = 63 THEN 165
155 PRINT: PRINT "INVALID NUMBER OF OBSTA-
    CLES . . ."
160 PRINT TAB(5);"TRY AGAIN.": GOTO 145
165 HOME : PRINT "THERE WILL BE ";CQ;" CREATURES"
170 PRINT "AND" ;TQ;"OBSTACLES";
175 PRINT "IN THE COMMUNITY."
180 PRINT : INPUT "OK(Y/N)?";S$
185 IF S$ < > "Y" THEN 105
190 DIM AC(CQ,10)
195 DEF FN R(R) = INT (5 * RND (1)) — 2
200 HOME : GR : GOSUB 1000
205 COLOR= 15
210 FOR N = 1 TO TQ
215 TX = INT (38 * RND (1)) + 1:TY = INT (35 * RND (1)) + 1
220 IF SCRN(TX,TY) < > 0 THEN 215
225 PLOT TX,TY: NEXT N
230 FOR CN = 1 TO CQ
235 AC(CN,2) = INT (38 * RND (1)) + 1
240 AC(CN,3) = INT (35 * RND (1)) + 1
245 IF SCRN (AC(CN,2),AC(CN,3)) < > 0 THEN 235
250 COLOR = CN: PLOT AC(CN,2),AC(CN,3)
```

```
 255 AC(CN,10) = CN:NEXT CN
 260 FOR CN = 1 TO CQ:AC(CN,1) = 1: NEXT CN
 265 FOR CN = 1 TO CQ
 270 ON AC(CN,1) GOTO 280,295
 275 NEXT CN: GOTO 265
 280 FOR N = 6 TO 7:AC(CN,N) = FN R(0): NEXT N
 285 IF AC(CN,6) = 0 AND AC(CN,7) = 0 THEN 280
 290 AC(CN,1) = 2: GOTO 275
 295 REM
 300 PX = AC(CN,2):PY = AC(CN,3):CI = AC(CN,6):CJ =
     AC(CN,7)
 305 REM
 310 GOSUB 2000
 315 IF NOT (CX = 0 AND CY = 0) THEN AC(CN,1) = 1:
     GOTO 335
 320 COLOR= 0: PLOT PX,PY
 325 PX = NX:PY = NY
 330 COLOR= AC(CN,10): PLOT PX,PY:AC(CN,1) = 2
 335 AC(CN,2) = PX:AC(CN,3) = PY
 340 AC(CN,6) = CI:AC(CN,7) = CJ
 345 GOTO 275
 350 REM
 355 REM
1000 REM ** BORDER,V.1—APPLESOFT **
1005 COLOR= 15
1010 HLIN 0,39 AT 0: HLIN 0,39 AT 36
1015 VLIN 0,36 AT 0: VLIN 0,36 AT 39
1020 RETURN
1025 REM
1030 REM
2000 REM ** SEARCH AHEAD, V.1—APPLESOFT **
2005 NX = PX:NY = PY:CX = 0:CY = 0
2010 SI = SGN (CI):SJ = SGN (CJ):AI = ABS (CI):AJ = ABS
     (CJ)
2015 IF AI = 0 THEN 2040
2020 AI = AI − 1
2025 IF SI > 0 THEN NX = NX + 1: GOTO 2035
2030 NX = NX − 1
2035 CX = SCRN(NX,NY)
2040 IF AJ = 0 THEN 2065
2045 AJ = AJ − 1
2050 IF SJ > 0 THEN NY = NY + 1: GOTO 2060
```

```
2055 NY = NY – 1
2060 CY = SCRN(NX,NY)
2065 IF NOT (CX = 0 AND CY = 0) THEN RETURN
2070 IF AI = 0 AND AJ = 0 THEN RETURN
2075 GOTO 2015
2080 REM
2085 REM
```

When you RUN the program, appropriate messages will prompt you to enter the number of Alpha creatures and obstacles. If you want to see a lot of Alphas at work without complicating their lives with obstacles, simply respond to the HOW MANY OBSTA-CLES (0-63) message with a zero.

Each creature is assigned a different color code number. Creature number 1 gets code 1 (magenta), number 2 gets the code for dark blue, number 3 gets the code for light blue, and so on. The obstacles are all white (color code15).

Left on its own, the program will run indefinitely. Do a CTRL C to terminate it.

Theory of Operation

The variable list for this program is shown here as Table 7-2. Use that table in conjunction with the program listing and flowchart to work your way through the following line-by-line analysis.

Lines 105-130—User input the number of Alpha creatures to reside in the community. Make sure it is an integer value between 1 and 10. If it isn't, print an error message and go back to input another number.

Lines 135-160—User input the number of obstacles. Make sure it is an integer value between 0 and 63. If not, print an error message and go back to try again.

Lines 165-185—Summarize the user's specifications for the number of Alphas and obstacles. If not satisfied, start all over; otherwise, begin the real activity.

Lines 190-200—Dimension the creature variables, clear the screen, set the graphics mode, and draw the usual border figure.

Lines 205-225—Draw the specified number of obstacles at random places on the screen. If a point to be plotted is already occupied, pick another place for it.

Lines 230-260—Initialize the creature positions at random places on the screen. If a spot is occupied, put that

Table 7-2. Applesoft Variable List for SIMPLE ALPHA COMMUNITY.

CQ	Selected number of Alpha creatures (1-10)
TQ	Selected number of fixed obstacles (0-63)
N	General-purpose numerical variable
S$	General-purpose string variable
FN R(R)	Motion code generator function
TX	Horizontal component of an obstacle position
TY	Vertical component of an obstacle position
CN	Current creature number (1-CQ)
AC(CN,1)	Current operating phase for creature CN
AC(CN,2)	PX for creature CN
AC(CN,3)	PY for creature CN
AC(CN,4)	NX for creature CN
AC(CN,5)	NY for creature CN
AC(CN,6)	CI for creature CN
AC(CN,7)	CJ for creature CN
AC(CN,8)	CX for creature CN
AC(CN,9)	CY for creature CN
AC(CN,10)	Color code for creature CN
PX	Horizontal component of creature position
PY	Vertical component of creature position
NX	Horizontal component of new creature position
NY	Vertical component of new creature position
CI	Horizontal component of motion code
CJ	Vertical component of motion code
CX	Horizontal component of contact code
CY	Vertical component of contact code
SI	Sign value of CI
SJ	Sign value of CJ
AI	Absolute value of CI
AJ	Absolute value of CJ

creature somewhere else. Draw the creatures and assign their color codes. Set all creatures for doing phase-1 operations first.

Lines 265-275—Sequence the creature to be serviced, jumping to the appropriate operating phase in each case.

Lines 280-290—Phase-1 operations (selecting a random motion code for the current creature).

Lines 295-345—Phase-2 operations. Get the creature's relevant variables, do the search ahead routine, and move the creature if the path ahead is clear. If the path isn't clear, set for phase-1 operations. Restore variables before going back to service the next creature in line.

Lines 1000-1020—Border drawing subroutine.

Lines 2000-2075—Search ahead subroutine.

Suggested Modifications

If you would like to add some audio to the activity, patch in the following lines:

287 CALL -198

317 POKE -16336,0

Doing that, you will hear a beeping sound every time one of the creatures blunders into something—the border, one of the obstacles, or another creature. The addition at line 317 will cause a clicking sound each time one of the creatures makes a move on the screen.

All that beeping and clicking might drive you crazy, especially if you set the system for 10 creatures and 63 obstacles. But those are merely the sounds of a busy community of Alpha creatures.

Try rewriting line 320 to read:

320 COLOR=13:PLOT PX,PY

Then run with 10 creatures and no obstacles. If you aren't sure what will happen, give it a try.

Chapter 8
Killer Alpha Duel

Chapter 5 introduced the notion of giving Alpha creatures some aggressive fight responses in addition to the usual non-aggressive flight responses. When those creatures chose to use their aggressive mode of behavior, they could put a dent into the border figure or completely destroy any randomly placed "killable thing" within the environment.

Then Chapter 6 dealt with a technique for running more than one Alpha creature at a time. Now, the obvious temptation is to combine the two basic ideas to come up with a situation where two killer Alphas are running around in the same environment. Both are capable of killing the other.

Since both creatures in this experiment have identical response mechanisms, there is no telling in advance which will get to its opposite number first. If you like to bet with even odds, you might find the demonstration enjoyable. To be sure, one of the Alphas will emerge the victor every time.

When you run the program, you will see the usual border figure, 64 passive obstacles scattered randomly around within that environment, and two killer Alpha creatures. The creatures roam around within the environment, responding to contacts with the passive obstacles and border by either striking out at them or running away. When responding aggressively to one of the passive obstacles, it is deleted from the screen, and the creature moves freely through the space thus created. When making an aggressive response to a contact with the border figure, a "dent" appears in the border, but it cannot be deleted. The creature thus remains at the border until it comes up with a flight response that gets it away from the situation.

The real fun begins, however, when the two killer Alphas begin approaching one another. There is no telling exactly how the encounter will be resolved. The creature sensing the mutual contact first has the option of running away or striking out to destroy the other one. If that creature sensing the contact first makes its aggressive response, it will, for certain, kill its opponent. There is a 50-50 chance that will happen. But if the creature sensing the contact first makes a flight response, the outcome is far less predictable. There is even a chance that the creature attempting to escape the situation will be zapped by the other one.

When one of the creatures is killed by the other, the normal program loop opens to print a message stating which creature "won" the encounter. You can resume the program by striking a key, or else you can start all over by terminating the program and RUNning it again from the beginning.

FLOWCHART ANALYSIS

The flowchart in Fig. 8-1 represents the mainline portion of the DUAL KILLER DEMO program. The operations begin with the usual sequence of initialization steps:
clearing the screen, drawing the border figure, initializing the two creatures' screen positions and operating phases, and drawing the passive, or "killable," things.

The remaining part of the mainline flowchart deals with swapping computer time back and forth between the two creatures and directing attention to the appropriate operating phase.

As shown in the flowcharts in Fig. 8-2, the phase-1 operations merely select a random motion code whenever it is needed, the phase-2 operations do the search ahead routine and, if appropriate, moves the creature to a new position on the screen, and the phase-3 operations deal with the matter of killing (or not killing) an obstacle in the creature's path.

At any given moment, one of the two creatures is being serviced in one of the three possible operating phases.

The phase-1 block diagram is identical to the phase-1 diagrams for all previous multi-creature programs. There is little need to describe it again.

The phase-2 block diagram is nearly identical to its earlier versions. In this case, however, it sets up the creature for doing phase-3 operations (instead of phase-1) when it finds that the path ahead is not clear. The idea is to give the creature a chance to select a kill response to the encounter.

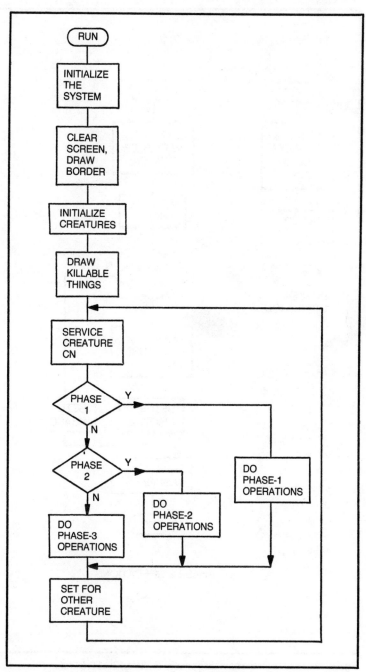

Fig. 8-1. Flowchart for the mainline portion of DUAL KILLER DEMO.

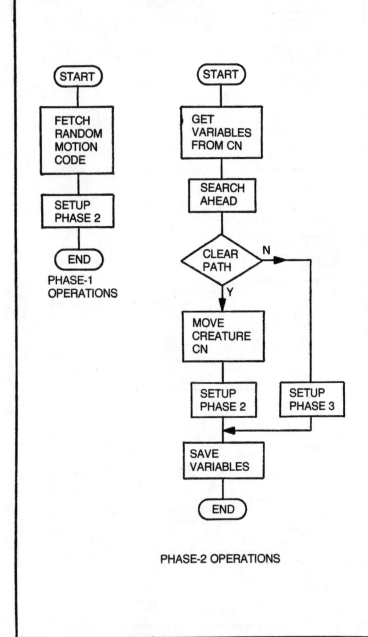

Fig. 8-2. Flowcharts for the operating phases of DUAL KILLER DEMO. Phase-1 for new motion code, Phase-2 for search ahead and move, Phase-3 for kill.

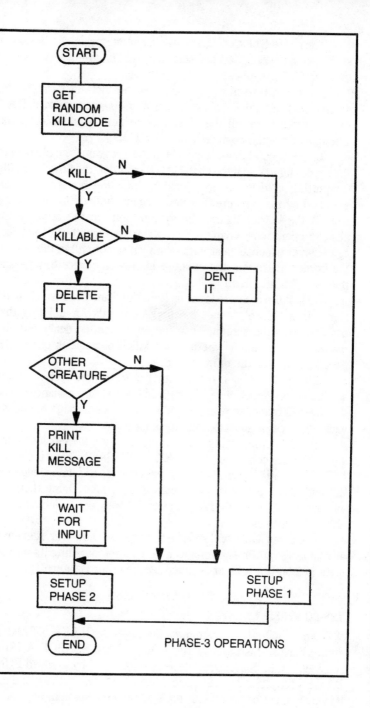

PHASE-3 OPERATIONS

91

The phase-3 block diagram calls for some special discussion. It starts out in the usual fashion, selecting a kill or no-kill response—a random, 50-50 response.

If the creature is not to "kill" the obstacle in its path, the system sets up for doing phase-1 operations on the next pass. But if the response is to kill the obstacle, the next question concerns whether or not the obstacle is a killable one.

The only non-killable obstacle in this program is an element of the border figure. So if the obstacle is the border, the flowchart calls for putting a "dent" in it—signalling that the border has been smacked by the creature, but never really "killed."After taking a shot at the border figure, the system sets up the creature for phase-2 operations, giving it a chance to see whether or not that aggressive response cleared the path. (It never will in the case of the border figure, but the creature is given a chance to try—and then see that it failed.)

Now, if the creature is set up for a "kill" and the obstacle in its sights is a "killable" one, the flowchart calls for deleting that obstacle from the screen. Then the next question deals with the matter of determining whether that killed obstacle is one of the passive things or the other creature.

If the killed thing is not the other creature, the system simply sets up phase-2 operations. That gives the creature a chance to see that the kill response worked, and it will move through the newly vacated space on the next multitasking cycle.

But if the killed thing is the other creature, the block diagram shows that the computer prints a KILL MESSAGE. Then it does an INPUT operation, waiting for the human user to acknowledge the kill and strike a key to get things going again. Doing that, the victorious creature will trample over the body of its victim and go about its business.

The killed Alpha will soon be resurrected, however. It eventually appears on the screen again, and begins pursuing its normal activities until it kills or is killed by the other creature again.

TRS-80 VERSION

The TRS-80 programming for DUAL KILLER DEMO is shown here as Listing 8-1. The BORDER and SEARCH AHEAD routines can be loaded from tape or disk if you have saved FUN-DAMENTAL ALPHA DEMO in that fashion. The entire mainline, however, must be typed into the system from scratch.

Listing 8-1. TRS-80 Programming for DUAL KILLER DEMO.

```
10 REM   DUAL KILLER DEMO
15 REM      TRS-80
20 REM
25 REM
100 REM ** ALPHA MAINLINE, V.6—TRS-80 **
105 DIM AC(2,8)
110 AC(1,8)=42:AC(2,8)=37
115 CLS:GOSUB 1000
120 FOR CN=1 TO 2
125 AC(CN,2)=15360+RND(831):IF PEEK(AC(CN,2))< >
    32 THEN 125
130 POKE AC(CN,2),AC(CN,8):AC(CN,1)=1:NEXT CN
135 FOR N=0 TO 63
140 TP=15360+RND(831):IF PEEK(TP)<> 32 THEN 140
145 POKE TP,191:NEXT N
150 FOR CN=1 TO 2
155 ON AC(CN,1) GOTO 165,180,210
160 NEXT CN:GOTO 150
165 FOR N=4 TO 5:AC(CN,N)=RND(5)−3:NEXT N
170 IF AC(CN,4)=0 AND AC(CN,5)=0 THEN 165
175 AC(CN,1)=2:GOTO 160
180 CP=AC(CN,2):CI=AC(CN,4):CJ=AC(CN,5)
185 GOSUB 2000
190 IF NOT (CX=32 AND CY=32) THEN  AC(CN,1)=3:
    GOTO 205
195 POKE CP,32
200 CP=NP:POKE CP,AC(CN,8):AC(CN,1)=2
205 AC(CN,2)=CP:AC(CN,3)=NP:GOTO 160
210 KC=RND(2)−1:IF KC=0 THEN AC(CN,1)=1:GOTO 160
215 PP=PEEK(AC(CN,3))
220 IF  PP>=129  AND  PP<= 176  THEN  POKE
    AC(CN,3),153:GOTO 230
225 POKE AC(CN,3),32
230 IF NOT(PP=AC(1,8) OR PP=AC(2,8)) THEN 250
235 PRINT @ 896,CHR$(AC(CN,8));"JUST  KILLED";
    CHR$(PP),
240 INPUT S$
245 PRINT @ 896,STRING$(32,32)
250 AC(CN,1)=2:GOTO 160
255 REM
260 REM
```

```
1000  REM ** BORDER, V.1—TRS-80 **
1005  F0=15360:F1=15423:F2=16128:F3=16191
1010  FOR N=F0 TO F1:POKE N,176:NEXT N
1015  FOR N=F2 TO F3:POKE N,131:NEXT N
1020  FOR N=F0 TO F2 STEP 64:POKE N,170:NEXT
1025  FOR N=F1 TO F3 STEP 64:POKE N,149:NEXT
1030  POKE F0,160:POKE F1,144:POKE F2,130:POKE
      F3,129
1035  RETURN
1040  REM
1045  REM
2000  REM ** SEARCH AHEAD, V.1—TRS-80 **
2005  NP=CP:CX=32:CY=32
2010  SI=SGN(CI):SJ=SGN(CJ):AI=ABS(CI):AJ=ABS(CJ)
2015  IF AI=0 THEN 2030 ELSE AI=AI−1
2020  IF SI>0 THEN NP=NP+1 ELSE NP=NP−1
2025  CX=PEEK(NP)
2030  IF AJ=0 THEN 2045 ELSE AJ=AJ−1
2035  IF SJ>0 THEN NP=NP+64 ELSE NP=NP−64
2040  CY=PEEK(NP)
2045  IF NOT(CX=32 AND CY=32) THEN RETURN
2050  IF AI=0 AND AJ=0 THEN RETURN ELSE GOTO 2015
2055  REM
2060  REM
```

Theory of Operation

Use the flowcharts in Figs. 8-1 and 8-2 and the summary of variables in Table 8-1 as guides for working through the following line-by-line analysis of DUAL KILLER DEMO.

Lines 105-110—Dimension the array, specify creature 1 as an asterisk (graphic 42) and creature 2 as a percent sign (graphic 37).

Line 115—Clear the screen and draw the border figure.

Lines 120-130—Initialize the random positions for the two creatures, and draw them on the screen. Make sure they don't overlap one another. Set both for starting with phase-1 operations.

Lines 135-145—Select random, non-overlapping positions for the killable obstacles (graphic 191). Draw them.

Lines 150-160—Select the creature to be serviced, calling upon the appropriate phase to be executed. Alternate the creature to be serviced after doing each phase.

Table 8-1. TRS-80 Listing for DUAL KILLER DEMO.

CN	Creature currently being serviced (1 or 2)
AC(CN,1)	Operating phase for creature CN (1-3)
AC(CN,2)	CP for creature CN
AC(CN,3)	NP for creature CN
AC(CN,4)	CI for creature CN
AC(CN,5)	CJ for creature CN
AC(CN,6)	CX for creature CN
AC(CN,7)	CY for creature CN
AC(CN,8)	Graphic code for creature CN
CP	Current screen position
NP	Next screen position
CI	Horizontal component of motion code
CJ	Vertical component of motion code
CX	Horizontal component of contact code
CY	Vertical component of contact code
SI	Sign value of CI
SJ	Sign value of CJ
AI	Absolute value of CI
AJ	Absolute value of CJ
TP	Screen position of a killable thing
N	General-purpose numerical variable
S$	General-purpose string variable
PP	Graphic code for an object about to be killed
KC	Kill code (0 for no-kill, 1 for kill)
F0	Upper-left corner of the border figure
F1	Upper-right corner of the border figure
F2	Lower-left corner of the border figure
F3	Lower-right corner of the border figure

Lines 165-175—Do phase-1 operations. Leave with the creature set for doing phase-2 operations.

Lines 180-205—Do phase-2 operations. Search ahead. If there is contact, set for phase-3 operations; otherwise, set the current creature for doing phase-2 operations again.

Lines 210-250—Do phase-3 operations. Get a random kill code. If it means don't kill, return with a setup for doing phase-1 operations. Otherwise, kill or "dent" the obstacle. Interrupt the program if the other creature is killed. Return to phase-2 operations if the kill response is carried out.

Lines 1000-1035—Border drawing subroutine.

Lines 2000-2050—Search ahead routine.

Running the Program

The primary purpose of this program is to show how the TRS-80 can multiplex the function of two killer Alpha creatures. To be sure, one creature will ultimately kill the other.

The chances of selecting the victor in this arena of combat are strictly 50-50. It can be used as a two-player game of chance; it is something a bit more involved and exciting than simply tossing a coin.

The loser in the battle generally ends up in that predicament because it has become tangled up in a contact situation while its opponent is running free. So after a kill takes place and you respond by striking the ENTER key, the vanquished creature might not appear on the screen again for several phase cycles—not until it finds its way out of the contact situation that spelled its doom in the first place. Rarely will the victor hang around to strike at its opponent the moment it is resurrected.

APPLESOFT VERSION

The Applesoft programming for DUAL KILLER DEMO is shown in Listing 8-2. The BORDER and SEARCH AHEAD routines can be loaded from tape or disk if you have saved FUNDAMENTAL ALPHA DEMO as suggested. The entire mainline, however, must be typed into the system from scratch.

Listing 8-2. Applesoft Programming for DUAL KILLER DEMO.

```
 10 REM   DUAL KILLER DEMO
 20 REM      APPLESOFT
 25 REM
 30 REM
100 REM ** ALPHA MAINLINE, V.6—APPLESOFT **
105 DIM AC(2,10)
110 DEF FN R(R) = INT (5 * RND (1)) − 2
115 DEF FN P(P) = (INT (P * RND (1)) + 1
120 AC(1,10) = 9:AC(2,10) = 7
125 HOME : GR : GOSUB 1000
130 FOR CN = 1 TO 2
135 AC(CN,2) = FN P(38):AC(CN,3) = FN P(35)
140 IF SCRN( AC(CN,2),AC(CN,3)) < > 0 THEN 135
145 COLOR= AC(CN,10)
150 PLOT AC(CN,2),AC(CN,3)
155 AC(CN,1) = 1: NEXT CN
160 COLOR= 13: FOR N = 0 TO 63
165 TX = FN P(38):TY = FN P(35)
170 IF SCRN(TX,TY) < > 0 THEN 165
175 PLOT TX,TY:NEXT N
180 FOR CN = 1 TO 2
```

```
185  ON AC(CN,1) GOTO 195,215,270
190  NEXT CN: GOTO 180
195  FOR N = 6 To 7
200  AC(CN,N) = FN R(0): NEXT N
205  IF AC(CN,6) = 0 AND AC(CN,7) = 0 THEN 195
210  AC(CN,1) = 2: GOTO 190
215  PX = AC(CN,2):PY = AC(CN,3)
220  CI = AC (CN,6):CJ = AC(CN,7)
225  GOSUB 2000
230  IF NOT (CX = 0 AND CY = 0) THEN AC(CN,1) = 3:
     GOTO 255
235  COLOR= 0: PLOT PX,PY
240  PX = NX:PY = NY
245  COLOR= AC(CN,10): PLOT PX,PY
250  AC(CN,1) = 2
255  AC(CN,2) = PX:AC(CN,3) = PY
260  AC(CN,4) = NX:AC(CN,5) = NY
265  GOTO 190
270  KC = INT (RND (1) + .5)
275  IF KC = 0 THEN AC(CN,1) = 1: GOTO 190
280  PP = SCRN(AC(CN,4),AC(CN,5))
285  IF PP < 14 THEN 300
290  COLOR= 14: PLOT AC(CN,4),AC(CN,5)
295  GOTO 330
300  COLOR= 0: PLOT AC(CN,4),AC(CN,5)
305  IF NOT (PP = AC(1,10) OR PP = AC(2,10)) THEN 330
310  IF PP = 9 THEN S$ = "ORANGE":T$ = "BLUE": GOTO
     320
315  S$ = "BLUE":T$ = "ORANGE"
320  HOME : PRINT T$; "HAS JUST KILLED";S$
325  INPUT S$: HOME
330  AC(CN,1) = 2: GOTO 190
335  REM
340  REM
1000 REM ** BORDER,V.1—APPLESOFT **
1005 COLOR= 15
1010 HLIN 0,39 AT 0: HLIN 0,39 AT 36
1015 VLIN 0,36 AT 0: VLIN 0,36 AT 39
1020 RETURN
1025 REM
1030 REM
2000 REM ** SEARCH AHEAD, V.1—APPLESOFT **
```

```
2005 NX = PX:NY = PY:CX = 0:CY = 0
2010 SI = SGN (CI):SJ = SGN (CJ):AI = ABS (CI):AJ = ABS
     (CJ)
2015 IF AI = 0 THEN 2040
2020 AI = AI − 1
2025 IF SI > 0 THEN NX = NX + 1: GOTO 2035
2030 NX = NX − 1
2035 CX = SCRN(NX,NY)
2040 IF AJ = 0 THEN 2065
2045 AJ = AJ − 1
2050 IF SJ > 0 THEN NY = NY + 1: GOTO 2060
2055 NY = NY − 1
2060 CY = SCRN(NX,NY)
2065 IF NOT (CX = 0 AND CY = 0) THEN RETURN
2070 IF AI = 0 AND AJ = 0 THEN RETURN
2075 GOTO 2015
2080 REM
2085 REM
```

Theory of Operation

Use the flowcharts in Figs. 8-1 and 8-2, and the summary of variables in Table 8-2 as guides for working your way through the following line-by-line analysis of DUAL KILLER DEMO.

Lines 105-120—Dimension the array, define the functions for selecting a random motion code and random screen position, and set the color codes for the creatures (orange for creature 1 and light blue for creature 2).

Line 125—Clear the screen, set the graphic mode, and draw the border figure.

Lines 130-155—Select different random initial positions for both creatures. Plot their images and set them up for starting with phase-1 operations.

Lines 160-175—Plot the 64 killable obstacles at random, non-overlapping positions on the screen.

Lines 180-190—Select the creature to be serviced, calling on the appropriate phase to be executed. Alternate the creature to be serviced after each phase is done.

Lines 195-210—Phase-1 operations. Select a random motion code and leave with the current creature set for doing phase-2 operations next.

Lines 215-265—Phase-2 operations. Search ahead. If contact occurs, set for phase-3 operations; otherwise, set the current creature for doing phase 2 again.

Lines 270-330—Phase-3 operations. Get a random kill code. If it means "don't kill," return with the creature set for doing phase-1 operations. Otherwise kill, or attempt to kill, the obstacle. Interrupt the program if the other creature is killed. In any event, return with the creature set for doing phase-2 operations next.

Lines 1000-1020—Border drawing subroutine.

Lines 2000-2075—Search ahead subroutine.

Running the Program

The primary purpose of this program is to demonstrate how Applesoft BASIC can multiplex the function of two killer Alpha creatures. The fact that one ultimately kills the other makes it something of a game.

Table 8-2. Applesoft Listing for DUAL KILLER DEMO.

FN R(R)	Random motion code function
FN P(P)	Random screen position function
CN	Creature being serviced (1 or 2)
AC(CN,1)	Operating phase for creature CN (1-3)
AC(CN,2)	PX for creature CN
AC(CN,3)	PY for creature CN
AC(CN,4)	NX for creature CN
AC(CN,5)	NY for creature CN
AC(CN,6)	CI for creature CN
AC(CN,7)	CJ for creature CN
AC(CN,8)	CX for creature CN
AC(CN,9)	CY for creature CN
AC(CN,10)	Color code for creature CN
PX	Horizontal component of screen position
PY	Vertical component of screen position
NX	Horizontal component of next screen position
NY	Vertical component of next screen position
CI	Horizontal component of motion code
CJ	Vertical component of motion code
CX	Horizontal component of contact code
CY	Vertical component of contact code
SI	Sign value of CI
SJ	Sign value of CJ
AI	Absolute value of CI
AJ	Absolute value of CJ
TX	Horizontal component of a killable thing position
TY	Vertical component of a killable thing position
N	General-purpose numerical variable
S$	General-purpose string variable
T$	Killer message string variable
KC	Killer code (0 for no-kill, 1 for kill)
PP	Color code of object about to be killed

The chances of selecting the victor in this battle are strictly 50-50. The loser generally ends up in that situation because it has become tangled up in a contact routine while the opponent is still running free. So after a kill takes place and you respond by striking the RETURN key to resume the action, the vanquished creature might not appear on the screen for several operating phases—not until it finds its way out of the contact situation that spelled its doom in the first place. Rarely will the victor hang around to strike at its opponent the moment it is resurrected.

Chapter 9
A Killer Alpha in
a Community of Non-killers

Upon running this program, you will see the screen initialized with one killer Alpha, four non-killer Alphas, and 15 fixed, killable obstacles. As you might suspect, the killer Alpha roams the environment, eventually killing off all the non-killer creatures and wiping out the obstacles. That is one purpose of the project; *it demonstrates that a killer among non-killers will eventually rid the environment of the more docile creatures and fixed obstacles that might fall into its path.*

From a technical viewpoint, the program demonstrates two additional features. First, it shows how creatures with unlike characteristics can be worked into a multitasking scheme. The non-killer Alphas use just two operating phases, while the killer uses three of them.

And second, the program shows how it is possible to build a killer that permanently disables other creatures. In the earlier killer programs, a killed creature is cleared from the screen, but is resurrected with its full range of behavior after it has gotten out of its trapped situation. Here, the killed creatures are permanently wiped out of the picture.

Incidentally, this program marks the end of the initial series of fundamental Alpha creature demonstrations. Alphas will be used in later programs, but it will then be assumed you already understand their essential characteristics on the basis of this series of projects.

FLOWCHART FOR ALPHA COMBO DEMO

The flowcharts for this program, ALPHA COMBO DEMO, are shown in Figs. 9-1 and 9-2. Figure 9-1 shows the overall flow of the

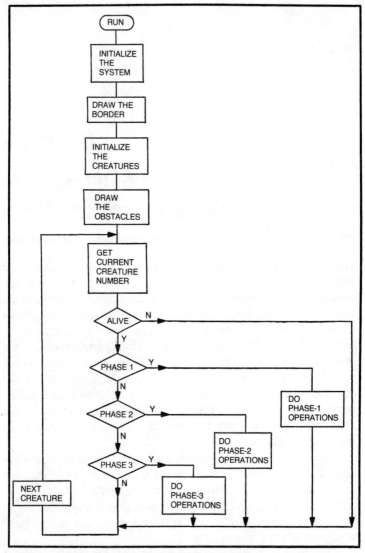

Fig. 9-1. Overall flowchart for ALPHA COMBO DEMO.

program, including the creature-select and phase-select operations. Figure 9-3 shows the three phases of operation in greater detail.

Referring to Fig. 9-1, the program begins in the usual fashion, initializing the system, drawing the border figure, drawing the creatures, and drawing the fixed obstacles onto the screen. The remaining operations in that particular flowchart deal with the matters of selecting the creature to be serviced and applying the appropriate operating phase to it.

The creatures to be serviced are numbered 1 through 5, with creature number 1 being the killer Alpha. Creatures 2 through 5 are the non-killing Alphas. The operations between GET CURRENT CREATURE NUMBER and NEXT creature take place in a cycling fashion, servicing the five creatures in turn, one at a time.

Once a creature number is selected, conditional ALIVE determines whether or not that particular creature has been killed at some earlier time during the course of the experiment. If it has been killed, the system jumps down to select the next creature in line. Killed creatures are simply not serviced at all.

But if it turns out that the creature being serviced at the moment is a live one, the next operation is to determine which operating phase it should undergo. If it is supposed to undergo phase-1 operations (selecting a random motion code) that is done, and the system selects the next creature in line. Phase-2 and phase-3 operations are selected and executed in a similar fashion. Phase-2 operations do the search ahead routine and, if the path ahead is found to be clear, it moves the creature to its next location on the screen. Phase-3 operations are performed only by the killer creature. Those operations are responsible for the kill or no-kill routines that have already been described in previous killer Alpha projects.

Referring to the phase-1 flowchart in Fig. 9-2A, there is nothing really new about it. It simply finds a valid random motion code for the creature being serviced, and it sets that creature for doing phase-2 operations the next time it is to be serviced.

The phase-2 flowchart includes a KILLER conditional operation that, as you probably suspect, determines if the creature being serviced is the number-1 killer creature. If that is the case, the creature is set for doing phase-3 operations on the next cycle. But if the creature being serviced is *not* the killer, it is set up for phase-1 operations. This is the sequence of steps that allow only creature number 1—the killer creature—to get into the phase-3 routine.

The phase-3 routine illustrated in Fig. 9-2C follows the usual pattern for a kill/no-kill operations. If the creature decides not to kill the obstacles (including other creatures and portions of the border figure), it is set for phase-1 operations; set for picking a random motion code to get it away from the contact situation. But if the killer decides to take a shot at the obstacle, it either "dents" it (if it is an element of the border figure), or wipes it out altogether (if

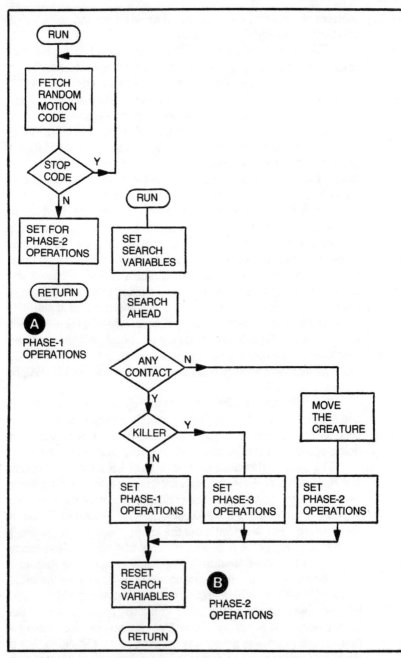

Fig. 9-2. Flowcharts of individual operating phases. (A) Phase-1 operations. (B) Phase-2 operations. (C) Phase-3 operations.

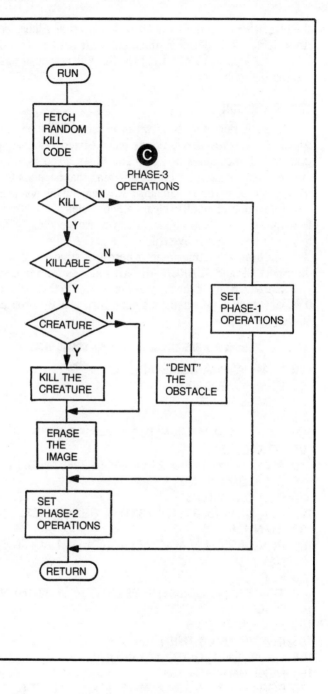

105

the object is one of the fixed obstacles or other Alpha creatures).
After doing a kill operation, the creature is set for phase-2 operations. The idea is to see whether the kill response has indeed
cleared the path ahead.

TRS-80 VERSION

The killer creature is drawn as an asterisk, the four non-killer
Alphas are shown as percent signs, and the fixed obstacles appear as
graphic-191 rectangles of light. The killer wanders through the
environment, sometimes killing anything that happens to get into
its way, and sometimes bouncing away, leaving the obstacle intact.

Eventually, the killer clears all obstacles and other creatures
from the screen. The program, however, runs endlessly, so it is up
to you to terminate it by striking the BREAK key.

The program listing is shown here as Listing 9-1. You can enter
the BORDER and SEARCH AHEAD routines from tape or disk if
you have saved any of the previous programs in that fashion. Doing
that, you can then type in the mainline portion of the program, lines
10 through 265.

Listing 9-1. TRS-80 Listing for ALPHA COMBO DEMO.

```
10 REM    ALPHA COMBO DEMO
15 REM       TRS-80
20 REM
25 REM
100 REM ** ALPHA MAINLINE, V.7—TRS-80 **
105 DIM AC(5,8)
110 AC(1,8)=42:FOR N=2 TO 5:AC(N,8)=37:NEXT N
115 CLS:GOSUB 1000
120 FOR CN=1 TO 5
125 AC(CN,2)=15360+RND(831):IF  PEEK(AC(CN,2))< >
    32 THEN 125
130 POKE AC(CN,2),AC(CN,8):AC(CN,1)=1:AC(CN,6)=1:
    NEXT CN
135 FOR N=0 TO 15
140 TP=15360+RND(831):IF PEEK(TP)< > 32 THEN 140
145 POKE TP,191:NEXT N
150 FOR CN=1 TO 5
155 IF AC(CN,6)=0 THEN 165
160 ON AC(CN,1) GOTO 170,185,220
165 NEXT CN:GOTO 150
170 FOR N=4 TO 5:AC(CN,N)=RND(5)-3:NEXT N
```

106

```
175 IF AC(CN,4)=0 AND AC(CN,5)=0 THEN 170
180 AC(CN,1)=2:GOTO 165
185 CP=AC(CN,2):CI=AC(CN,4):CJ=AC(CN,5)
190 GOSUB 2000
195 IF CX=32 AND CY=32 THEN 210
200 IF CN=1 THEN AC(CN,1)=3 ELSE AC(CN,1)=1
205 GOTO 215
210 POKE CP,32:CP=NP:POKE CP,AC(CN,8):AC(CN,1)=2
215 AC(CN,2)=CP:AC(CN,3)=NP:GOTO 165
220 KC=RND(2)−1:IF KC=0 THEN AC(CN,1)=1:GOTO 165
225 PP=PEEK(AC(CN,3))
230 IF PP>129 AND PP<=176 THEN POKE AC(CN,3),
    153:GOTO 255
235 FOR N=2 TO 5
240 IF AC(CN,3)=AC(N,2) THEN AC(N,6)=0:GOTO 250
245 NEXT N
250 POKE AC(CN,3),32
255 AC(CN,1)=2:GOTO 165
260 REM
265 REM
1000 REM ** BORDER, V.1—TRS-80 **
1005 F0=15360:F1=15423:F2=16128:F3=16191
1010 FOR N=F0 TO F1:POKE N,176:NEXT N
1015 FOR N=F2 TO F3:POKE N,131:NEXT N
1020 FOR N=F0 TO F2 STEP 64:POKE N,170:NEXT
1025 FOR N=F1 TO F3 STEP 64:POKE N,149:NEXT
1030 POKE F0,160:POKE F1,144:POKE F2,130:POKE
     F3,129
1035 RETURN
1040 REM
1045 REM
2000 REM ** SEARCH AHEAD, V.1—TRS-80 **
2005 NP=CP:CX=32:CY=32
2010 SI=SGN(CI):SJ=SGN(CJ):AI=ABS(CI):AJ=ABS(CJ)
2015 IF AI=0 THEN 2030 ELSE AI=AI−1
2020 IF SI>0 THEN NP=NP+1 ELSE NP=NP−1
2025 CX=PEEK(NP)
2030 IF AJ=0 THEN 2045 ELSE AJ=AJ−1
2035 IF SJ>0 THEN NP=NP+64 ELSE NP=NP−64
2040 CY=PEEK(NP)
2045 IF NOT(CX=32 AND CY=32) THEN RETURN
2050 IF AI=0 AND AJ=0 THEN RETURN ELSE GOTO 2015
2055 REM
```

The variable list for ALPHA COMBO DEMO is shown in Table 9-1. Use that list in conjunction with Figs. 9-1 and 9-2 as you work through the following analysis of the program listing.

Lines 105-110—Dimension the creature array, and set the creatures' graphic codes.

Line 115—Clear the screen and draw the border figure.

Lines 120-130—Initialize the creature figures at random, non-overlapping places on the screen.

Lines 135-145—Draw the fixed obstacles figures at random, non-overlapping places on the screen.

Lines 150-165—Select the creature to be serviced and direct it to the designated phase of operation.

Lines 170-180—Phase-1 operations.

Lines 185-215—Phase-2 operations.

Lines 220-255—Phase-3 operations.

Lines 1000-1035—Border drawing subroutine.

Lines 2000-2050—Search ahead subroutine.

Table 9-1. TRS-80 Variable List for ALPHA COMBO DEMO.

CN	Creature currently being serviced (1 through 5)
AC(CN,1)	Operating phase for creature CN (1 through 3)
AC(CN,2)	CP for creature CN
AC(CN,3)	NP for creature CN
AC(CN,4)	CI for creature CN
AC(CN,5)	CJ for creature CN
AC(CN,6)	Dead-or-alive code for creature CN (0-dead, 1-alive)
AC(CN,7)	CY for creature CN
AC(CN,8)	Graphic code for creature CN
CP	Current creature screen position
NP	Next screen position
CI	Horizontal component of motion code
CJ	Vertical component of motion code
CX	Horizontal component of contact code
CY	Vertical component of contact code
SI	Sign value of CI
SJ	Sign value of CJ
AI	Absolute value of CI
AJ	Absolute value of CJ
TP	Screen position of an obstacle
N	General-purpose numeric variable
PP	Graphic code for an object about to be killed
KC	Kill code (0 for no-kill, 1 for kill)
F0	Upper-left corner of border figure
F1	Upper-right corner of border figure
F2	Lower-left corner of border figure
F3	Lower-right corner of border figure

APPLESOFT VERSION

The killer creature in this project is bright orange, the four non-killer Alphas are light blue, and the obstacles are yellow. The killer wanders through the environment, sometimes killing anything that happens to get into its way, and sometimes bouncing away, leaving the obstacle intact. Whenever the killer attempts to take a bite out of an element of the border figure, the element turns a sickly green, but remains intact.

The killer eventually clears all obstacles and other creatures from the environment. The program, however, runs endlessly; so it is up to you to terminate it by doing a CTRL C operation at the keyboard.

The program listing is shown here as Listing 9-2. You can enter the usual BORDER and SEARCH AHEAD routines from tape or disk if you have saved any of the earlier programs in that fashion. Doing that, you can then type in the mainline portion of the program, lines 10 through 325.

Listing 9-2. Applesoft Listing for ALPHA COMBO DEMO.

```
 10 REM   ALPHA COMBO DEMO
 20 REM       APPLESOFT
 25 REM
 30 REM
100 REM ** ALPHA MAINLINE, V.7—APPLESOFT **
105 DIM AC(5,10)
110 DEF FN R(R) = INT (5 * RND (1)) − 2
115 DEF FN P(P) = INT (P * RND (1)) + 1
120 AC(1,10) = 9: FOR N = 2 TO 5:AC(N,10) = 7: NEXT N
125 HOME : GR : GOSUB 1000
130 FOR CN = 1 TO 5
135 AC(CN,2) = FN P(38):AC(CN,3) = FN P(35)
140 IF SCRN(AC(CN,2),AC(CN,3)) < > 0 THEN 135
145 COLOR= AC(CN,10)
150 PLOT AC(CN,2),AC(CN,3)
155 AC(CN,1) = 1:AC(CN,8) = 1: NEXT CN
160 COLOR= 13: FOR N = 0 TO 15
165 TX = FN P(38):TY = FN P(35)
170 IF SCRN(TX,TY) < > 0 THEN 165
175 PLOT TX,TY: NEXT N
180 FOR CN = 1 TO 5
185 IF AC(CN,8) = 0 THEN 195
190 ON AC(CN,1) GOTO 200,215,275
```

```
195  NEXT CN: GOTO 180
200  FOR N = 6 TO 7:AC(CN,N) = FN R(0):NEXT N
205  IF AC(CN,6) = 0 AND AC(CN,7) = 0 THEN 200
210  AC(CN,1) = 2: GOTO 195
215  PX = AC(CN,2):PY = AC(CN,3)
220  CI = AC(CN,6):CJ = AC(CN,7)
225  GOSUB 2000
230  IF CN = 0 AND CY = 0 THEN AC(CN,1) = 2: GOTO 245
235  IF CN = 1 THEN AC(CN,1) = 3: GOTO 260
240  AC(CN,1) = 1: GOTO 260
245  COLOR= 0: PLOT PX,PY
250  PX = NX:PY = NY
255  COLOR= AC(CN,10): PLOT PX,PY
260  AC(CN,2) = PX:AC(CN,3) = PY
265  AC(CN,4) = NX:AC(CN,5) = NY
270  GOTO 195
275  KC = INT (RND (1) + .5)
280  IF KC = 0 THEN AC(CN,1) = 1: GOTO 195
285  IF SCRN(AC(CN,4),AC(CN,5)) < 14 THEN 295
290  COLOR= 14: PLOT AC(CN,4),AC(CN,5): GOTO 315
295  FOR N = 2 TO 5
300  IF AC(CN,4) = AC(N,2) AND AC(CN,5) = AC(N,3) THEN
     AC(N,8) = 0
305  NEXT N
310  COLOR= 0: PLOT AC(CN,4),AC(CN,5)
315  AC(CN,1) = 2: GOTO 195
320  REM
325  REM
1000  REM ** BORDER, V.1—APPLESOFT **
1005  COLOR= 15
1010  HLIN 0,39 AT 0: HLIN 0,39 AT 36
1015  VLIN 0,36 AT 0: VLIN 0,36 AT 39
1020  RETURN
1025  REM
1030  REM
2000  REM ** SEARCH AHEAD, V.1—APPLESOFT **
2005  NX = PX:NY = PY:CX = 0:CY = 0
2010  SI = SGN (CI):SJ = SGN (CJ):AI = ABS (CI):AJ = ABS
      (CJ)
2015  IF AI = 0 THEN 2040
2020  AI = AI − 1
2025  IF SI > 0 THEN NX = NX + 1: GOTO 2035
```

```
2030 NX = NX − 1
2035 CX = SCRN(NX,NY)
2040 IF AJ = 0 THEN 2065
2045 AJ = AJ − 1
2050 IF SJ > 0 THEN NY = NY + 1: GOTO 2060
2055 NY = NY − 1
2060 CY = SCRN(NX,NY)
2065 IF NOT (CX = 0 AND CY = 0) THEN RETURN
2070 IF AI = 0 AND AJ = 0 THEN RETURN
2075 GOTO 2015
2080 REM
2085 REM
```

The Applesoft variable list for ALPHA COMBO DEMO is shown in Table 9-2. Use that list in conjunction with Figs. 9-1 and 9-2 as you work through the following analysis of the program listing.

Table 9-2. Applesoft Variable List for ALPHA COMBO DEMO.

FN R(R)	Random motion code function
FN P(P)	Random screen position function
CN	Creature being serviced (1 through 5)
AC(CN,1)	Operating phase for creature CN (1 through 3)
AC(CN,2)	PX for creature CN
AC(CN,3)	PY for creature CN
AC(CN,4)	NX for creature CN
AC(CN,5)	NY for creature CN
AC(CN,6)	CI for creature CN
AC(CN,7)	CJ for creature CN
AC(CN,8)	Dead-or-alive code for creature CN (0-dead, 1-alive)
AC(CN,9)	CY for creature CN
AC(CN,10)	Color code for creature CN
PX	Horizontal component of creature position
PY	Vertical component of creature position
NX	Horizontal component of next position
NY	Vertical component of next position
CI	Horizontal component of motion code
CJ	Vertical component of motion code
CX	Horizontal component of contact code
CY	Vertical component of contact code
SI	Sign value of CI
SJ	Sign value of CJ
AI	Absolute value of CI
AJ	Absolute value of CJ
TX	Horizontal component of obstacle position
TY	Vertical component of obstacle position
N	General-purpose numeric variable
KC	Killer code (0 for no-kill, 1 for kill)
PP	Color code of object about to be killed

Lines 105-115—Dimension the creature array, and define the
functions for getting a random motion code and random
screen postions.

Line 120—Set the color codes for the creatures.

Line 125—Clear the screen, set the graphics mode, and draw
the border figure.

Lines 130-155—Select random, non-overlapping positions for
the creatures; draw them.

Lines 160-175—Draw the 15 yellow, fixed obstacles in random, non-overlapping positons on the screen.

Lines 180-195—Select the creature to be serviced and direct it
to the appropriate operating phase.

Lines 200-210—Phase-1 operations.

Lines 215-270—Phase-2 operations.

Lines 275-315—Phase-3 operations.

Lines 1000-1020—Border drawing subroutine.

Lines 2000-2075—Search ahead subroutine.

Chapter 10
Fundamental Beta Demonstration

The Beta creature introduced in this chapter is different from all the Alphas in one important respect; the Beta can remember previous successful responses and call upon them immediately whenever they are needed at a later time. The difference in creature behavior here is a significant and quite noticeable one.

Upon running the program, you will see the usual border figure and a creature roaming around within it. This particular version makes the creature leave behind a trail that it cannot sense at all. As far as the creature is concerned, the trail is no different from a segment of clear screen.

You will see the creature rebounding from contacts with the border figure. At first, the responses will be purely random, suggesting that an Alpha-like mechanism is at work. But given some time and a number of border-contact situations, the Beta spends less time dealing with contact situations and more time running freely within its environment.

In fact, the most significant feature of the whole demonstration is seeing the Beta creature establish a habit pattern of motion—going through a series of motions that fall into a predictable pattern. That habit pattern of motion is the hallmark of a Beta creature dealing with a static environment.

There is no telling how long it will take a Beta to establish a habit pattern, and there is no telling how simple or complex its pattern will be. But there will be a habit pattern of motion that reflects the workable responses that have grown up in the Beta's working memory.

During the initial process of exploring its environment and establishing a habit pattern of motion, the Beta will leave random trails all over the place. To rid the screen of that confusion, simply strike the ENTER or RETURN key. You will see the screen clear, the border figure redrawn, and the Beta creature drawing a new trail pattern.

This screen-clearing feature does not affect the Beta programming at all. The creature retains its motion code and screen position, and there is absolutely no change in the content of the Beta memory. It is simply a convenience for the user, and it lets you view the habit pattern of motion without the clutter of trails left by the initial learning phases of the Beta's life.

It must be emphasized that the Beta creature is programming its own responses as it goes along. The mechanism is adaptive and self-correcting, and in a later experiment, you will have a chance to observe the Beta's behavior in an environment that is far more complicated and dynamic than this one. But for now, it is sufficient to note how the Beta learns its way around the environment without using a lot of elaborate sensory mechanisms that typify more conventional approaches to a similar situation. Just look for that habit pattern of motion.

FLOWCHART ANALYSIS

The general flowchart for FUNDAMENTAL BETA DEMO is shown here as Fig. 10-1. It is divided into two sections for clarity; section B is really just an expanded version of the DO BETA ROUTINE operation shown in section A.

Section A in Fig. 10-1 represents the operations for initializing the system and running the creature as long as it is not sensing a contact. There are basically three parts to it; initialize things, run the creature, and see about clearing the trail from the screen.

The initialization phase is rather straightforward. INITIALIZE BETA SYSTEM dimensions the Beta's memory array, and sets the memory so that all responses are the stop-code response—an invalid one in the context of our work here. Finding that stop code in a memory location suggests that the situation that called up that memory location has never been encountered or resolved successfully.

The INITIALIZE CREATURE and CLEAR AND DRAW BORDER operations are vitually identical to those used in earlier Alpha programs.

The next major part of section A does the search ahead operation and moves the creature if the next spot on the screen is clear. That is generally the same clear-path operations used by all the previous Alpha programs. The only difference is the action taken in response to finding the path is not clear. An Alpha would deal with the situation by picking up a random motion code and trying it out. A Beta, however, deals with a contact situation by shifting over to the Beta memory routine—the one diagrammed here in section B.

Before looking at the Beta routine in more detail, it is necessary to complete the analysis of section A.

Whether the PATH CLEAR conditional in section A calls the Beta routine or not, the next step is to move the creature to its next position on the screen. The system as it is presented here will always return from the Beta routine with a successful solution to a contact situation.

Finally, there is the CLEAR TRAIL conditional. It is worked into the program in such a way that it does not normally interrupt the ongoing program. The operation simply scans the keyboard. If there is no key depression, the program loops back to SEARCH AHEAD to continue the action without interruption. But if the CLEAR TRAIL operation finds that a key is depressed, it loops the program back to CLEAR AND DRAW BORDER. The creature and its Beta memory are unaffected by the trail-clearing operation. The only effect is that of clearing away all previously drawn trails, giving the creature a fresh start with regard to its "footprints."

The primary objective of the Beta routine in section B of Fig. 10-1 is to come up with a workable response to a contact situation. Equally important is the notion that the response should come from the Beta memory—it should be a response that has been tried before and proven to be a successful one. But if it turns out that the Beta creature has never encountered a particular situation, or it has encountered it but never resolved it successfully, the memory is of no use, and the creature is forced to resort to a more primitive form of Alpha reflex behavior. In any event, the system leaves the Beta routine with a new motion code that will lead the creature away from the contact situation that called the Beta routine in the first place.

The Beta routine opens with an operation that is labeled SET BETA VARIABLES. The idea here is to transform the current motion code from a pair of integers between -2 and 2 into a pair of positive integers between 0 and 4. That is accomplished by simply adding 2 to the CI and CJ elements of the creature's current motion code. The reason for that conversion is that elements of an array—

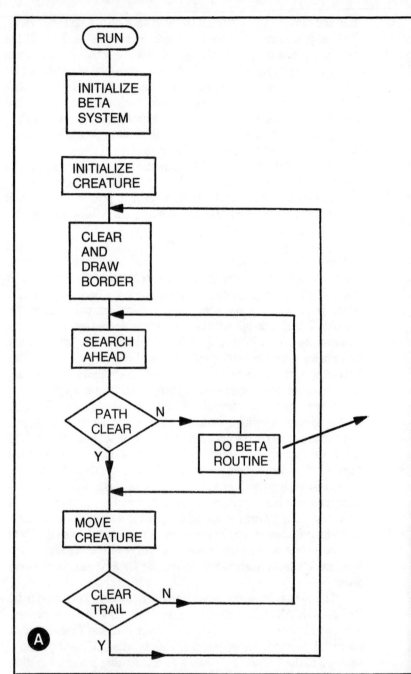

Fig. 10-1. General flowchart for FUNDAMENTAL BETA DEMO.

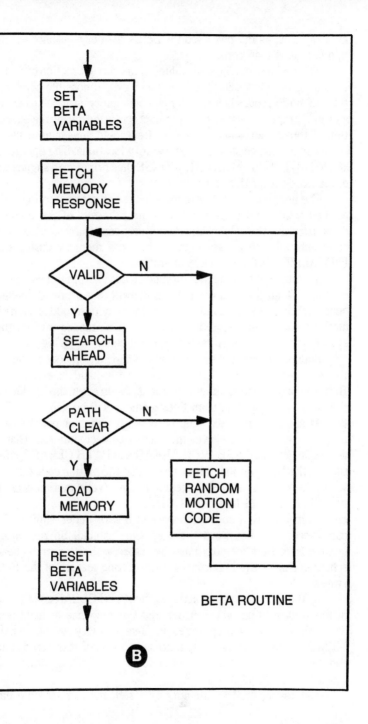

BETA ROUTINE

B

117

an array such as the one used for Beta's memory—cannot accept numbers less than zero.

The revised, or adjusted, values of the current motion code are then used for addressing the Beta memory. All possible combinations of motion codes have an element of memory assigned to them, and an appropriate response to a contact occurring during the execution of those addressing motion codes should appear as data—a response motion code—in those memory locations. The operation labeled FETCH MEMORY RESPONSE thus brings up a suggested motion code from Beta memory.

The next step is to determine whether or not the motion code fetched from memory is valid. For the purposes of the present demonstration, the only invalid motion response is a stop code—the code entered into all sections of the Beta memory during the INITIALIZE BETA SYSTEM operation.

If it turns out that the motion code picked up from Beta memory is invalid (a stop code), the system resorts to a bit of Alpha-like behavior and picks up a randomly generated motion code. That new motion code is then tested for validity. If it, too, is invalid, the system picks up another random motion code.

Sooner or later, the system finds a valid motion-code response to the current contact situation. The more first-hand experience the Beta has undergone in its environment, the greater the likelihood the response picked up from Beta memory will be valid.

At any rate, the next step is to see whether or not the new motion code actually resolves the current contact situation. That is accomplished via the SEARCH AHEAD and PATH CLEAR operations in the Beta routine. If it turns out that the motion code doesn't work, the system resorts to picking another valid motion code at FETCH RANDOM MOTION CODE.

Even a motion code that worked before under similar circumstances will not work the next time around. So responses fetched from Beta memory must be tested with the search ahead scheme. This is the important self-correcting feature of the Beta system.

By the time the system satisfies the PATH CLEAR conditional in the Beta routine, you can bet that the response at hand is a workable one. It is then saved in Beta memory at the LOAD MEMORY operation. At what address is it saved? It is saved at an address determined by the motion code that existed the moment the contact situation occurred.

Addressing in Beta memory is a reflection of sensible environmental conditions that exist when a contact occurs. The data in those address locations is either an invalid stop code (a response never tried), or a motion code response that represents a solution to the situation that worked at some previous time.

The final operation in the Beta routine resets the motion codes back to their standard negative and positive format.

TRS-80 VERSION

The programming for the TRS-80 version of FUNDAMEN-TAL BETA DEMO is shown in Listing 10-1. The entire listing can be entered from scratch at the keyboard, or you can save yourself some time by loading FUNDAMENTAL ALPHA DEMO from tape or disk, and making the following modifications:

● Delete the old mainline and replace it with BETA MAIN-LINE, V.1

● Modify lines 2000 and 2045 of the SEARCH AHEAD sub-routine to conform to the version shown here.

Listing 10-1. TRS-80 Program for FUNDAMENTAL BETA DEMO.

```
10 REM   FUNDAMENTAL BETA DEMO
15 REM       TRS-80
20 REM
25 REM
100 REM ** BETA MAINLINE, V.1—TRS-80 **
105 DIM M(4,4,2)
110 FOR MI=0 TO 4:FOR MJ=0 TO 4:FOR KL=1 TO 2
115 M(MI,MJ,KL)=2:NEXT KL,MJ,MI
120 TC=191:CP=15776+RND(5)−3+64*(RND(5)−3)
125 CI=RND(5)−3:CJ=RND(5)−3:IF CI=0 AND CJ=0
    THEN 125
130 CLS:GOSUB 1000:POKE CP,42
135 GOSUB 2000
145 IF (CX=32 OR CX=TC) AND (CY=32 OR CY=TC)THEN
    190
150 MI=CI+2:MJ=CJ+2
155 CI=M(MI,MJ,1):CJ=M(MI,MJ,2)
160 IF NOT(CI=2 AND CJ=2) THEN 170
165 CI=RND(5)−1:CJ=RND(5)−1:GOTO 160
170 CI=CI−2:CJ=CJ−2:GOSUB 2000:CI=CI+2:CJ=CJ+2
175 IF NOT((CX=32 OR CX=TC) AND (CY=32 OR
    CY=TC)) THEN 165
180 M(MI,MJ,1)=CI:M(MI,MJ,2)=CJ
```

119

```
185 CI=CI-2:CJ=CJ-2
190 POKE CP,TC
195 CP=NP:POKE CP,42
200 IF INKEY$<>"" THEN 130
205 GOTO 135
210 REM
215 REM
1000 REM ** BORDER,V.1-TRS-80 **
1005 F0=15360:F1=15423:F2=16128:F3=16191
1010 FOR N=F0 TO F1:POKE N,176:NEXT N
1015 FOR N=F2 TO F3:POKE N,131:NEXT N
1020 FOR N=F0 TO F2 STEP 64:POKE N,170:NEXT
1025 FOR N=F1 TO F3 STEP 64:POKE N,149:NEXT
1030 POKE F0,160:POKE F1,144:POKE F2,130:POKE
     F3,129
1035 RETURN
1040 REM
1045 REM
2000 REM ** SEARCH AHEAD, V.2-TRS-80 **
2005 NP=CP:CX=32:CY=32
2010 SI=SGN(CI):SJ=SGN(CJ):AI=ABS(CI):AJ=ABS(CJ)
2015 IF AI=0 THEN 2030 ELSE AI=AI-1
2020 IF SI>0 THEN NP=NP+1 ELSE NP=NP-1
2025 CX=PEEK(NP)
2030 IF AJ=0 THEN 2045 ELSE AJ=AJ-1
2035 IF SJ>0 THEN NP=NP+64 ELSE NP=NP-64
2040 CY=PEEK(NP)
2045 IF NOT((CX=32 OR CX=TC) AND (CY=32 OR
     CY=TC)) THEN RETURN
2050 IF AI=0 AND AJ=0 THEN RETURN ELSE GOTO 2015
2055 REM
2060 REM
```

Theory of Operation

The TRS-80 variable list for FUNDAMENTAL BETA DEMO
is shown in Table 10-1. It is important to realize that the Beta
memory is handled as a $4 \times 4 \times 2$ array. Values MI and MJ are the
adjusted values of the current motion code (MI=CI+2 and
MJ=CJ+2). Thus, the content of M(MI,MJ,1) points to the
suggested CI portion of the remembered response, and M(MI,MJ,2)
points to the CJ value.

Lines 105-115—Initialize the Beta system. Dimension the

Table 10-1. TRS-80 Variable List for FUNDAMENTAL BETA DEMO.

MI	Value of stimulus CI (adjusted to range of 0-4)
MJ	Value of stimulus CJ (adjusted to range of 0-4)
KL	Memory pointer (1 for response CI, 2 for response CJ)
M(MI,MJ,1)	Memory value of response CI (adjusted to 0-4)
M(MI,MJ,2)	Memory value of response CJ (adjusted to 0-4)
TC	Trail graphic code number
CI	Horizontal component of motion code
CJ	Vertical component of motion code
CX	Horizontal component of contact code
CY	Vertical component of contact code
CP	Current creature screen position
NP	Next screen position for the creature
SI	Sign value of CI
SJ	Sign value of CJ
AI	Absolute value of CI
AJ	Absolute value of CJ
M	General-purpose numeric variable
N	General-purpose numeric variable
F0	Upper-left corner of border figure
F1	Upper-right corner of border figure
F2	Lower-left corner of border figure
F3	Lower-right corner of border figure

memory array and set all elements of the Beta memory to the invalid stop code (adjusted motion code values 2,2).

Lines 120-125—Initialize the creature. Set the trail code to graphic 191, set the initial position near the middle of the screen, and get the initial motion code.

Line 130—Clear the screen, draw the border and creature figures.

Lines 135-145—Do the search ahead routine. If the path is clear, then jump down to move the creature at line 190. Otherwise, run the Beta routine.

Lines 150-155—Set the Beta variables and fetch the memory response.

Line 160—The VALID conditional.

Line 165—Fetch a new, random motion code, then test its validity by looping back to line 160.

Line 170—Do the search ahead routine, adjusting the motion code values before and after.

Line 175—PATH CLEAR conditional for the Beta routine.

Lines 180-185—Load the new motion code to memory and adjust the new values to their standard range.

Lines 190-195—Move the creature, leaving a trail of graphics TC.

Lines 200-205—Scan the keyboard for any key depression. If there is none, loop back to line 130. Otherwise, go back to the search ahead routine at line 135.

Operating Instructions

Upon running the program, you will first note a short delay while the system loads the Beta memory with 2,2 motion codes. Then the screen will clear, the border figure will appear, and the creature will begin moving around on the screen.

Since the program runs indefinitely, the most satisfactory way to stop it is by striking the BREAK key.

Whenever you want to clear out the old trail, just strike any key—the ENTER key works quite nicely.

Don't forget to watch for the Beta's habit pattern of motion. If you miss that feature of the project, you miss the only available criterion that Beta learning is taking place.

As mentioned earlier in the discussion, there is no way to predict how long it will take a given Beta to establish its habit pattern of motion. It might establish it within a dozen moves or less, or it might take a hundred moves to do it. You can be sure, however, that the pattern will be established sooner or later.

Then, too, there is no way to predict the nature of that habit pattern of motion. Sometimes it will be a simple repetitive bouncing pattern between two elements of the border figure. Other times, however, the Beta will establish a highly complex pattern.

You can know that the creature is working a habit pattern when you note that it no longer covers unused portions of its environment—when its activity keeps it covering nothing but sections of previously drawn trail.

When you suspect the creature has established its habit pattern of motion, strike the ENTER key to delete the trail marks. If, indeed, the Beta has completed its learning task, the trail it then draws represents its habit pattern of motion.

Once the pattern is established, there is no way to alter it. (Techniques for upsetting the habit pattern of motion are introduced later.) The best thing to do at that point is to BREAK the program and RUN again from scratch. That will, in effect, kill the old Beta and give birth to a brand new one.

Suggested Modification

It is not always easy to determine whether or not a Beta has completed its learning task. The following additions to the listing will aid in your determination:

$$107 \text{ FC}=0$$
$$162 \text{ FC}=\text{FC}+1:\text{PRINT} @ 896,\text{FC}$$

Variable FC thus keeps track of the number of times the Beta routine calls for a new random motion code. Since the Beta resorts to this Alpha-like behavior only as long as the learning is incomplete. The number appears near the lower-left corner of the screen; and as long as it is incrementing at reasonably short intervals, you can know that the habit pattern of motion—the creature learning— is incomplete.

When a reasonable length of time passes without changing the FC number on the screen, you can be sure that the learning experiment is done.

Just how large that number grows before it stops incrementing is a reflection of how hard the Beta had to work in order to complete its unique learning task. The larger the value, the more difficult time the creature had.

APPLESOFT VERSION

The programming for the Applesoft version of FUNDAMENTAL BETA DEMO is shown as Listing 10-2. The entire listing can be entered from scratch at the keyboard, or you can save yourself some time by loading FUNDAMENTAL ALPHA DEMO from tape or disk, and making the following modifications:

●Delete the old mainline and replace it with BETA MAINLINE, V.1

●Modify lines 2000 and 2065 in the SEARCH AHEAD subroutine to conform to the version shown here.

Listing 10-2. Applesoft Program for FUNDAMENTAL BETA DEMO.

```
10 REM   FUNDAMENTAL BETA DEMO
15 REM     APPLESOFT
20 REM
25 REM
30 REM
100 REM ** BETA MAINLINE, V.1—APPLESOFT **
105 DIM M(4,4,2)
110 FOR M = 0 TO 4: FOR N = 0 TO 4: FOR KL = 1 TO 2
115 M(M,N,KL) = 2: NEXT KL,N,M
120 TC = 13: DEF FN R(R) = INT (5 * RND (1)) – 2
125 PX = 20 + FN R(0):PY = 20 + FN R(0)
```

```
130  CI = FN R(0):CJ = FN R(0): IF CI = 0 AND CJ = 0 THEN
     130
135  HOME : GR : GOSUB 1000
140  COLOR= 9: PLOT PX,PY
145  GOSUB 2000
150  IF (CX = 0 OR CX = TC) AND (CY = 0 OR CY = TC)
     THEN 195
155  MI = CI + 2:MJ = CJ + 2
160  CI = M(MI,MJ,1):CJ = M(MI,MJ,2)
165  IF NOT (CI = 2 AND CJ = 2) THEN 175
170  CI = FN R(0) + 2:CJ = FN R(0) + 2: GOTO 165
175  CI = CI – 2:CJ = CJ – 2: GOSUB 2000:CI = CI + 2:CJ =
     CJ + 2
180  IF NOT ((CX = 0 OR CX = TC) AND (CY = 0 OR CY =
     TC)) THEN 170
185  M(MI,MJ,1) = CI:M(MI,MJ,2) = CJ
190  CI = CI – 2:CJ = CJ – 2
195  COLOR= TC: PLOT PX,PY
200  PX = NX:PY = NY
205  COLOR= 9: PLOT PX,PY
210  N = PEEK ( – 16384): POKE – 16368,0
215  IF N > 127 THEN 135
220  GOTO 145
225  REM
230  REM
1000 REM ** BORDER,V.1—APPLESOFT **
1005 COLOR= 15
1010 HLIN 0,39 AT 0: HLIN 0,39 AT 36
1015 VLIN 0,36 AT 0: VLIN 0,36 AT 39
1020 RETURN
1025 REM
1030 REM
2000 REM ** SEARCH AHEAD, V.2—APPLESOFT **
2005 NX = PX:NY = PY:CX = 0:CY = 0
2010 SI = SGN (CI):SJ = SGN (CJ):AI = ABS (CI):AJ = ABS
     (CJ)
2015 IF AI = 0 THEN 2040
2020 AI = AI – 1
2025 IF SI > 0 THEN NX = NX + 1: GOTO 2035
2030 NX = NX – 1
2035 CX = SCRN(NX,NY)
2040 IF AJ = 0 THEN 2065
```

```
2045  AJ = AJ − 1
2050  IF SJ > 0 THEN NY = NY + 1: GOTO 2060
2055  NY = NY − 1
2060  CY = SCRN(NX,NY)
2065  IF NOT((CX = 0 OR CX = TC) AND (CY = 0 OR CY = TC))
      THEN RETURN
2070  IF AI = 0 AND AJ = 0 THEN RETURN
2075  GOTO 2015
2080  REM
1085  REM
```

Theory of Operation

The Applesoft variable list for FUNDAMENTAL BETA DEMO is shown in Table 10-2. It is important to realize that the Beta memory is handled as the 4×4×2 variable array. Values MI and MJ are the adjusted values of the current motion code. Thus, the content of M(MI,MJ,1) points to the remembered CI portion of the response, and M(MI,MJ,2) points to the CJ portion of that response motion code.

 Lines 105-115—Initialize the Beta system. Dimension the array and set all elements of the Beta memory to the invalid stop code (adjusted motion code values 2,2).

 Lines 120-130—Initialize the creature. Set the trail code to yellow, define the random motion code function, establish the initial position and motion code.

Table 10-2. Applesoft Variable List for FUNDAMENTAL BETA DEMO.

MI	Value of stimulus CI (adjusted to range 0-4)
MJ	Value of stimulus CJ (adjusted to range 0-4)
KL	Memory pointer (1 for response CI, 2 for response CJ)
M(MI,MJ,1)	Memory value of response CI (0-4)
M(MI,MJ,2)	Memory value of response CJ (0-4)
TC	Trail color code number
CI	Horizontal component of motion code
CJ	Vertical component of motion code
CX	Horizontal component of contact code
CY	Vertical component of contact code
PX	Horizontal component of creature position
PY	Vertical component of creature position
NX	Horizontal component of next creature position
NY	Vertical component of next creature position
SI	Sign value of current CI
SJ	Sign value of current CJ
AI	Absolute value of current CI
AJ	Absolute value of current CJ
M,N	General-purpose numeric variables

Lines 135-140—Clear the screen, draw the border and creature figures.

Lines 145-150—Do the search ahead routine. If the path is clear, jump to move the creature at line 195. Otherwise, begin the Beta routine.

Lines 155-165—Set the Beta variables and fetch the memory response. If the fetched response is a valid one (not the adjusted stop code), then try it at line 175. Otherwise, fetch a random motion code.

Line 170—Fetch a random motion code, then jump back to line 165 to test its validity. Otherwise try it out.

Line 175—Do the search ahead routine, adjusting the motion code values before and after.

Line 180—PATH CLEAR conditional for the Beta routine.

Lines 185-190—Load the new motion code into memory and adjust the new values to their standard negative-and-positive range.

Lines 195-205—Move the creature, leaving a trail of color TC.

Lines 210-220—Scan the keyboard for any key depression. If there is none, loop back to line 145 to continue normal motion. Otherwise, loop back to line 135 to clear the old trail pattern.

Operating Instructions

Upon running the program, you will note a short time delay while the system initializes the Beta memory with 2,2 motion codes. Then the screen will clear, the border figure will appear, and then the creature will begin moving around on the screen.

Whenever you want to clear out the old trail, just strike any key—the RETURN key works nicely.

Since the program runs indefinitely, the most satisfactory way to stop it is by the control-C keyboard operation. Running the program again lets you start with a brand new Beta and a blank memory.

Don't forget about watching for Beta's habit pattern of motion. That is why the trail-drawing features are built into this program. If you miss the habit pattern idea, you miss the only available criterion that Beta-type learning is taking place.

As mentioned earlier in the discussion, there is no way to predict how long it will take a given Beta creature to establish its habit pattern of motion. It might establish the pattern within a dozen moves or less, or it might take a hundred moves to do it. You can be sure, however, that the pattern will be established sooner or later.

Then, too, there is no way to predict the shape of that habit pattern of motion. Sometimes it will be a simple repetitive bouncing pattern between two elements of the border figure. Other times, however, the Beta will establish a highly complex and hard-to-trace pattern.

One way to know that the creature is working a habit pattern of motion is by noting that it no longer covers blank portions of the screen—it keeps itself running along previously drawn trails.

When you suspect that the creature has established its habit pattern of motion, strike the RETURN key to delete the old trail marks. If, indeed, the Beta has completed its learning task, the new trail represents that resulting habit pattern.

Once the pattern is established, there is no way to alter it. (Techniques for upsetting the habit pattern are introduced later.) The best thing to do at this point is to CTRL C the program and RUN it again from the beginning. That will, in effect, kill the old Beta and give birth to a new one.

Suggested Modification

It is not always easy to determine whether or not a Beta creature has completed its learning task and entered a habit pattern of motion. The following additions to the listing will aid in your determination:

107 FC=0

172 FC=FC+1:HOME:PRINT FC

Variable FC keeps track of the time of times the Beta system has to resort to an Alpha-type selection of a random motion code. The less frequently Beta resorts to picking a random motion code, the better its learning is shaping up. When a reasonable period of time passes without showing an increase in that FC value near the bottom of the screen, you can be sure the Beta has completed its learning operations.

Just how large that number grows before it stops incrementing is a reflection of how hard the Beta creature had to work in order to complete its learning task. The larger the final value, the more difficult time the creature had.

Chapter 11
Fundamental Beta
with Obstacle Options

The program in the previous chapter clearly demonstrates that a Beta creature freely explores its new environment, learning the proper responses to contact situations, and eventually coming up with enough sure-fire responses to set up a habit pattern of motion.

Upon running the program in this chapter, you will immediately notice one big difference: the environment is dotted with 64 randomly placed obstacles. Having to deal with this relatively complicated, yet static, environment, tends to foster more complex habit patterns of motion. But there is more to this project than simply throwing a Beta creature into a cluttered environment.

This program lets the experimenter tamper with various characteristics of the creature and its environment in an online fashion. The purpose is to observe the Beta mechanism adapting to sudden changes in the environment.

Table 11-1 shows the user-operated key functions that affect the program while it is running. They are all inline functions, so the program, as such, is not interrupted.

The Beta creature always leaves behind a visible trail. It cannot sense its own trail, so it does not influence the system activity. It's there for your benefit.

As in the previous program, you can delete all sections of the previously drawn trail by striking the ENTER (TRS-80) or RETURN (Apple) key. Even through the entire display is erased initially, the border figure, obstacles and creature are all redrawn in the positions they held prior to the trail-erasing command.

Table 11-1. Summary of Keyboard Commands for Experimenting with Beta Adaptive Behavior.

A	Abort the present Beta memory, but continue with the same environment and creature variables.
K	Kick the creature out of its present path, but continue with the same environment and screen position.
D	Displace the creature from its present position, but continue with the same environment and creature motion code.
E	Generate a new environment, but retain the present creature variables.
ENTER or RETURN	Clear old trail; continue with the same environment and retain the current Beta memory and creature variables.

An additional, and far more significant keyboard command, comes about by striking the *D* key. That command instantly displaces the creature to some other randomly generated screen position. The trail, obstacle and border figures are unaffected.

The purpose of the delete command is to deal with this question; *Once a Beta establishes a habit pattern of motion, what happens if it is disturbed by suddenly placing it somewhere else in the environment?*

A Beta, you see, will set up a habit pattern of motion that is partly dictated by the geometry in its immediate surroundings. Perhaps it is more correct to say that the geometry of the immediate surroundings has a lot to do with the creature's habit pattern of motion. If that geometry—the relative positions of obstacles and elements of the border figure—have a lot to do with the creature's habit pattern of motion, some insight into the essence of Beta behavior can be found by putting the creature into a somewhat different geometrical situation. That is done in this case by displacing the creature.

You will find that the creature can, indeed, adapt to such a sudden change. Sometimes it locks almost immediately into a habit pattern that is nearly identical to the previous one. Other times, the creature undergoes a short period of retraining, coming up with a different habit pattern (but one that retains at least a few elements of the original).

Striking the *K* key gives the creature a kick away from its present course. Actually, it gives the creature a new, randomly generated motion code. The idea here is to let the creature set up a habit pattern of motion, then kick it off track. You might be surprised how well the simple Beta adapts to that sort of disturbance. The first few times you try it, the creature clearly undergoes a period of adaptive trauma—dashing about wildly, attempting to set up a habit pattern of motion. But after kicking it off track a number of times (allowing a habit pattern to develop in the meantime), you will notice that the creature spends less time trying to adjust. *The Beta learns how to deal with these kicks.* The more often it is kicked around, the less time it spends in confusion.

Most often, a kick does not change the original habit pattern very much. The position of the pattern might change, but the general shape does not, Occasionally, the Beta will change its habit pattern to some extent.

Striking the *E* key completely alters the geometry of the obstacle part of the environment. The Beta memory remains intact, and the creature holds its present motion code and position on the screen. But a whole new set of randomly positioned obstacles are placed on the screen.

Carrying its previous knowledge to the new environment, the Beta is fairly well equipped to deal with it in an effective manner. There will most likely be a short period of adaptive trauma, but the Beta will settle into its new environment in a fairly short time— usually a shorter time than was required for adapting to the original environment.

Finally, striking the *A* key aborts the entire Beta memory, wiping out all previously learned responses. In effect, this command amounts to starting a new Beta creature.

Rather than dwelling on lengthy descriptions and scenarios about how the Beta responds to these disturbances, I suggest you load the program and try it for yourself. If you have been following the general flow of information in this book, and if you have a sense of curiosity about these matters, you will certainly have more fun making up your own experiments with this program than reading about mine.

There is little need to describe a flowchart for this program. It follows the diagram in Fig. 10-1 rather closely. The main difference is the command-select operations that are included here. It is a rather simple and straightforward routine, and the line-by-line listing of them ought to be sufficient for understanding how they work the way they do.

TRS-80 VERSION

The TRS-80 version of FUNDAMENTAL BETA DEMO WITH OBSTACLE OPTIONS is shown in Listing 11-1. The mainline has to be entered from scratch at the keyboard, but you can get the border and search ahead routines into place by loading FUN-DAMENTAL BETA DEMO (Listing 10-1) from tape or disk.

Listing 11-1. TRS-80 Listing for FUNDAMENTAL BETA DEMO WITH OBSTACLE OP-TIONS.

```
10 REM FUNDAMENTAL BETA DEMO
15 REM WITH OBSTACLE OPTIONS
20 REM TRS-80
25 REM
30 REM
100 REM ** BETA MAINLINE, V.2—TRS-80 **
105 NT=64:DIM M(4,4,2):DIM TM(NT):TC=132:TT=191
110 FOR MI=0 TO 4:FOR MJ=0 TO 4:FOR KL=1 TO 2
115 M(MI,MJ,KL)=2:NEXT KL,MJ,MI
120 CLS:GOSUB 1000
125 FOR N=0 TO NT
130 TP=15360+RND(831):IF PEEK(TP)<>32 THEN 130
135 POKE TP,TT:TM(N)=TP:NEXT N
140 CP=15360+RND(831):IF PEEK(CP)<>32 THEN 140
145 POKE CP,42
150 CI=RND(5)−3:CJ=RND(5)−3:IF CI=0 AND CJ=0
    THEN 150
155 GOSUB 2000
160 IF (CX=32 OR CX=TC) AND (CY=32 OR CY=TC)
    THEN 205
165 MI=CI+2:M J=CJ+2
170 CI=M(MI,MJ,1):CJ=M(MI, MJ,2)
175 IF NOT(CI=2 AND CJ=2) THEN 185
180 CI=RND(5)−1:CJ=RND(5)−1:GOTO 175
185 CI=CI−2:CJ=CJ−2:GOSUB 2000:CI=CI+2:CJ=CJ+2
190 IF NOT((CX=32 OR CX=TC) AND (CY=32 OR
    CY=TC)) THEN 180
195 M(MI,MJ,1)=CI:M(MI,MJ,2)=CJ
200 CI=CI−2:CJ=CJ−2
205 POKE CP,TC
210 CP=NP:POKE CP,42
215 S$=INKEY$:IF S$=" " THEN 155
220 IF S$<>"A" THEN 235
```

```
 225 FOR MI=0 TO 4:FOR MJ=0 TO 4:FOR KL=1 TO 2
 230 M(MI,MJ,KL)=2:NEXT KL,MJ,MI:GOTO 155
 235 IF S$="K" THEN 150
 240 IF S$<>"D" THEN 260
 245 POKE CP,32
 250 CP=15360+RND(831):IF PEEK(CP)<>32 THEN 250
 255 POKE CP,42:GOTO 155
 260 CLS:GOSUB 1000
 265 IF S$<>"E" THEN 295
 270 POKE CP,42
 275 FOR N=0 TO NT
 280 TP=15360+RND(831):IF PEEK(TP)<>32 THEN 280
 285 POKE TP,TT:TM(N)=TP
 290 NEXT N:GOTO 155
 295 FOR N=0 TO NT:POKE TM(N),TT:NEXT N:GOTO 155
 300 REM
 305 REM
1000 REM ** BORDER, V.1—TRS-80 **
1005 F0=15360:F1=15423:F2=16128:F3= 16191
1010 FOR N=F0 TO F1:POKE N,176:NEXT N
1015 FOR N=F2 TO F3:POKE N,131:NEXT N
1020 FOR N=F0 TO F2 STEP 64:POKE N,170:NEXT
1025 FOR N=F1 TO F3 STEP 64:POKE N,149:NEXT
1030 POKE F0,160:POKE F1,144:POKE F2,130:POKE
     F3,129
1035 RETURN
1040 REM
1045 REM
2000 REM ** SEARCH AHEAD, V.2—TRS-80 **
2005 NP=CP:CX=32:CY=32
2010 SI=SGN(CI):SJ=SGN(CJ):AI=ABS(CI):AJ=ABS(CJ)
2015 IF AI=0 THEN 2030 ELSE AI=AI—1
2020 IF SI>0 THEN NP=NP+1 ELSE NP =NP—1
2025 CX=PEEK(NP)
2030 IF AJ=0 THEN 2045 ELSE AJ=AJ—1
2035 IF SJ>0 THEN NP=NP+64 ELSE NP=NP—64
2040 CY=PEEK(NP)
2045 IF NOT ((CX=32 OR CX=TC) AND (CY=32 OR
     CY=TC)) THEN RETURN
2050 IF AI=0 AND AJ=0 THEN RETURN ELSE GOTO 2015
2055 REM
2060 REM
```

Theory of Operation

Use the variable list in Table 11-2 as a guide for working through this analysis of the program listing.

Line 105—Dimension arrays and set the values for fixed variables.

Lines 110-115—Set all elements of the Beta memory array to the stop code 2,2.

Line 120—Clear the screen and draw the border figure.

Lines 130-135—Fix the random positions of the obstacle figures. Assign their positions to the obstacle-position array, and draw them on the screen.

Lines 140-145—Get a random position for the creature. If the spot is already occupied by an obstacle, get a different position. Draw the creature figure on the screen.

Line 150—Fetch a random motion code for the creature. If it is the stop code, get another one.

Line 155—Do the search ahead routine.

Line 160—If there is no contact, jump to line 205 (move the creature); otherwise, start the Beta routine.

**Table 11-2. TRS Variable List for FUNDA-
MENTAL BETA DEMO WITH OBSTACLE OPTIONS.**

NT	Number of obstacles in the environment
TM(N)	Screen position of obstacle N (N=O through NT)
TC	Creature trail graphic code
TT	Obstacle graphic code
MI	Value of stimulus CI (adjusted to range 0-4)
MJ	Value of stimulus CJ (adjusted to range 0-4)
M(MI,MJ,1)	Memory value of response CI (adjusted to 0-4)
M(MI,MJ,2)	Memory value of response CJ (adjusted to 0-4)
KL	Memory response pointer (1 for CI, 2 for CJ)
CI	Horizontal component of motion code
CJ	Vertical component of motion code
CX	Horizontal component of contact code
CY	Vertical component of contact code
CP	Creature's current screen position
NP	Creature's next screen position
SI	Sign value of CI
SJ	Sign value of CJ
AI	Absolute value of CI
AJ	Absolute value of CJ
M, N	General-purpose numeric variables
S$	General-purpose string variable
F0	Upper-left corner of border figure
F1	Upper-right corner of border figure
F2	Lower-left corner of border figure
F3	Lower-right corner of border figure

Beta routine occupies lines 165 through 200

Lines 165-170—Adjust the current motion code and fetch the response from memory.

Line 175—If the code is valid (not a stop code), jump to line 185 (search ahead routine). Otherwise, get a new motion code.

Line 180—Pick a random motion code and test its validity by jumping back to line 175.

Line 185—Do the search ahead routine, adjusting the motion code range before and after.

Line 190—If the suggested motion code results in a contact situation, jump back to line 180 to pick another random motion code.

Lines 195-200—Remember the motion code response that works, adjust it before moving the creature.

Lines 205-210—Move the creature to its new position, leaving behind a trail.

Line 215—Scan the keyboard. If no key is depressed, jump back to do the next search ahead routine at line 155.

Special command routines occupy lines 220 through 295

Lines 220-230—If the *A* key is depressed, clear the Beta memory to the stop code (2,2). Then go back to line 155 to do the next search ahead routine.

Line 235—If the *K* key is depressed, jump back to pick up a random motion code from line 150. Resume operations from there.

Lines 240-250—If the *D* key is depressed, erase the current creature image, pick a new spot for it, print it, and jump back to line 155 to resume normal operations.

Line 260—Clear the screen and draw the border figure.

Lines 265-290—Select new random positions for the obstacles. Draw them on the screen and remember their positions in the obstacle position array.

Line 295—Command default line. If any key but *A, D, K* or *E* is depressed, this line redraws the obstacle figures at the positions contained in the obstacle position array. Generally speaking, this line is used for erasing old trail lines when you strike the ENTER key. In any event, operations loop back to line 155 to resume normal Beta action.

Lines 1000-1035—Border drawing subroutine.

Lines 2000-2050—Search ahead subroutine.

Running the Program

As listed here, the obstacles are drawn as graphic 191 characters, the creature is an asterisk, and the creature trail is a small
square of light (graphic code 132). You can alter the appearance of
the obstacles or creature trail by changing their values assigned in
line 105. Do not, however, assign the trail (variable TC) any one of
the graphic codes used in the BORDER, V.1 subroutine.

The program sets up 64 obstacles. You can change that, too, by
altering the value assigned to variable NT in line 105.

The program is set up to run endlessly. When you want to
interrupt it, use the BREAK key. But if you want to create the effect
of starting a new Beta creature, use the *A* control option—strike the
A key to get a fresh memory. If you want, you can then get a new
obstacle field by striking the *E* key.

The real purpose of this program is to give you an opportunity
to experiment with Beta adaptive behavior. There is more to this
demonstration than meets the eye, and if you aren't sure about what
is really happening, perhaps you should review Chapter 1 again.

APPLESOFT VERSION

The Applesoft version of FUNDAMENTAL BETA DEMO
WITH OBSTACLE OPTIONS is shown as Listing 11-2. The mainline has to be entered from scratch at the keyboard, but you can get
the border and search ahead subroutines into place by loading them
from FUNDAMENTAL BETA DEMO (Listing 10-2) as saved on
tape or disk.

**Listing 11-2. Applesoft Listing for FUNDA-
MENTAL BETA DEMO WITH OBSTACLE OPTIONS.**

```
10  REM   FUNDAMENTAL BETA DEMO
15  REM   WITH OBSTACLE OPTIONS
20  REM     APPLESOFT
25  REM
30  REM
35  REM
100 REM ** BETA MAINLINE,V.2—APPLESOFT 00
105 NT = 64: DIM M(4,4,2): DIM TM(NT,2):TC = 13:TT = 15
110 DEF FN R(R) = INT (5 * RND (1)) − 2
115 DEF FN P(P) = INT (P * RND (1)) + 1
120 FOR MI = 0 TO 4: FOR MJ = 0 TO 4: FOR KL = 1 TO 2
125 M(MI,MJ,KL) = 2: NEXT KL,MJ,MI
```

```
130 HOME : GR : GOSUB 1000
135 COLOR= TT$
140 FOR N = 0 TO NT
145 TX = FN P(38):TY = FN P(35)
150 IF SCRN(TX,TY) < > 0 THEN 145
155 PLOT TX,TY:TM(N,1) = TX:TM(N,2) = TY
160 NEXT N
165 PX = FN P(38):PY = FN P(35)
170 IF SCRN(PX,PY) < > 0 THEN 165
175 COLOR= 9: PLOT PX,PY
180 CI = FN R(0):CJ = FN R(0): IF CI = 0 AND CJ = 0 THEN
    180
185 GOSUB 2000
190 IF (CX = 0 OR CX = TC) AND (CY = 0 OR CY = TC)
    THEN 235
195 MI = CI + 2:MJ = CJ + 2
200 CI = M(MI,MJ,1):CJ = M(MI,MJ,2)
205 IF NOT (CI = 2 AND CJ = 2) THEN 215
210 CI = FN R(0) + 2:CJ = FN R(0) + 2: GOTO 205
215 CI = CI - 2:CJ = CJ - 2: GOSUB 2000:CI = CI + 2: CJ =
    CJ + 2
220 IF NOT ((CX = 0 OR CX = TC) AND (CY = 0 OR CY =
    TC)) THEN 210
225 M(MI,MJ,1) = CI:M(MI,MJ,2) = CJ
230 CI = CI - 2:CJ = CJ - 2
235 COLOR= TC: PLOT PX,PY
240 PX = NX:PY = NY
245 COLOR= 9: PLOT PX,PY
250 S = PEEK (- 16384): POKE - 16368,0
255 IF S< = 127 THEN 185
260 IF S < > 193 THEN 275
265 FOR MI = 0 TO 4: FOR MJ = 0 TO 4: FOR KL = 1 TO 2
270 M(MI,MJ,KL) = 2: NEXT KL,MJ,MI: GOTO 185
275 IF S = 203 THEN 180
280 IF S < > 196 THEN 300
285 COLOR = 0: PLOT PX,PY
290 PX = FN P(38):PY = FN P(35): IF SCRN(PX,PY) < > 0
    THEN 290
295 COLOR=9: PLOT PX,PY: GOTO 185
300 TEXT : HOME: GR : GOSUB 1000
305 IF S < > 197 THEN 335
310 COLOR= 9: PLOT PX,PY
315 FOR N = 0 TO NT
```

```
320 TX = FN P(38):TY = FN P(35): IF SCRN(TX,TY) < > 0
    THEN 320
325 COLOR= TT: PLOT TX,TY:TM(N,1) = TX:TM(N,2) = TY
330 NEXT N: GOTO 185
335 COLOR= TT
340 FOR N = 0 TO NT: PLOT TM(N,1),TM(N,2): NEXT N
345 GOTO 185
350 REM
355 REM
1000 REM ** BORDER,V.1—APPLESOFT **
1005 COLOR= 15
1010 HLIN 0,39 AT 0: HLIN 0,39 AT 36
1015 VLIN 0,36 AT 0: VLIN 0,36 AT 39
1020 RETURN
1025 REM
1030 REM
2000 REM ** SEARCH AHEAD, V.2—APPLESOFT **
2005 NX = PX:NY = PY:CX = 0:CY = 0
2010 SI = SGN (CI):SJ = SGN (CJ):AI = ABS (CI):AJ = ABS
     (CJ)
2015 IF AI = 0 THEN 2040
2020 AI = AI − 1
2025 IF SI > 0 THEN NX = NX + 1: GOTO 2035
2030 NX = NX − 1
2035 CX = SCRN(NX,NY)
2040 IF AJ = 0 THEN 2065
2045 AJ = AJ − 1
2050 IF SJ > 0 THEN NY = NY + 1: GOTO 2060
2055 NY = NY − 1
2060 CY = SCRN(NX,NY)
2065 IF NOT ((CX = 0 OR CX = TC) AND (CY = 0 OR CY =
     TC)) THEN RETURN
2070 IF AI = 0 AND AJ = 0 THEN RETURN
2075 GOTO 2015
2080 REM
2085 REM
```

Theory of Operation

Use the variable list in Table 11-3 as a guide for working through this analysis of the program listing.

Line 105—Dimension the arrays and set the fixed values for

the number of obstacles, trail color code and obstacle color code.

Lines 110-115—Define the functions for random motion code and random screen positions.

Lines 120-125—Clear the Beta memory to the stop code (2,2).

Line 130—Clear the screen, set the graphics mode and draw the border figure.

Lines 135-160—Get random positions for the obstacles. If one piles on top of another, get another position. Plot the obstacles and save their positions in the obstacle position array.

Lines 165-175—Get a random, initial position for the creature. Plot it if it doesn't overlap an obstacle figure.

Line 180—Get an initial random motion code. If it is the stop code (0,0), get another one.

Line 185—Do the search ahead routine.

Line 190—If there is no contact, jump to line 235 (move the creature); otherwise, begin the Beta routine.

The Beta routine occupies lines 195 through 230

Lines 195-200—Adjust the motion code variables and fetch the response code from Beta memory array.

Line 205—Test the response for the adjusted stop code (2,2). If it is not the stop code—if the code is a valid one—go to the search ahead operation at line 215. Otherwise, pick a random motion code.

Line 210—Fetch a random motion code. Jump back to test its validity at line 205.

Line 215—Do the search ahead routine, adjusting the range of the motion code before and after.

Line 220—If a contact situation occurs, go back to line 210 to pick a new random motion code.

Lines 225-230—Remember the successful reponse and adjust the motion code range before moving the creature.

Lines 235-245—Move the creature, leaving behind a trail.

Lines 250-255—Scan the keyboard. If no key is depressed, jump back to line 185 to resume normal Beta activity.

Special command routines occupy lines 260 through 345

Lines 260-270—If the A key (key code 193) is depressed, clear the current Beta memory to stop codes; then jump back to resume normal activity from line 185.

Line 275—If the K key (key code 203) is depressed, get a new random motion code by jumping back to line 180 and

NT	Number of obstacles in the environment
TX	Horizontal component of an obstacle position
TY	Vertical component of an obstacle position
TM(N,1)	TX value for obstacle N
TM(N,2)	TY value for obstacle N
MI	Value of stimulus (CI (adjusted to range 0-4)
MJ	Value of stimulus CJ (adjusted to range 0-4)
M(MI,MJ,1)	Memory value of CI (adjusted to range 0-4)
M(MI,MJ,2)	Memory value of CJ (adjusted to range 0-4)
TC	Creature's trail color code
TT	Obstacle color code
FN R(R)	Random motion code function
FN P(P)	Random screen position function
KL	Memory response pointer (1 or 2)
CI	Horizontal component of motion code
CJ	Vertical component of motion code
PX	Horizontal component of creature's position
PY	Vertical component of creature's position
NX	Horizontal component of creature's next position
NY	Vertical component of creature's next position
SI	Sign value of CI
SJ	Sign value of CJ
AI	Absolute value of CI
AJ	Absolute value of CJ
N,S	General-purpose numeric variables

resuming normal activity from that point.

Lines 280-295—If the *D* key (key code 196) is depressed, erase the creature figure from the screen, get a new random creature position that doesn't fall on an obstacle figure, redraw the creature in its new position, and resume normal Beta activity from line 195.

Line 300—Clear the screen and redraw the border figure.

Lines 305-330—If the *E* key (key code 197) is depressed, plot the creature figure, get new positions for the obstacles—draw them and remember them in the obstacle position array. Resume activity from line 185.

Lines 335-345—Redraw the obstacles at the positions held in the obstacle position array. Resume normal activity from line 185.

Lines 1000-1020—Border drawing subroutine.

Lines 2000-2075—Search ahead subroutine.

Running the Program

As listed here, the obstacles are white, the creature is orange, and the creature's trail is yellow. You can change those colors by adjusting the color codes assigned in line 105. Do not, however, assign white (color code 15) to the trail (variable TC). That will allow the creature to roam through the border and escape.

The program sets up 64 obstacles. You can change the number of obstacles by altering the value assigned to variable NT in line 105.

The program runs endlessly. Whenever you want to interrupt it, do the CTRL C operation. But if you really want to start a new creature, use the *A* key control feature built into the program. That will give the creature a whole new, blank memory. If you wish, you can then get a new obstacle field by striking the *E* key.

This is one of the most significant programs in this book. Its primary purpose is to give you an opportunity to experiment with Beta adaptive behavior. There is much more to the demonstration than meets the eye, but if you aren't sure about what is really happening, perhaps you should review Chapter 1.

Chapter 12
Killer Beta
Demonstration

The next logical step in the evolution of a Beta creature is to build one that has an extended response mechanism. This chapter shows how to give the Beta the option of striking out at an obstacle, and if that aggressive sort of response clears the path ahead, Beta will remember that striking out at obstacles under similar conditions is a workable response.

Bear in mind, however, that a Beta creature acts very much like an Alpha creature during the early part of its experiences with the environment. The Beta makes a good many random, reflex-like responses to contact situations. But with experience, the responses come more from memory than from the basic Alpha mechanisms. If killing an obstacle worked at some time in the past, it will probably work again. Beta gives it a try.

There is still just a 50-50 chance that a Beta will adapt an aggressive "kill" response to a contact situation. Once the creature finds that the kill response works, it will use it under the same contact situation in the future.

The program suggested here fills the screen with 64 randomly positioned obstacles. The Beta creature is placed at some random position in that field and given a randomly generated, initial motion code.

Of course the Beta memory is cleared to the invalid stop codes when the program is started, so the creature begins its experiences without the least notion of how to respond effectively to contact situations. The initial contact with an obstacle on an element of the border figure will elicit a reflex, random response. It might or might not include a "kill" quality. Once the creature finds a workable

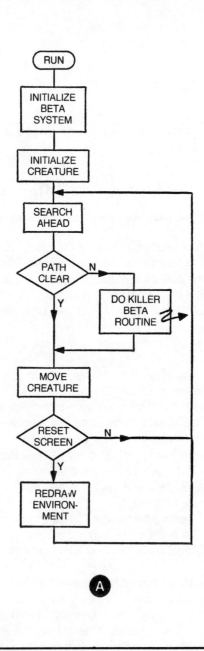

Fig. 12-1. Flowchart for KILLER BETA DEMO.

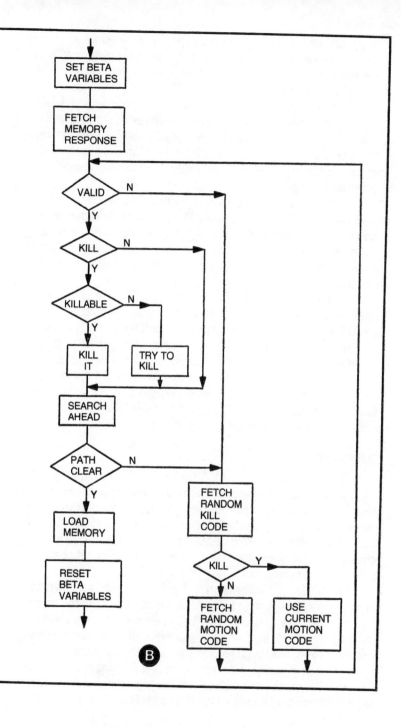

143

response—one that either generates a motion code that lets it run away from the obstacle or one that lets the creature kill the obstacle—it remembers it, and calls upon it immediately when needed in the future.

When the creature kills an obstacle, that obstacle is deleted from the environment, and the creature moves on with the motion code that existed the moment the contact occurred. The creature will attempt to "kill" sections of the border figure, but that must never be allowed to happen. The border figure can be "dented," but never hacked open.

Begin a habit-forming Beta creature. You will find it soon develops a habit pattern of motion. The program is designed so that the creature leaves behind a trail of light. The trail, itself, if insensible as far as the creature is concerned, and its only purpose is to help you determine whether or not the creature has fallen into its habit pattern.

Striking the ENTER (TRS-80) or RETURN (Apple) key deletes the old trail pattern and replaces any obstacles that might have been killed at an earlier time. The experiment is especially interesting when the Beta's habit pattern includes some spaces originally occupied by an obstacle or two. Once the creature deletes them, the pattern takes no account of them. Clearing away the old trail and replacing all original obstacles, however, gives you a chance to see how the Beta deals with resurrected obstacles. The outcome is not always entirely predicatable.

FLOWCHART ANALYSIS

The flowchart for KILLER BETA DEMO is shown in Fig. 12-1. It is divided into two sections for the sake of clarity. Section A shows the initializing operations and the operations normally used when the creature is running freely across the screen. The RESET SCREEN conditional in that section of the flowchart gives you the chance to clear up the old trail and replace any deleted obstacles after every creature move.

The section of the flowchart in Fig. 12-1B is used whenever the Beta creature encounters an obstacle or an element of the border figure. Whenever that happens, the system calls upon the Beta memory to see whether or not the contact situation has occurred before. If so—if the VALID conditional is answered with a "Y"—the next question concerns the matter of killing the obstacle. If, in the past experience, the creature solved the contact situation by making a kill response, it either kills the obstacle or attempts to kill a

144

portion of the border figure. In any event, the motion code from memory is tried by the SEARCH AHEAD operation. If the remembered response works again this time, the path is clear and the response—including the 1 or 0 kill response—is loaded into Beta memory for future reference.

If the initial response does not work or if the particular contact situation has never been encountered before, the creature resorts to the Alpha-like behavior that is represented here by operations that fetch a random kill code and, possibly, a new random motion code. After doing that, the system loops back to the VALID test and runs through the series of Beta responses.

TRS-80 VERSION

The program for KILLER BETA DEMO is shown in Listing 12-1. You can save yourself a bit of programming time by loading FUNDAMENTAL BETA DEMO from tape or disk, deleting its mainline programming, then replacing it with BETA MAINLINE, V.3—lines 10 through 265.

Listing 12-1. Programming for the TRS-80 Version of KILLER BETA DEMO.

```
10 REM   KILLER BETA DEMO
15 REM        TRS-80
20 REM
25 REM
100 REM ** BETA MAINLINE, V.3—TRS-80 **
105 DIM M(4,4,3):DIM TM(63):TC=45:TT=191
110 FOR MI=0 TO 4:FOR MJ=0 TO 4:FOR KL=1 TO 3
115 M(MI,MJ,KL)=2:NEXT KL,MJ,MI
120 CLS:GOSUB 1000
125 FOR N=0 TO 63
130 TP=15360+RND(831):IF PEEK(TP)<> 32 THEN 130
135 POKE TP,TT:TM(N)=TP:NEXT N
140 CP=15360+RND(831):IF PEEK(CP)<> 32 THEN 140
145 POKE CP,42
150 CI= RND(5)—3:CJ=RND(5)—3:IF  CI=0  AND  CJ=0
    THEN 150
155 GOSUB 2000
160 IF (CX=32 OR CX=TC) AND (CY=32 OR CY=TC)
    THEN 230
165 MI=CI+2:MJ=CJ+2
170 CI=M(MI,MJ,1):CJ=M(MI,MJ,2):KC=M(MI,MJ,3)
175 IF NOT((CI=2 AND CJ=2) OR KC>1) THEN 195
```

```
180 KC=RND(2)-1
185 IF KC=1 THEN CI=MI:CJ=MJ:GOTO 195
190 CI=RND(5)-1:CJ=RND(5)-1:GOTO 175
195 IF KC=0 THEN 210
200 IF PEEK(NP)>=129 AND PEEK(NP)<=176 THEN
    POKE NP,153:GOTO 210
205 POKE NP,TC
210 CI=CI-2:CJ=CJ-2:GOSUB 2000:CI=CI+2:CJ=CJ+2
215 IF NOT((CX=32 OR CX=TC) AND (CY=32 OR
    CY=TC)) THEN 180
220 M(MI,MJ,1)=CI:M(MI,MJ,2)=CJ:M(MI,MJ,3)=KC
225 CI=CI-2:CJ=CJ-2
230 POKE CP,TC
235 CP=NP:POKE CP,42
240 IF INKEY$="" THEN 155
245 CLS:GOSUB 1000
250 FOR N=0 TO 63:POKE TM(N),TT:NEXT N
255 GOTO 155
260 REM
265 REM
1000 REM ** BORDER, V.1-TRS-80 **
1005 F0=15360:F1=15423:F2=16128:F3=16191
1010 FOR N=F0 TO F1:POKE N,176:NEXT N
1015 FOR N=F2 TO F3:POKE N,131:NEXT N
1020 FOR N=F0 TO F2 STEP 64:POKE N,170:NEXT
1025 FOR N=F1 TO F3 STEP 64:POKE N,149:NEXT
1030 POKE F0, 160:POKE F1,144:POKE F2,130:POKE
    F3,129
1035 RETURN
1040 REM
1045 REM
2000 REM ** SEARCH AHEAD, V.2-TRS-80 **
2005 NP=CP:CX=32:CY=32
2010 SI=SGN(CI):SJ=SGN(CJ):AI=ABS(CI):AJ=ABS(CJ)
2015 IF AI= 0 THEN 2030 ELSE AI=AI-1
2020 IF SI>0 THEN NP=NP+1 ELSE NP=NP-1
2025 CX=PEEK(NP)
2030 IF AJ=0 THEN 2045 ELSE AJ=AJ-1
2035 IF SJ>0 THEN NP=NP+64 ELSE NP=NP-64
2040 CY=PEEK(NP)
2045 IF NOT((CX=32 OR CX=TC) AND (CY=32 OR
    CY=TC)) THEN RETURN
```

```
2050  IF AI=0 AND AJ=0 THEN RETURN ELSE GOTO 2015
2055  REM
```

Theory of Operation

Use the variable list in Table 12-1 as a guide for studying the following line-by-line analysis of the program. Of course the flow-chart in Fig. 12-1 will be helpful as well.

Line 105—Dimension the arrays and fix the trail code and obstacle graphic code.

Lines 110-115—Set the entire Beta memory to the invalid motion code (2,2) and an invalid kill code (2).

Line 120—Clear the screen and draw the border figure.

Lines 125-135—Select positions for the 64 randomly placed obstacle figures. If one falls on top of another, pick another position. Remember the positions in the TM array.

Table 12-1. TRS-80 Variable List for KILLER BETA DEMO.

MI	Memory version of CI (range of 0-4)
MJ	Memory version of CJ (range of 0-4)
KL	Memory data pointer: 1 response CI
	2 response CJ
	3 response KC
M(MI,MJ,1)	Response CI
M(MI,MJ,2)	Response CJ
M(MI,MJ,3)	Response KC
CI	Horizontal component of motion code
CJ	Vertical component of motion code
KC	Kill response: 0 for no kill, 1 for kill
TP	Screen position of an obstacle
TM(N)	Screen position of obstacle N
TC	Creature trail graphic code
TT	Obstacle graphic code
CP	Creature's current screen position
NP	Creature's next screen position
N	General-purpose numeric variable
SI	Sign value of CI
SJ	Sign value of CJ
AI	Absolute value of CI
AJ	Absolute value of CJ
CX	Horizontal component of contact code
CY	Vertical component of contact code
F0	Upper-left corner of border figure
F1	Upper-right corner of border figure
F2	Lower-left corner of border figure
F3	Lower-right corner of border figure

Lines 140-145—Pick a random clear spot for the creature's initial position. Draw the creature figure.

Line 150—Get a random motion code for the creature.

Lines 155-160—Do not search ahead routine. Move the creature (jump to line 230) if the path is clear. Otherwise, begin the Beta routine at line 165.

Lines 165-175—Adjust the motion code to the range of 0-4, fetch the response from memory and test its validity. If the remembered response is valid, then try it (beginning at line 195); otherwise, get some random responses.

Lines 180-190—Get a random kill code. If it calls for trying the kill response, retain the same motion code and see if the kill works (by trying it at line 195). If the kill is not to take place, fetch a run-away response—a new random motion code—and jump back to line 175 to check its validity.

Lines 195-205—If the creature is not to attempt a kill, then do the search ahead at line 210. Otherwise test to see whether or not the thing in its path is killable. If it is an element of the border figure, just "dent" it with code 153; otherwise, kill it by replacing it with the trail code graphic.

Line 210—Do the search ahead routine, adjusting the motion code variables before and after.

Lines 215-225—If a contact situation still exists, loop back to line 180 to try something else. Otherwise readjust the Beta variables and get ready to move the creature.

Lines 230-235—Move the creature.

Lines 240—Scan the keyboard for a possible key depression. If no key is depressed, continue normal activity by looping back to the search ahead routine at line 155.

Lines 245-255—Clear the screen, draw the border figure, and replace all the obstacles in their original positions. Loop back to line 155 to resume normal activity.

Running the Program

As listed here, the creature appears as an asterisk figure, its trail is a hyphen (graphic 45), and the obstacle figures are rectangles of light (graphic 191).

The program runs endlessly, and becomes quite monotonous once the Beta establishes its habit pattern of motion. Striking the ENTER key will clear up old trail figures and possibly extend the interest of the routine by throwing an old obstacle back into the creature's path. Eventually the creature will learn to deal with every situation you can offer it, and at that time, it is best to strike the BREAK key to end the experiment. The program featured in the next chapter offers a few more options.

APPLESOFT VERSION

The program for KILLER BETA DEMO is shown here as Listing 12-2. You can save yourself a bit of keyboard time by loading FUNDAMENTAL BETA DEMO from tape or disk, deleting its mainline program, then replacing it with BETA MAINLINE, V.3—lines 10 through 315.

Listing 12-2. Applesoft Listing for KILLER BETA DEMO.

```
10 REM   KILLER BETA DEMO
15 REM       APPLESOFT
20 REM
25 REM
30 REM
100 REM ** BETA MAINLINE, V.3—APPLESOFT **
105 DIM M(4,4,3): DIM TM(63,2):TC = 13:TT = 2
110 DEF FN R(R) = INT (5 * RND (1)) − 2
115 DEF FN P(P) = INT (P * RND (1)) + 1
120 FOR MI = 0 TO 4: FOR MJ = 0 TO 4: FOR KL = 1 TO 3
125 M(MI,MJ,KL) = 2: NEXT KL,MJ,MI
130 HOME : GR : GOSUB 1000
135 COLOR= TT
140 FOR N= 0 TO 63
145 TX = FN P(38):TY = FN P(35)
150 IF SCRN(TX,TY) < > 0 THEN 145
155 PLOT TX,TY:TM(N,1) = TX:TM(N,2) = TY
160 NEXT N
165 PX = FN P(38):PY = FN P(35)
170 IF SCRN(PX,PY) < > 0 THEN 165
175 COLOR= 9: PLOT PX,PY
180 CI = FN R(0):CJ = FN R(0): IF CI = 0 AND CJ = 0 THEN
    180
185 GOSUB 2000
190 IF (CX = 0 OR CX = TC) AND (CY = 0 OR CY = TC)
    THEN 265
195 MI = CI + 2:MJ = CJ + 2
200 CI = M(MI,MJ,1):CJ = M(MI,MJ,2):KC = M(MI,MJ,3)
205 IF NOT ((CI = 2 AND CJ = 2) OR KC > 1) THEN 225
```

149

```
210  KC = INT (RND (1) + .5)
215  IF KC = 1 THEN CI = MI:CJ = MJ: GOTO 205
220  CI = FN R(0) + 2:CJ = FN R(0) + 2: GOTO 205
225  IF KC = 0 THEN 245
230  IF SCRN(NX,NY) < 14 THEN 240
235  COLOR= 14: PLOT NX,NY: GOTO 245
240  COLOR= 0: PLOT NX, NY
245  CI = CI – 2:CJ = CJ – 2: GOSUB 2000:CI = CI + 2:CJ =
     CJ + 2
250  IF NOT ((CX = 0 OR CX = TC) AND (CY = 0 OR CY =
     TC)) THEN 210
255  M(MI,MJ,1) = CI:M(MI,MJ,2) = CJ:M(MI,MJ,3) = KC
260  CI = CI – 2:CJ = CJ – 2
265  COLOR= TC: PLOT PX,PY
270  PX = NX:PY = NY
275  COLOR= 9: PLOT PX,PY
280  S = PEEK ( – 16384): POKE – 16368,0
285  IF S < = 127 THEN 185
290  TEXT : HOME : GR : GOSUB 1000
295  COLOR= TT
300  FOR N = 0 TO 63: PLOT TM(N,1),TM(N,2): NEXT N
305  GOTO 185
310  REM
315  REM
1000 REM ** BORDER,V.1—APPLESOFT **
1005 COLOR= 15
1010 HLIN 0,39 AT 0: HLIN 0,39 AT 36
1015 VLIN 0,36 AT 0: VLIN 0,36 AT 39
1020 RETURN
1025 REM
1030 REM
2000 REM ** SEARCH AHEAD, V.2—APPLESOFT **
2005 NX = PX:NY = PY:CX = 0:CY = 0
2010 SI = SGN (CI):SJ = SGN (CJ):AI = ABS (CI):AJ = ABS
     (CJ)
2015 IF AI = 0 THEN 2040
2020 AI = AI – 1
2025 IF SI > 0 THEN NX = NX + 1: GOTO 2035
2030 NX = NX – 1
2035 CX = SCRN(NX,NY)
2040 IF AJ = 0 THEN 2065
2045 AJ = AJ – 1
```

```
2050  IF SJ > 0 THEN NY = NY + 1: GOTO 2060
2055  NY = NY − 1
2060  CY = SCRN(NX,NY)
2065  IF NOT ((CX = 0 OR CX = TC) AND (CY = 0 OR CY =
      TC)) THEN RETURN
2070  IF AI=0 AND AJ= 0 THEN RETURN
2075  GOTO 2015
2080  REM
2085  REM
```

Theory of Operation

Use the variable list in Table 12-2 and the flowchart in **Fig.**
12-1 as guides for following this line-by-line analysis of the program.

Lines 105-115—Dimension the arrays, set the trail and obstacle color codes, and define the motion code and random position functions.

Table 12-2. Applesoft Variable List for KILLER BETA DEMO.

MI	Memory version of CI (range of 0-4)
MJ	Memory version of CJ (range of 0-4)
KL	Memory data pointer: 1 response CI
	2 response CJ
	3 response KC
M(MI,MJ,1)	Response CI
M(MI,MJ,2)	Response CJ
M(MI,MJ,3)	Response KC
KC	Kill response: 1 kill
	2 no kill
TM(N,1)	Horizontal component of obstacle N's screen position
TM(N,2)	Vertical component of obstacle N's screen position
FN R(R)	Random motion code function
FN P(P)	Random screen position function
CI	Horizontal component of motion code
CJ	Vertical component of motion code
PX	Horizontal component of creature position
PY	Vertical component of creature position
TC	Creature trail color code
TT	Obstacle figure color code
NX	Horizontal component of new creature position
NY	Vertical component
N,S	General-purpose numeric variables
SI	Sign value of CI
SJ	Sign value of CJ
AI	Absolute value of CI
AJ	Absolute value of CJ
CX	Horizontal component of contact code
CY	Vertical component of contact code

Lines 120-125—Initialize the Beta memory with invalid motion codes (2,2) and invalid kill codes (2).

Line 130—Clear the screen, set the graphic mode and draw the border figure on the screen.

Lines 135-160—Select positions for the 64 obstacle figures. If one falls on top of another, pick another random position for it. Save the positions in array TM and draw those obstacles on the screen.

Lines 165-175—Find a random, unused screen position for starting the creature. Draw its figure.

Line 180—Get a random initial motion code.

Lines 185-190—Do the search ahead routine. If the path is clear, move the creature by jumping to line 265. Otherwise begin the Beta routine.

Lines 195-205—Set the Beta variables, check the content of the Beta memory, and test the validity of that remembered response. If the response is valid, try it out by jumping to line 225; otherwise get a new response.

Lines 210-220—Fetch a random kill code. If it is the kill code then use the present motion code and doublecheck its validity by looping back to line 205. If it is not a kill code, get a new random motion code.

Lines 225-240—If the response does not call for a kill, then jump to search the path ahead. If the response is a kill, but the obstacle is a non-killable one, "dent" it by replacing it with color code 14. If the obstacle is a killable one, delete it with a color code 0.

Line 245—Search the path ahead, adjusting the range of motion codes before and after.

Lines 250-260—If the path ahead is still obstructed, loop back to line 210 to begin all over. Otherwise remember the response and ready the motion codes for moving the creature to its new position on the screen.

Lines 265-275—Move the creature.

Lines 280-285—Scan the keyboard. If no key is depressed, loop to line 185 to resume normal activity.

Lines 290-305—Clear the screen, redraw the border figure, and replace all obstacles to their original positions. Go back to line 185 to resume normal activity.

Running the Program

As listed here, the creature appears as an orange figure, its trail is yellow, and the obstacle figures are dark blue.

The program runs endlessly, and becomes rather monotonous once the Beta creature establishes its habit pattern of motion. Striking the RETURN key clears up the old trail patterns and repairs any damage the creature has done to the obstacles and border figure.

Eventually, the creature will learn to cope with its environment, even after redrawing it. At that time, the best thing to do is a CTRL C. Do a RUN to start the whole operation from scratch again. The program featured in the next chapter offers a few more options.

Chapter 13
Killer Beta with Alterable Conditions

A killer Beta can be a nasty little creature at times. It appears to kill off most obstacles that get into its way, and once it builds up a killer habit, it uses those responses to keep itself running in its habit pattern of motion. The previous killer Beta demonstration, however, had no provisions for proving that the creature can retain its killer responses and implement them again when necessary.

The program featured in this chapter begins running much like the program suggested in Chapter 12. Here, however, you have the option of manipulating the environment and creature codes via keys on the computer keyboard assembly. The main idea is to show how well a killer Beta can survive changes in its environment.

Table 13-1 summarizes the key controls. They are nearly indentical to similar functions built into an earlier Beta experiment in Chapter 11. Striking the *A* key clears out the Beta memory and forces the creature to begin learning its way around from scratch. Striking the *K* key gives the creature a little kick out of its present path; actually generating a new random motion code. The *D* key lets you displace the creature to a new, randomly generated position on the screen, and the *E* key generates a whole new set of randomly positioned obstacles. Striking the ENTER (TRS-80) or RETURN (Apple) key clears out the old creature trail and redraws all the obstacles in their original positions, including those that were killed by the creature at some earlier time. The latter feature represents the main difference between these key functions and those offered in Chapter 11.

The most meaningful demonstration of killer Beta behavior begins by letting the creature establish its habit pattern of motion.

Table 13-1. Table of Key Controls of Experimenting with the Killer Beta Creature.

A	Abort the present Beta memory, but continue with the same environment and creature variables.
K	Kick the creature out of its present path, but continue with the same environment and screen position.
D	Displace the creature from its present position, but continue with the same environment and creature motion code.
E	Generate a whole new environment, but retain all the present creature variables.
ENTER or RETURN	Clear the old trail and replace any killed obstacles; retain the present BETA memory and creature variables.

In doing so, it usually kills a few obstacles to make way for a clear habit path. Once that habit pattern is established, there will be no further need for killing anything—the path is void of obstacles that require killing.

Once the habit pattern is established, you can attempt to upset it by striking the ENTER or RETURN key. If the path originally contained an obstacle, it will be replaced and the creature will be forced to deal with it—either killing it in an attempt to re-establish the same habit pattern of motion, or bouncing away from it to set up its habit pattern elsewhere on the screen. No matter how the creature responds to replacing all previously killed obstacles, it will eventually adapt to the situation.

It is also quite interesting to let the creature establish a habit pattern of motion, then kick it out of its present path by striking the *K* key. The adaptive effort in that case can be more traumatic for the creature, often causing it to alter its habit pattern. You will also notice a tendency to set up simpler habit patterns each time the creature is kicked out of its current pattern of motion. It doesn't always happen, but doing a number of kicks in succession (allowing the creature to set up a new habit pattern between each kick) produces successively simpler habit patterns. If, indeed, there is some validity to this particular observation, it means that simpler habits are more adaptive to variety than complex habits are. This must be proven by doing some carefully planned psychological experiments, however.

FLOWCHART ANALYSIS

The flowchart for the main flow of operations is shown in Fig. 13-1. After initializing the system, clearing the Beta memory to invalid stop codes (2,2) clearing the screen, drawing the border figure and initializing the creature position on the screen, the actual running begins by picking a random motion code. After that, the creature searches the path ahead. If the path is clear, the creature moves to its next position on the screen and the system scans the keyboard for a key depression.

If the A key is depressed, the ABORT conditional is satisfied, and the system responds by clearing the Beta memory to the invalid stop codes. That literally wipes out anything the creature might have learned through past experiences. If the K key is depressed, the KICK conditional loops operations back to the point in the program where the creature selects a new random motion code. If the D key is depressed, the DISPLACE conditional causes the system to fetch a new random screen position on the screen. Finally, if some key is depressed, but it isn't one of the keys just mentioned, the system clears the screen, draws a fresh border figure, and looks to see whether or not the E key is depressed. If it is, the NEW OBSTACLES conditional is satisfied, and the system draws a whole new set of randomly positioned obstacles. Otherwise, the assumption is that the ENTER or RETURN key is depressed, and the old obstacles are all replaced in their original positions.

Whenever the creature does a search ahead routine and finds that the path ahead is *not* clear, it switches over to the killer Beta routine. That routine is shown in detail in Fig. 13-2.

The flowchart in this case is virtually identical to the one in Fig. 12-1. Assuming you studied the matter thoroughly in that earlier chapter, there is no need for going into great detail here. Briefly, the system uses the current motion code as an address for the Beta memory. If the memory contains some information from a previous encounter of the same type, it is considered VALID information, and it is tried. And if that previous response works—if it is found that the response clears the path ahead—it is simply remembered again, and the system returns to the main running loop in Fig. 13-1.

But if the remembered response doesn't work for some reason, or if the content of the memory is invalid, the system fetches a random kill code. If it is a kill instruction, the creature retains its current motion code, doublechecks the validity of its new response, and gives it a try. If the system happens to select a random no-kill response, the creature fetches a new motion code and gives it a try.

Ultimately, the system returns to the main sequence of opera-

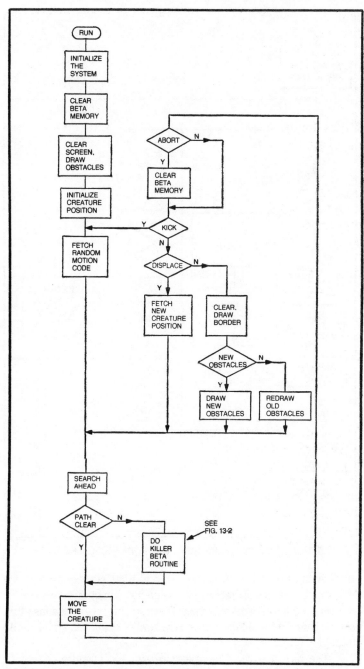

Fig. 13-1. Main program loop for KILLER BETA WITH OBSTACLE OPTIONS.

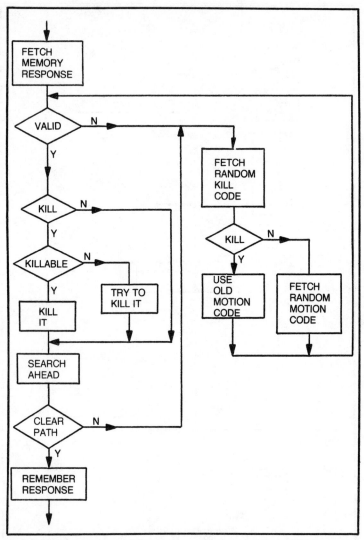

Fig. 13-2. Beta routine for KILLER BETA WITH OBSTACLE OPTIONS.

tions with a workable response saved in the Beta memory. Every encounter with an obstacle (not including elements of the border figure) produces a workable response in memory—a response that can be called up immediately when a similar condition arises in the future.

The fact that the Beta creature can successfully cope with unexpected changes in its environment has nothing at all to do with changing any part of the basic Beta function. The creature programs itself to adapt to changes in the environment, altering its Beta memory as necessary to do the job.

TRS-80 VERSION

The programming for KILLER BETA DEMO WITH OBSTA-CLE OPTIONS is shown as Listing 13-1. The BORDER and SEARCH AHEAD routines can be loaded from tape or disk if you have saved the listing from Chapter 12 in that fashion. Doing so, you can delete the old mainline and replace it with BETA MAINLINE, V.4 shown here.

The killer creature appears as an asterisk figure, its trail is a series of hyphens, and the killable obstacles shown up as graphic-191 rectangles of light. "Dents" the creature makes in the border figure appear as graphic 153 figures.

The program runs endlessly; so when you want to run a new creature, you can do one of two things. First, you can strike the *A* key to abort the current Beta memory, and then strike the *E* key to build a new environment. Otherwise, you can simply strike the BREAK key and do a RUN to start the whole program from the beginning.

Listing 13-1. TRS-80 Programming for KILLER BETA WITH OBSTACLE OPTIONS.

```
10 REM  KILLER BETA DEMO
15 REM  WITH OBSTACLE OPTIONS
20 REM    TRS-80
25 REM
30 REM
100 REM ** BETA MAINLINE, V.4—TRS-80 **
105 NT=63:DIM M(4,4,3):DIM TM(63):TC=45:TT=191
110 FOR MI=0 TO 4:FOR MJ=0 TO 4:FOR KL=1 TO 3
115 M(MI,MJ,KL)=2:NEXT KL,MJ,MI
120 CLS:GOSUB 1000
125 FOR N=0 TO 63
130 TP=15360+RND(831):IF PEEK(TP)<>32 THEN 130
135 POKE TP,TT:TM(N)=TP:NEXT N
140 CP=15360+RND(831):IF PEEK(CP)<>32 THEN 140
145 POKE CP,42
150 CI=RND(5)−3:CJ=RND(5)−3:IF CI=0 AND CJ=0
    THEN 150
155 GOSUB 2000
160 IF (CX=32 OR CX=TC) AND (CY=32 OR CY=TC)
    THEN 230
```

```
165  MI=CI+2:MJ=CJ+2
170  CI=M(MI,MJ,1):CJ=M(MI,MJ,2):KC=M(MI,MJ,3)
175  IF NOT((CI=2 AND CJ=2) OR KC>1) THEN 195
180  KC=RND(2)-1
185  IF KC=1 THEN CI=MI:CJ=MJ:GOTO 195
190  CI=RND(5)-1:CJ=RND(5)-1:GOTO 175
195  IF KC=0 THEN 210
200  IF PEEK(NP)>=129 AND PEEK (NP)<=176 THEN
     POKE NP,153:GOTO 210
205  POKE NP,TC
210  CI=CI-2:CJ=CJ-2:GOSUB 2000:CI=CI+2:CJ=CJ+2
215  IF NOT((CX=32 OR CX=TC) AND (CY=32 OR
     CY=TC)) THEN 180
220  M(MI,MJ,1)=CI:M(MI,MJ,2)=CJ:M(MI,MJ,3)=KC
225  CI=CI-2:CJ=CJ-2
230  POKE CP,TC
235  CP=NP:POKE CP,42
240  S$=INKEY$:IF S$="" THEN 155
245  IF S$<>"A" THEN 260
250  FOR MI=0 TO 4:FOR MJ=0 TO 4:FOR KL=1 TO 3
255  M(MI,MJ,KL)=2:NEXT KL,MJ,MI:GOTO 155
260  IF S$="K" THEN 150
265  IF S$<>"D" THEN 285
270  POKE CP,32
275  CP=15360+RND(831):IF PEEK(CP)<>32 THEN 275
280  POKE CP,42:GOTO 155
285  CLS:GOSUB 1000
290  IF S$<>"E" THEN 320
295  POKE CP,42
300  FOR N=0 TO NT
305  TP=15360+RND(831):IF PEEK(TP)<>32 THEN 305
310  POKE TP,TT:TM(N)=TP
315  NEXT N:GOTO 155
320  FOR N=0 TO NT:POKE TM(N), TT:NEXT N:GOTO 155
325  REM
330  REM
1000 REM ** BORDER, V.1-TRS-80 **
1005 F0=15360:F1=15423:F2=16128:F3=16191
1010 FOR N=F0 TO F1:POKE N,176:NEXT N
1015 FOR N=F2 TO F3:POKE N,131:NEXT N
1020 FOR N=F0 TO F2 STEP 64:POKE N,170:NEXT
```

```
1025 FOR N=F1 TO F3 STEP 64:POKE N,149:NEXT
1030 POKE F0,160:POKE F1,144:POKE F2,130:POKE
     F3,129
1035 RETURN
1040 REM
1045 REM
2000 REM ** SEARCH AHEAD, V.2—TRS-80 **
2005 NP=CP:CX=32:CY=32
2010 SI=SGN(CI):SJ=SGN(CJ):AI=ABS(CI):AJ=ABS(CJ)
2015 IF AI=0 THEN 2030 ELSE AI=AI−1
2020 IF SI>0 THEN NP=NP+1 ELSE NP=NP−1
2025 CX=PEEK(NP)
2030 IF AJ=0 THEN 2045 ELSE AJ=AJ−1
2035 IF SJ>0 THEN NP=NP+64 ELSE NP=NP−64
2040 CY=PEEK(NP)
2045 IF NOT((CX=32 OR CX=TC) AND (CY=32 OR
     CY=TC)) THEN RETURN
2050 IF AI=0 AND AJ=0 THEN RETURN ELSE GOTO 2015
2055 REM
2060 REM
```

The more you experiment with this program, the more ideas you will get about devising further experiments.

The variable list is shown in Table 13-2. Use that list in conjunction with Figs. 13-1 and 13-2 as you work your way through the following line-by-line analysis of the program.

Line 105—Dimension the arrays and define the essential graphic codes.

Lines 110-115—Clear the Beta memory to invalid motion codes and kill codes.

Line 120—Clear the screen and draw the border figure.

Lines 125-135—Find random, non-overlapping positions for the 64 obstacle figures; draw them on the screen and save their positions in array TM.

Lines 140-150—Initialize the creature position and motion code.

Lines 155-160—Do the search ahead routine. If the path is clear or composed of the creature's own trail, jump down to line 230 to move the creature.

Lines 165-175—Look at the Beta memory. If the content is valid, try the response from line 195.

Lines 180-190—Fetch a random kill code. If it calls for doing a kill, retain the present motion code and try it from line 195. If it is a no-kill code, fetch a new random motion code and check its validity from line 175.

Lines 195-205—If the creature is to attempt a kill, check to see whether or not the obstacle is a portion of the border figure. If it is, then "dent" it with a graphic 153 and jump down to see whether or not that response cleared the path (which it never will). If the obstacle is not an element of the border figure, wipe it out.

Lines 210-225—Search the path ahead. IF it is not clear, jump back to line 180 to fetch some random elements of behavior. Otherwise, remember the response and get ready to move.

Lines 230-235—Move the creature.

Line 240—Scan the keyboard. If no key is depressed, loop back to line 155 for the next search ahead cycle.

Lines 245-320—Take action relevant to the key that is depressed, ultimately looping back to line 155 to resume activity.

Table 13-2. TRS-80 Variable List for KILLER BETA WITH OBSTACLE OPTIONS.

NT	Number of obstacles in the environment
TM(N)	Screen position of obstacle N (N=0 through NT)
TC	Creature's trail graphic code
TT	Obstacle graphic code
MI	Memory version of stimulus CI
MJ	Memory version of stimulus CJ
M(MI,MJ,1)	Memory version of response CI
M(MI,MJ,2)	Memory version of response CJ
M(MI,MJ,3)	Memory of kill code
KL	Memory response pointer (1 for CI, 2 for CJ, 3 for Kill code)
CI	Horizontal component of motion code
CJ	Vertical component of motion code
CP	Creature's current screen position
NP	Creature's next screen position
CX	Horizontal component of contact code
CY	Horizontal component of contact code
KC	Kill code (0 for no-kill, 1 for kill)
N	General-purpose numeric variable
S$	General-purpose string variable
SI	Sign value of CI
SJ	Sign value of CJ
AI	Absolute value of CI
AJ	Absolute value of CJ
F0	Upper-left corner of border figure
F1	Upper-right corner of border figure
F2	Lower-left corner of border figure
F3	Lower-right corner of border figure

Lines 1000-1030—Border drawing subroutine.
Lines 2000-2050—Search ahead subroutine.

APPLESOFT VERSION

The programming for KILLER BETA DEMO WITH OBSTA-
CLE OPTIONS is shown for the Applesoft system in Listing 13-2.
The BORDER and SEARCH AHEAD subroutines can be loaded
from tape or disk if you have saved the listing from Chapter 12 in
that fashion. After loading that program, you can delete the old
mainline and replace it with BETA MAINLINE, B.4 shown here.

The killer creature appears as a bright orange square, its trail
is yellow, and the killable obstacles are dark blue. "Dents" that the
creature makes in the white border figure appear green.

The program runs endlessly, so when you want to run a new
creature, you can do one of two things. First, you can strike the A
key to abort the current Beta memory, and then strike the E key to
build a brand-new environment. Otherwise, you can simply do a
CTRL C operation, followed by a RUN. In either case, you end up
running a new creature in a fresh environment.

Listing 13-2. Applesoft Programming for KILLER BETA WITH OBSTACLE OPTIONS.

```
 10 REM   KILLER BETA DEMO
 15 REM   WITH OBSTACLE OPTIONS
 20 REM      APPLESOFT
 25 REM
 30 REM
 35 REM
100 REM ** BETA MAINLINE, V.4—APPLESOFT **
105 NT = 63: DIM M(4,4,3): DIM TM(NT,2):TC = 13:TT = 2
110 DEF FN R(R) = INT (5 * RND (1)) − 2
115 DEF FN P(P) = INT (P* RND (1)) + 1
120 FOR MI = 0 TO 4: FOR MJ = 0 TO 4: FOR KL = 1 TO 3
125 M(MI,MJ,KL) = 2: NEXT KL,MJ,MI
130 HOME : GR : GOSUB 1000
135 COLOR= TT
140 FOR N = 0 TO 63
145 TX = FN P(38):TY = FN P(35)
150 IF SCRN(TX,TY) <> 0 THEN 145
155 PLOT TX,TY:TM(N,1) = TX:TM(N,2) = TY
160 NEXT N
165 PX = FN P(38):PY = FN P(35)
```

163

```
170 IF SCRN(PX,PY) <> φ THEN 165
175 COLOR= 9: PLOT PX,PY
180 CI = FN R(0):CJ = FN R(0): IF CI = 0 AND CJ
    = 0 THEN 180
185 GOSUB 2000
190 IF (CX = 0 OR CX = TC) AND (CY = 0 OR CY = TC)
    THEN 265
195 MI = CI + 2:MJ = CJ + 2
200 CI = M(MI,MJ,1):CJ = M(MI,MJ,2):KC = M(MI,MJ,3)
205 IF NOT ((CI = 2 AND CJ = 2) OR KC > 1) THEN 225
210 KC = INT (RND (1) + .5)
215 IF KC = 1 THEN CI = MI:CJ = MJ: GOTO 205
220 CI = FN R(0) + 2:CJ = FN R(0) + 2: GOTO 205
225 IF KC = 0 THEN 245
230 IF SCRN(NX,NY) < 14 THEN 240
235 COLOR= 14: PLOT NX,NY: GOTO 245
240 COLOR= 0: PLOT NX,NY
245 CI = CI - 2:CJ = CJ - 2: GOSUB 2000:CI = CI + 2:CJ =
    CJ + 2
250 IF NOT ((CX = 0 OR CX = TC) AND (CY = 0 OR CY =
    TC)) THEN 210
255 M(MI,MJ,1) = CI:M(MI,MJ,2) = CJ:M(MI,MJ,3) = KC
260 CI = CI - 2:CJ = CJ - 2
265 COLOR= TC: PLOT PX,PY
270 PX = NX:PY = NY
275 COLOR= 9: PLOT PX,PY
280 S = PEEK ( - 16384): POKE - 16368,0
285 IF S < = 127 THEN 185
290 IF S < > 193 THEN 305
295 FOR MI = 0 TO 4: FOR MJ = 0 TO 4: FOR KL = 1 TO 3
300 M(MI,MJ,KL) = 2: NEXT KL,MJ,MI: GOTO 185
305 IF S = 203 THEN 180
310 IF S < > 196 THEN 330
315 COLOR= 0: PLOT PX,PY
320 PX = FN P(38):PY = FN P(35): IF SCRN(PX,PY) < > 0
    THEN 320
325 COLOR= 9: PLOT PX,PY: GOTO 185
330 TEXT : HOME : GR : GOSUB 1000
335 IF S < > 197 THEN 360
340 FOR N = 0 TO NT
345 TX = FN P(38):TY = FN P(35): IF SCRN(TX,TY) < > 0
    THEN 345
```

```
350  COLOR=TT:PLOT TX,TY:TM(N,1) = TX:TM(N,2) = TY
355  NEXT N:GOTO 185
360  COLOR=TT
365  FOR N = 0 TO NT: PLOT TM(N,1),TM(N,2): NEXT N
370  GOTO 185
375  REM
380  REM
1000  REM ** BORDER,V.1—APPLESOFT **
1005  COLOR= 15
1010  HLIN 0,39 AT 0: HLIN 0,39 AT 36
1015  VLIN 0,36 AT 0: VLIN 0,36 AT 39
1020  RETURN
1025  REM
1030  REM
2000  REM ** SEARCH AHEAD, V.2—APPLESOFT **
2005  NX = PX:NY = PY:CX = 0:CY = 0
2010  SI = SGN (CI):SJ = SGN (CJ):AI = ABS (CI):AJ = ABS
      (CJ)
2015  IF AI = 0 THEN 2040
2020  AI = AI − 1
2025  IF SI > 0 THEN NX = NX + 1: GOTO 2035
2030  NX = NX − 1
2035  CX = SCRN(NX,NY)
2040  IF AJ = 0 THEN 2065
2045  AJ = AJ − 1
2050  IF SJ > 0 THEN NY = NY + 1: GOTO 2060
2055  NY = NY − 1
2060  CY = SCRN(NX,NY)
2065  IF NOT ((CX = 0 OR CX = TC) AND (CY = 0 OR CY =
      TC)) THEN RETURN
2070  IF AI = 0 AND AJ = 0 THEN RETURN
2075  GOTO 2015
2080  REM
2085  REM
```

The variable list for the program is shown in Table 13-3. Use it in conjunction with Figs. 13-1 and 13-2 as you work your way through the following line-by-line analysis of the scheme.

 Lines 105-115—Dimension the arrays, set the critical color codes, and define the necessary functions.

 Lines 120-125—Clear the Beta memory to invalid motion and kill codes.

Line 130—Clear the screen, set the graphics mode, and draw the border figure.

Lines 135-160—Select random, non-overlapping positions for the 64 killable obstacle figures. Draw them and save their positions in array TM.

Lines 165-180—Select a random initial position and motion code for the creature.

Lines 185-190—Do the search ahead routine. If the path ahead is clear, jump down to line 265 to move the creature.

Lines 195-205—Get the memory response. If it is valid, then jump down to line 225 to try it out.

Lines 210-220—Get a random kill code. If it calls for a kill operation, use the current motion code and jump back to line 205 to doublecheck its validity. If it is not a kill code, fetch a new random motion code and check its validity.

Lines 225-240—If the creature is not to kill anything, jump to line 245 to do a search ahead routine. If the obstacle is an element of the border figure, "dent" it by replacing it

Table 13-3. Applesoft Variable List for KILLER BETA WITH OBSTACLE OPTIONS.

NT	Number of obstacles in the environment
TX	Horizontal component of obstacle position
TY	Vertical component of obstacle position
TM(N,1)	TX value for obstacle N
TM(N,2)	TY value for obstacle N
MI	Memory version of stimulus CI
MJ	Memory version of stimulus CJ
M(MI,MJ,1)	Memory version of response CI
M(MI,MJ,2)	Memory version of response CJ
M(MI,MJ,3)	Memory of kill code
KL	Memory response pointer (1 for CI, 2 for CJ, 3 for kill code)
TC	Creature's trail color code
TT	Obstacle color code
FN R(R)	Function for generating random motion code
FN P(P)	Function for generating random screen positions
CI	Horizontal component of motion code
CJ	Vertical component of motion code
PX	Horizontal component of creature position
PY	Vertical component of creature position
NX	Horizontal component of creature's next position
NY	Vertical component of creature's next position
KC	Kill code (0 for no-kill, 1 for kill)
SI	Sign value of CI
SJ	Sign value of CJ
AI	Absolute value of CI
AJ	Absolute value of CJ
S, N	General-purpose numeric variables

with a green spot. If the object is a killable creature, delete it from the screen by replacing it with color code 0.

Lines 245-250—Do a search ahead. If the path is not clear or not made up of the creature's own trail, loop back to line 210 to pick up some random response elements.

Lines 255-260—Remember the response that works.

Lines 265-275—Move the creature.

Lines 280-285—Scan the keyboard. If no key is depressed, loop back to line 185 to resume normal activity.

Lines 290-370—Take appropriate action based on the key that is depressed.

Lines 1000-1020—Border drawing subroutine.

Lines 2000-2075—Search ahead subroutine.

Chapter 14
Beta Duel

Putting two killer Beta creatures onto the same screen is a matter of combining the multitasking procedures already described for Alpha creatures with the programming for killer Betas just described. With this program, you will see two Beta creatures, each having a different appearance, drawn into a plain, bordered environment. They roam the environment, each developing their own ideas about how to deal with their surroundings. Their memory systems are entirely independent of one another.

They are killer Betas, and that means there is a chance that they will attempt to kill anything that gets in their way—a segment of the border figure or the other creature. They can take bites out of the border, but cannot actually chomp through it. When one Beta is killed by the other, the routine continues, with the killed Beta being resurrected as soon as it recovers from a trapped situation that might have spelled its doom in the first place.

The program can be used as a two-player betting game. Each player can bet that his or her Beta creature will kill the other first. But the real point of the program is to demonstrate the way Beta creatures, specifically killer Beta creatures, can adapt to the presence of another live creature in the environment. Here is a sample scenario.

The two killer Betas explore their environment. They just happen to stay away from one another for some length of time; perhaps long enough to set up a habit pattern of motion. Now once that habit pattern is established, there is a chance that it will remain in force indefinitely—as long as the other Beta doesn't eventually work its way into the habit-pattern territory. If and when the two creatures do come into contact, there's no telling what will happen. It all depends on each creature's previous learning experiences. If both creatures learned to bounce away from an obstacle under the contact situation that prevails at the moment, that is exactly what will happen when they encounter each other. Perhaps they will then run into each other again, at a later time and under a different combination of contact codes. Then there is the chance that one or the other will make a kill response.

I would like to be able to say that one creature will always end up killing the other. But that isn't necessarily the case. It is probable, but not certain. The two Betas might establish habit patterns of motion that never cross. To keep things interesting, the program includes the "kick" featured described in a couple of earlier experiments. Striking the K key "kicks" both creatures out of their current path; it gives both of them a new, randomly selected motion code. By working the K key and observing the responses, it is possible to coax the two killers into a combat situation.

The program runs endlessly, so it is terminated by striking the BREAK key (TRS-80) or doing the CTRL C operation from the keyboard (Apple).

FLOWCHART ANALYSIS

The flowcharts for DUAL KILLER BETA DEMO are shown in Figs. 14-1 and 14-2. The one in Fig. 14-1 illustrates the main flow of operations, and those in Fig. 14-2 show how the four individual operating phases are organized.

Referring to Fig. 14-1, the program begins in the usual fashion, clearing the Beta memories, clearing the screen and drawing the border figure, and initializing the creatures' positions and motion codes. That particular set of operations is executed only when the program is first started. The remainder of the flowchart represents one bit operating loop.

The main operating loop begins by having the system scan the keyboard for a key depression; and if it happens that the user has just hit the K key, the system sets up both creatures for doing a phase-1 operation when its next turn comes around. Phase-1 operations, as described shortly, involve selecting a random motion code. Thus, striking the K key interrupts the current phasing of the creatures and forces them to phase 1.

After completing the kick phase of the job, the system executes one of the four main operating phases and after that, the system switches over to service the other creature.

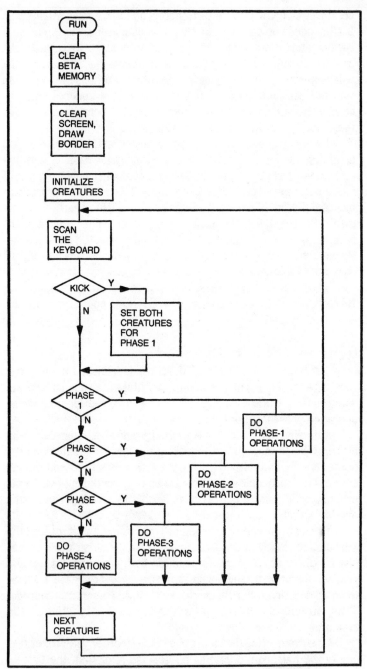

Fig. 14-1. Main program flowchart for DUAL KILLER BETA DEMO.

The main operating loop is thus run for the two creatures in turn. It is run for creature number 1, then for number 2, then back to number 1, and so on. Except immediately after doing the kick operation from the keyboard, the creatures aren't necessarily set for running the same phase of operation when their turn comes around. The scheme, in other words, is wholly asynchronous.

Figure 14-2 breaks down the four main operating phases of the program. Phase-1 operations merely fetch a valid (non-stopping) motion code. Phase-2 is mainly concerned with doing the search ahead routine and, if no contact occurs, moving the creature being serviced to its next position on the screen. But if a contact is sensed during the execution of the phase-2 operations, the system fetches the memory responses for that particular situation and that particular creature.

Phase-1 operations always conclude by setting up the creature for phase-2 operations. The creature leaves phase-2 operations pointed in one of two directions; either to phase-2 again (if no contact occurs) or phase-3 operations (if a contact does occur).

The phase-3 operations are concerned with the memory response task. It first tests the validity of the response pulled from the creature's Beta memory. If it is an invalid response (cleared or proven unworkable in the past), the system sets that creature for doing phase-4 operations on its next turn. Otherwise, the system looks to see whether or not the remembered response included a "kill" feature. If not, the creature searches the path ahead; otherwise, the system tests the obstacle to see whether or not it is a killable creature—something other than the border figure. If it is a portion of the border figure, the creature attempts to kill it, but only puts a "dent" in it. Otherwise, it wipes it out, doing a clean "kill."

Whether the creature actually kills or merely "dents" the obstacle, it does a search ahead. If the path is not clear (if the kill response failed to clear the path), the creature is set for phase-4 operations on its next turn. But if the path is clear after doing the kill response, the creature remembers that response, because it is a workable one, and is set for doing phase-2 operations next.

The creatures make a transition from phase-3 to phase-2 operations only after finding and remembering a workable response to a contact situation. The response might or might not include a kill feature.

The nature of the successful response is dictated by the workings of the phase-4 operations. Upon executing that phase, the creature picks up a random kill code, 0 or 1. If that response is a

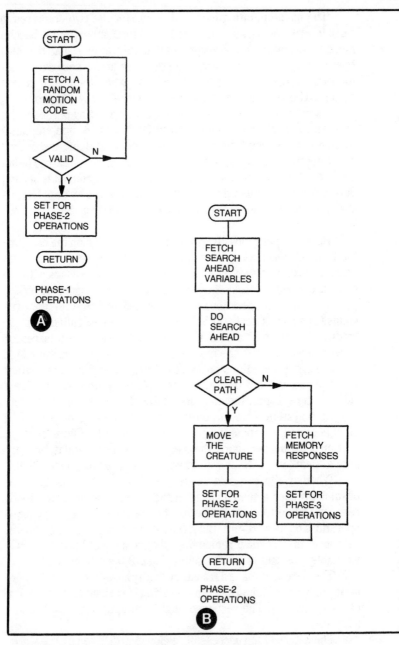

Fig. 14-2. DUAL KILLER BETA DEMO operations flowcharts. (A) (Phase-1 operations. (B) Phase-2 operations. (C) Phase-3 operations. (D) Phase-4 operations.

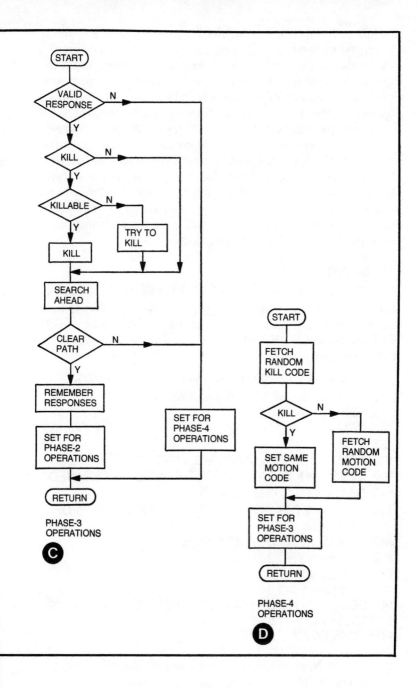

PHASE-3
OPERATIONS

C

PHASE-4
OPERATIONS

D

no-kill, or 0, response, it is subjected to the selection of a randomly generated motion code. The idea is to run away from the obstacle, rather than grapple with it in an aggressive fashion. But if the creature happens to pick a kill code, or 1, it retains the same motion code, presumably to kill the obstacle and trample over its body. In either case, the creature leaving phase-4 operations always returns phase 3 on its next turn. The idea is to try out the new response.

Phase 4 represents the real Alpha portion of the creatures' modes of behavior. The less trained the creatures are, the more frequent the references to the random, Alpha-like phase-4 operations. As the creatures become more experienced and they begin establishing successful habit patterns, there are far less references to phase-4 operations. Phase-3 operations dominate at that point; they are the distinctive Beta operations.

TRS-80 VERSION

The TRS-80 program for DUAL KILLER BETA DEMO is shown in Listing 14-1. Assuming you have saved an earlier Beta program on tape or disk, you can load the two subroutines, BORDER and SEARCH AHEAD, in that way. The mainline, however, has to be typed in from scratch.

Listing 14-1. TRS-80 Programming for DUAL KILLER BETA DEMO.

```
 10 REM   DUAL KILLER BETA DEMO
 15 REM      TRS-80
 20 REM
 25 REM
100 REM ** BETA MAINLINE, V.5—TRS-80 **
105 CLS:PRINT"BETA MEMORIES ARE BEING CLEARED"
110 DIM M(4,4,3,2):DIM BC(2,12)
115 FOR MI=0 TO 4:FOR MJ=0 TO 4:FOR KL=1 TO 3:FOR
    N= 1 TO 2
120 M(MI,MJ,KL,N)=2:NEXT N,KL,MJ,MI
125 BC(1,8)=42:BC(2,8)=37
130 CLS:GOSUB 1000
135 FOR CN=1 TO 2
140 BC(CN,2)=15360+RND(831):IF PEEK(BC(CN,2))<>32
    THEN 140
145 POKE BC(CN,2),BC(CN,8)
150 FOR N=4 TO 5
155 BC(CN,N)=RND(5)−3:IF BC(CN,4)=0 AND BC(CN,5) =
    0 THEN 155
```

```
160 NEXT N
165 BC(CN,1)=1:NEXT CN
170 FOR CN=1 TO 2
175 S$=INKEY$
180 IF S$<>"K" THEN 190
185 FOR N=1 TO 2:BC(N,1)=1:NEXT N
190 ON BC(CN,1) GOTO 200,215,265,330
195 NEXT CN:GOTO 170
200 FOR N=4 TO 5:BC(CN,N)=RND(5)-3:NEXT N
205 IF BC(CN,4)=0 AND BC(CN,5)=0 THEN 200
210 BC(CN,1)=2:GOTO 195
215 CP=BC(CN,2):CI=BC(CN,4):CJ=BC(CN,5)
220 GOSUB 2000
225 IF NOT(CX=32 AND CY=32)THEN 240
230 POKE CP,32:CP=NP:POKE CP,BC(CN,8)
235 BC(CN,2)=CP:BC(CN,1)=2:GOTO 195
240 BC(CN,10)=BC(CN,4)+2:BC(CN,11)=BC(CN,5)+2
245 BC(CN,4)=M(BC(CN,10),BC(CN,11),1,CN)
250 BC(CN,5)=M(BC(CN,10),BC(CN,11),2,CN)
255 BC(CN,12)=M(BC(CN,10),BC(CN,11),3,CN)
260 BC(CN,2)=CP:BC(CN,3)=NP:BC(CN,1)=3:GOTO 195
265 IF BC(CN,4)=2 AND BC(CN,5)=2 OR BC(CN,12)=2
    THEN BC(CN,1)=GOTO 195
270 IF BC(CN,12)=0 THEN 290
275 IF PEEK(BC(CN,3))<129 OR PEEK(BC(CN,3))>176
    THEN 285
280 POKE BC(CN,3),153:GOTO 290
285 POKE BC(CN,3),32
290 CP=BC(CN,2):CI=BC(CN,4)-2:CJ=BC(CN,5)-2
295 GOSUB 2000
300 BC(CN,3)=NP:BC(CN,4)=CI+2:BC(CN,5)=CJ+2
305 IF NOT(CX=32 AND CY=32) THEN BC(CN,1)=4:GOTO
    195
310 M(BC(CN,10),BC(CN,11),1,CN)=BC(CN,4)
315 M(BC(CN,10),BC(CN,11),2,CN)=BC(CN,5)
320 M(BC(CN,10),BC(CN,11),3,CN)=BC(CN,12)
325 BC(CN,4)=BC(CN,4)-2:BC(CN,5)=BC(CN,5)-2:BC
    (CN,1)=2:GOTO 195
330 BC(CN,12)=RND(2)-1
335 IF BC(CN,12) THEN BC(CN,4)=BC(CN,10):BC(CN,5)
    =BC(CN,11):GOTO 345
```

```
340  FOR N=4 TO 5:BC(CN,N)=RND(5)-1:NEXT N
345  BC(CN,1)=3:GOTO 195
350  REM
355  REM
1000 REM ** BORDER, V.1—TRS-80 **
1005 F0=15360:F1=15423:F2=16128:F3=16191
1010 FOR N=F0 TO F1:POKE N,176:NEXT N
1015 FOR N=F2 TO F3:POKE N,131:NEXT N
1020 FOR N=F0 TO F2 STEP 64:POKE N,170:NEXT
1025 FOR N=F1 TO F3 STEP 64:POKE N,149:NEXT
1030 POKE F0,160:POKE F1,144:POKE F2,130:POKE
     F3,129
1035 RETURN
1040 REM
1045 REM
2000 REM ** SEARCH AHEAD, V.2—TRS-80 **
2005 NP=CP:CX=32:CY=32
2010 SI=SGN(CI):SJ=SGN(CJ):AI=ABS(CI):AJ=ABS(CJ)
2015 IF AI=0 THEN 2030 ELSE AI=AI-1
2020 IF SI>0 THEN NP=NP+1 ELSE NP=NP-1
2025 CX=PEEK(NP)
2030 IF AJ=0 THEN 2045 ELSE AJ=AJ-1
2035 IF SJ> 0 THEN NP=NP+64 ELSE NP=NP-64
2040 CY=PEEK(NP)
2045 IF NOT((CX=32 OR CX=TC) AND (CY=32 OR
     CY=TC)) THEN RETURN
2050 IF AI=0 AND AJ=0 THEN RETURN ELSE GOTO 2015
2055 REM
2060 REM
```

Functionally speaking, the two Beta creatures are identical. They have different appearances on the screen, however. One is drawn as an asterisk and the other as a percent sign.

Theory of Operation

The variable list for the program is shown in Table 14-1. The program makes extensive use of multi-dimensioned arrays, and you should study their definitions in that list before attempting the following analysis of the program. In view of the fact that most of the procedures have been used and described in connection with previous experiments, the line-by-line analysis is comparitively brief in nature.

Table 14-1. TRS-80 Variable List for DUAL KILLER BETA DEMO.

Arrays

M(MI,MJ,1,CN)	Memory CI for Beta creature CN
M(MI,MJ,2,CN)	Memory CJ for Beta creature CN
M(MI,MJ,3,CN)	Memory kill code for Beta creature CN
BC(CN,1)	Operating phase for creature CN
BC(CN,2)	CP for creature CN
BC(CN,3)	NP for creature CN
BC(CN,4)	CI for creature CN
BC(CN,5)	CJ for creature CN
BC(CN,6)*	CX for creature CN
BC(CN,7)*	CY for creature CN
BC(CN,8)	Character code for creature CN
BC(CN,9)*	Dead-or-alive code for creature CN
BC(CN,10)	Working MI for creature CN
BC(CN,11)	Working MJ for creature CN
BC(CN,12)	Working kill code for creature CN

*Array variable not used in the current program; reserved for future expansion.

Simple Variables

CP	Current creature's screen position
NP	Current creature's next screen position
CI	Horizontal component of motion code
CJ	Vertical component of motion code
CX	Horizontal component of contact code
CY	Vertical component of contact code
KL,N	General-purpose numeric variables
S$	General-purpose string variable
CN	Current creature number: 1 or 2
MI	Memory version of current CI
MJ	Memory version of current CJ
SI	Sign value of CI
SJ	Sign value of CJ
AI	Absolute value of CI
AJ	Absolute value of CJ
TC	Trail code number
F0	Upper-left corner of border figure
F1	Upper-right corner of border figure
F2	Lower-left corner of border figure
F3	Lower-right corner of border figure

Lines 105-120—Set all 3 elements of both Beta memories to 2; that is the "invalid" state. Print a message to let you know that the relatively long pause doesn't spell some sort of bug in the programming.

Line 125—Set the graphic code for the two creatures.

Line 130—Clear the screen and draw the border figure.

Lines 135-165—Execute this series of statements twice, once for each creature. Initialize the creature position in such

177

a way that it doesn't fall onto an obstacle of any sort. Draw the creature figure. Initialize its motion code, and set it up for starting with phase-1 operations.

Lines 170-195—This is the main operating loop. See that loop in Fig. 14-1.

Lines 200-210—Phase-1 operations. See Fig. 14-2A.

Lines 215-260—Phase-2 operations. See Fig. 14-2B.

Lines 265-325—Phase-3 operations. See Fig. 14-2C.

Lines 330-345—Phase-4 operations. See Fig. 14-2D.

Lines 1000-1035—Border drawing subroutine.

Lines 2000-2050—Search ahead subroutine.

Let me stress the importance of understanding the meaning of the array variables. Each one can be related to a simple variable used in the single killer Beta experiment in Chapter 13. By using arrays in this fashion, both creatures can use the same programming lines. Without using arrays in these multi-tasking programs, the program length would be multipled by at least one half.

Some Possible Modifications

If you would like to add in some killable obstacle figures (graphic 191s, for instance), take an obstacle-drawing routine from one of the earlier programs and write it as a subroutine beginning at line 1500. Then patch it into the system by inserting a GOSUB 1500 at line 132.

It is possible to have the creatures leave behind a trail. Since array variables BC(CN,6) and BC(CN,7) aren't used in this program, they can be assigned trail code graphic numbers. Perhaps you'd like creature 1 to leave behind a trail of hyphens and creature 2 to make a trail of periods. Two steps are necessary. First, define the trail codes by adding this line:

127 BC(1,6)=45:BC(2,6)=46

Then change line 285 to read:

285 POKE BC(CN,3),BC(CN,6)

Now the creatures will leave behind trails that neither can penetrate without "killing" the trail element first. It tends to produce some pretty nasty creatures; creatures that are prone to learn kill responses rather than the more passive flight responses.

It is a bit more troublesome to make the creatures insensible to contacts with the trails. If you want a given creature to be insensitive to its own trail, but have to deal with the other creature's trail as an obstacle, make these additional changes:

217 TC=BC(CN,6)

292 TC=BC(CN,6)

225 IF NOT((CX=32 OR CX=TC) AND (CY=32 OR CY=TC)) THEN 240

305 IF NOT((CX=32 OR CX=TC) AND (CY=32 OR CY=TC)) THEN BC(CN,1)=4:GOTO 195

With those modifications, one creature will tend to block the other into a corner. Things are perhaps a bit more exciting to watch.

APPLESOFT VERSION

The Applesoft program for DUAL KILLER BETA DEMO is shown in Listing 14-2. Assuming you have saved an earlier Beta program on tape or disk, you can load the two subroutines, BORDER and SEARCH AHEAD, in that way. The mainline, however, has to be typed in from scratch.

Listing 14-2. Applesoft Programming for DUAL KILLER BETA DEMO.

```
10 REM   DUAL KILLER BETA DEMO
15 REM      APPLESOFT
20 REM
25 REM
100 REM ** BETA MAINLINE, V.5—APPLESOFT **
105 TEXT : HOME : PRINT "BETA MEMORIES ARE BEING
    CLEARED"
110 DIM M(4,4,3,2): DIM BC(2,14)
115 DEF FN R(R) = INT (5 * RND (1)) − 2
120 FOR MI = 0 TO 4: FOR MJ = 0 TO 4: FOR KL = 1 TO 3:
    FOR N = 1 TO 2
125 M(MI,MJ,KL,N) = 2: NEXT N,KL,MJ,MI
130 BC(1,10) = 9:BC(2,10) = 13
135 HOME : GR : GOSUB 1000
140 FOR CN = 1 TO 2
145 BC(CN,2) = INT (38 * RND (1)) + 1
150 BC(CN,3) = INT (35 * RND (1)) + 1
155 IF SCRN(BC(CN,2),BC(CN,3)) < > 0 THEN 145
160 COLOR= BC(CN,10): PLOT BC(CN,2),BC(CN,3)
165 FOR N = 6 TO 7:BC(CN,N) = FN R(0):NEXT N
170 IF BC(CN,6) = 0 AND BC(CN,7) = 0 THEN 165
175 BC(CN,1) = 1: NEXT CN
180 REM **** MULTIPLEXING DRIVER ****
185 FOR CN = 1 TO 2
190 S = PEEK ( − 16384):POKE − 16368,0
195 IF S < > 203 THEN 205
```

179

```
200 FOR N = 1 TO 2:BC(N,1) = 1: NEXT N
205 ON BC(CN,1) GOTO 215,235,300,385
210 NEXT CN: GOTO 185
215 REM **** PHASE-1 OPERATIONS ****
220 FOR N = 6 TO 7:BC(CN,N) = FN R(0):NEXT N
225 IF BC(CN,6) = 0 AND BC(CN,7) = 0 THEN 220
230 BC(CN,1) = 2: GOTO 210
235 REM **** PHASE-2 OPERATIONS ****
240 PX = BC(CN,2):PY = BC(CN,3):CI = BC(CN,6):CJ =
    BC(CN,7)
245 GOSUB 2000
250 IF NOT (CX = 0 AND CY = 0) THEN 265
255 COLOR= 0: PLOT PX,PY:PX = NX:PY = NY: COLOR=
    BC(CN,10):PLOT PX,PY
260 BC(CN,2) = PX:BC(CN,3) = PY:BC(CN,1) = 2: GOTO
    210
265 BC(CN,12) = BC(CN,6) + 2:BC(CN,13) = BC(CN,7) + 2
270 BC(CN,6) = M(BC(CN,12),BC(CN,13),1,CN)
275 BC(CN,7) = M(BC(CN,12),BC(CN,13),2,CN)
280 BC(CN,14) = M(BC(CN,12),BC(CN,13),3,CN)
285 BC(CN,2) = PX:BC(CN,3) = PY
290 BC(CN,4) = NX:BC(CN,5) = NY
295 BC(CN,1) = 3: GOTO 210
300 REM **** PHASE-3 OPERATIONS ****
305 IF NOT (BC(CN,6) = 2 AND BC(CN,7) = 2 OR
    BC(CN,14) = 2) THEN 315
310 BC(CN,1) = 4: GOTO 210
315 IF BC(CN,14) = 0 THEN 335
320 IF SCRN(BC(CN,4),BC(CN,5)) < 14 THEN 330
325 COLOR= 14: PLOT BC(CN,4),BC(CN,5): GOTO 335
330 COLOR= 0: PLOT BC(CN,4),BC(CN,5)
335 PX = BC(CN,2):PY = BC(CN,3):CI = BC(CN,6) – 2:CJ =
    BC(CN,7) – 2
340 GOSUB 2000
345 BC(CN,4) = NX:BC(CN,5) = NY:BC(CN,6) = CI +
    2:BC(CN,7) = CJ +
350 REM
355 IF NOT (CX = 0 AND CY = 0) THEN BC(CN,1) = 4:
    GOTO 210
360 M(BC(CN,12),BC(CN,13),1,CN) = BC(CN,6)
365 M(BC(CN,12),BC(CN,13),2,CN) = BC(CN,7)
370 M(BC(CN,12),BC(CN,13),3,CN) = BC(CN,14)
```

```
 375 BC(CN,6) = BC(CN,6) − 2:BC(CN,7) = BC(CN,7) − 2
 380 BC(CN,1) = 2: GOTO 210
 385 REM **** PHASE-4 OPERATIONS ****
 390 BC(CN,14) = INT (RND (1) + .5)
 395 IF BC(CN,14) = 0 THEN 405
 400 BC(CN,6) = BC(CN,12):BC(CN,7) = BC(CN,13): GOTO
     410
 405 FOR N = 6 TO 7:BC(CN,N) = FN R(0) + 2: NEXT N
 410 BC(CN,1) = 3: GOTO 210
 415 REM
 420 REM
1000 REM ** BORDER,V.1—APPLESOFT **
1005 COLOR= 15
1010 HLIN 0,39 AT 0: HLIN 0,39 AT 36
1015 VLIN 0,36 AT 0: VLIN 0,36 AT 39
1020 RETURN
1025 REM
1030 REM
2000 REM ** SEARCH AHEAD, V.2—APPLESOFT **
2005 NX = PX:NY = PY:CX = 0:CY = 0
2010 SI = SGN (CI):SJ = SGN (CJ):AI = ABS (CI):AJ = ABS
     (CJ)
2015 IF AI = 0 THEN 2040
2020 AI = AI − 1
2025 IF SI > 0 THEN NX = NX + 1: GOTO 2035
2030 NX = NX − 1
2035 CX = SCRN(NX,NY)
2040 IF AJ = 0 THEN 2065
2045 AJ = AJ − 1
2050 IF SJ > 0 THEN NY = NY + 1: GOTO 2060
2055 NY = NY − 1
2060 CY = SCRN(NX,NY)
2065 IF NOT ((CX = 0 OR CX = TC) AND (CY = 0 OR CY =
     TC)) THEN RETURN
2070 IF AI = 0 AND AJ = 0 THEN RETURN
2075 GOTO 2015
2080 REM
2085 REM
```

Functionally speaking, the two Beta creatures are identical.
They have different colors; one is bright orange and the other is
yellow.

Theory of Operation

The variable list for the program is shown in Table 14-2. The program makes extensive use of multi-dimensioned arrays, and you must study the definitions in that list before attempting the following analysis of the program. Each array variable can be related to a simple variable used here and in all the earlier Beta experiments. By using arrays in this fashion, both creatures can use the same lines of programming. Without using arrays in these multi-tasking

Table 14-2. Applesoft Variable List for DUAL KILLER BETA DEMO.

Arrays

M(MI,MJ,1),CN)	Memory CI for Beta creature CN
M(MI,MJ,2,CN)	Memory CJ for Beta creature CN
M(MI,MJ,3,CN)	Memory kill code for Beta creature CN:
	0 for no-kill, 1 for kill
BC(CN,1)	Operating phase for creature CN
BC(CN,2)	PX for creature CN
BC(CN,3)	PY for creature CN
BC(CN,4)	NX for creature CN
BC(CN,5)	NY for creature CN
BC(CN,6)	CI for creature CN
BC(CN,7)	CJ for creature CN
BC(CN,8)*	CX for creature CN
BC(CN,9)*	CY for creature CN
BC(CN,10)	Color code for creature CN
BC(CN,11)*	Dead-or-alive code for creature CN
BC(CN,12)	Working MI for creature CN
BC(CN,13)	Working MJ for creature CN
BC(CN,14)	Working kill code for creature CN

*Array variable not used in the current program; reserved for future expansion.

Simple Variables

PX	Horizontal component of creature's screen position
PY	Vertical component of creature's screen position
NX	Horizontal component of next screen position
NY	Vertical component of next screen position
CI	Horizontal component of motion code
CJ	Vertical component of motion code
CX	Horizontal component of contact code
CY	Vertical component of contact code
KL,N,S	General-purpose numeric variables
CN	Current creature number:1 or 2
MI	Memory version of current CI
MJ	Memory version of current CJ
SI	Sign value of CI
SJ	Sign value of CJ
AI	Absolute value of CI
AJ	Absolute value of CJ
TC	Trail color code

programs, the program length would be multiplied by at least one half.

Lines 105-125—Dimension the arrays, define the random motion code function, and clear the Beta memories to the "invalid" state. Write a simple message to let you know that the long pause is not caused by a program bug.

Line 130—Define the creature colors.

Line 135—Clear the screen, set the graphics mode, and draw the border figure.

Lines 140-175—Carry out the following operations for the two creatures in turn. Initialize the screen position at some random place that does not fix a creature onto the border or the other creature. Get a running motion code and set for phase-1 operations.

Lines 180-210—This is the program's main operating loop. See that loop detailed in Fig. 14-1.

Lines 215-230—Phase-1 operations. See Fig. 14-2A

Lines 235-295—Phase-2 operations. See Fig. 14-2B.

Lines 300-380—Phase-3 operations. See Fig. 14-2C.

Lines 385-410—Phase-4 operations. See Fig. 14-2D.

Lines 1000-1020—Border drawing subroutine.

Lines 2000-2075—Search ahead subroutine.

Some Possible Modifications

If you would like to add some killable obstacles to the field (brown color 8, for instance), take an obstacle-drawing routine from one of the earlier programs and write it as a subroutine beginning at line 1500. Then patch it into this system by inserting a GOSUB 1500 at line 137.

It is possible to have the creatures leave behind some trails wherever they go. Since array variables BC(CN,8) and BC(CN,9) aren't used here, one can be assigned to the creatures' trail codes. Perhaps you would like creature 1 to leave behind a dark blue (code 2) footprints and creature 2 to make light blue (code 7) trails. Two steps are necessary. First, define the trail code by adding this line:

132 BC(1,8)=2:BC(2,8)=7

Then change line 255 to read:

255 COLOR BC(CN,8):PLOT PX,PY:PX=NX: PY=NY: COLOR=BC(CN,10):PLOT PX,PY

Now the creature will leave behind trails that neither can penetrate without "killing" that trail element first. It tends to produce some pretty nasty creatures; creatures that are prone to learning kill responses rather than the more passive sorts of flight responses.

It is a bit more troublesome to make the creatures insensible to contacts with trail elements. If you want a given creature to be insensitive to its own trail, but have to deal with the other's trail as an obstacle, make these additional changes in the programming:

```
242 TC=BC(CN,8)
337 TC=BC(CN,8)
250 IF NOT((CX=0 OR CX=TC) AND (CY=0 OR CY=TC))
    THEN 265
355 IF NOT((CX=0 OR CX=TC) AND (CY=0 OR CY=TC))
    THEN BC(CN,1)=4:GOTO 210
```

With those modifications, one creature will tend to block the other into a corner. Things are perhaps a bit more exciting to watch.

Chapter 15
A Community of
Killer Alphas and Betas

This is the final program in the current series of Alpha and Beta demonstrations. There are four creatures initially; 2 killer Alphas and 2 killer Betas. As the program is shown here, there are no obstacles in the environment, but they can be added as an option.

Initially the four creatures roam the environment, behaving in ways that characterize their underlying adaptive mechanisms. The Alphas wander around, responding to contact situations by making purely random, Alpha-like responses. The Betas start out behaving like Alpha creatures, but gradually build up a file of workable responses based on their past experiences. Whether or not the Betas have a chance to develop some clear-cut habit patterns of motion depends on how long they are allowed to survive.

It is certainly a vicious little community. All four creatures are fully capable of killing off any of the others. The program is designed so that a killed creature, whether an Alpha or Beta, remains dead. There is no resurrection feature in this case. So the population of creatures gradually diminishes until there is just one victor. And there's no telling in advance which creature will survive.

Upon making contact with another creature, an Alpha always has a 50-50 chance of picking a kill response. The alternative is to attempt to flee the situation, selecting a purely random motion code that does not have any kill elements. But even when an Alpha picks a kill response, there is no guarantee it will hit its target; the target might have an opportunity to strike out and kill its adversary first or move away. So even though an Alpha will have an even chance of picking a kill response, the chances of making a successful kill are somewhat less.

It is not so easy to predict how one of the Beta creatures will respond to a contact with another creature. If the Beta has never encountered that particular sort of contact situation before, it will resort to its more primitive mode of behavior and select a random kill code that gives it an even 50-50 chance of picking a kill response. But if that Beta has encountered another creature under similar conditions, it will repond as it did before; it will either strike out to kill the adversary or flee from it, depending on which response worked in the past. In any event, there is no guarantee that a kill response, if it is used, will be successful. As in the case of an Alpha's attempt to kill another creature, it might be killed first or it might miss the target because it has an opportunity to get out of the way.

So the only thing that is wholly predictable about this program is that one creature will emerge as the ultimate victor.

There is some good reason to ask whether an Alpha or Beta creature has a better chance of emerging as the lone victor in this program. An experiment that is intended to answer that question is suggested in the closing section of this chapter. Be sure you study the hypothesis and suggested experiment if you would like to attempt to tie together some elements of creature psychology and social behavior.

The program is equipped with a Beta "kick" feature. Striking the K key interrupts the operating cycles for both Betas, effectively giving them a new, random motion code that promises to kick them off into a different direction. The important purpose is to break up habit patterns of motion that never allow the Betas to come into contact with one another. A more exciting application, however, is to force the Betas into a conflict situation with one another or either of the surviving Alpha creatures. (Just continue striking the K key until the Betas are set onto paths that lead to a conflict with another creature.) The "kick" feature does not affect either of the Alphas.

As the program is written here, the Alpha and Beta creatures have different appearances, but both Alphas look alike and so do both Betas. A minor modification of the programming allows it to select different images for all four creatures. Doing that, the program can be transformed into an exciting, 4-player game that reminds one of a Roman arena of gladiators.

FLOWCHART ANALYSIS

Figure 15-1 shows the flowchart for the main sequence of operations, and Fig. 15-2 illustrates the flowcharts for the 5 individual operating phases.

186

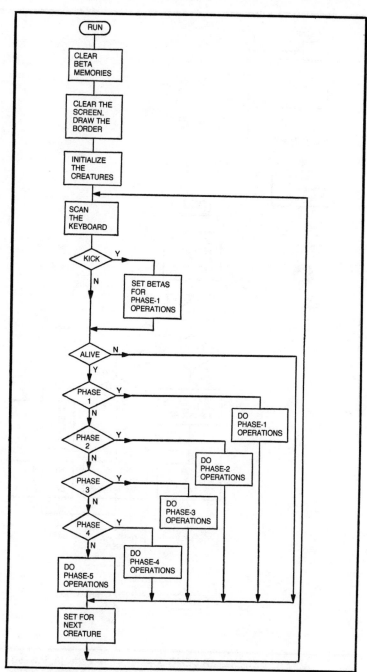

Fig. 15-1. Main program flowchart for ALPHA/BETA KILLER DEMO.

187

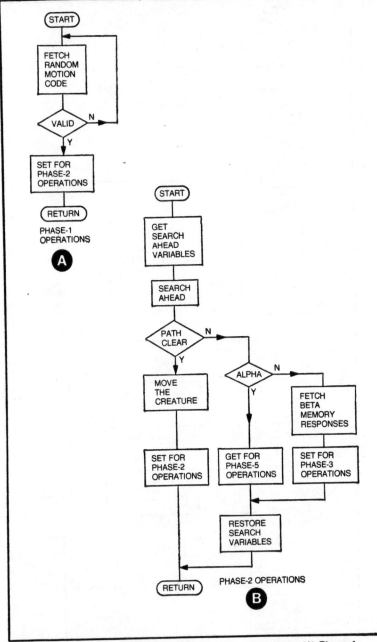

Fig. 15-2. ALPHA / BETA KILLER DEMO operations flowcharts. (A) Phase-1 operations. (B) Phase-2 operations. (C) Phase-3 operations. (D) Phase-4 operations. (E) Phase-5 operations.

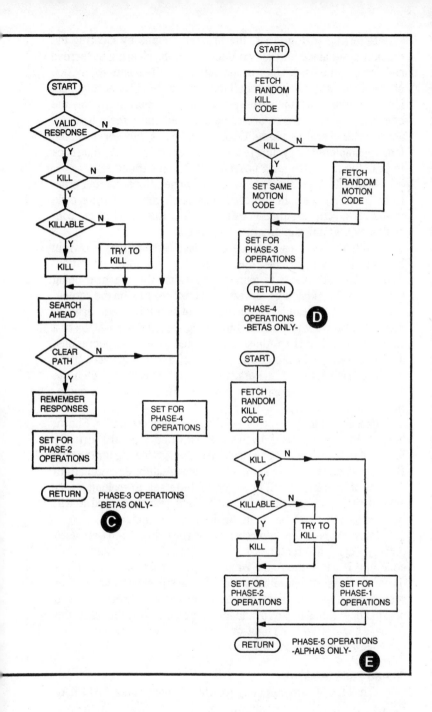

PHASE-3 OPERATIONS
-BETAS ONLY-
C

PHASE-4
OPERATIONS
-BETAS ONLY-
D

PHASE-5 OPERATIONS
-ALPHAS ONLY-
E

189

Referring to Fig. 15-1, the program begins by clearing the memories set aside for the two Beta creatures, clearing the screen and drawing the border figure, and initializing the positions, motion codes and operating phase for all four creatures. After accomplishing that set of tasks, the system enters it main operating loop—the one that selects the creature to be serviced and directs it to the appropriate operating phase. Once a creature is thus serviced, the loop is completed by cycling to the next creature and returning back to scan the keyboard for a possible "kick" operation.

Figure 15-2A represents the phase-1 operations. All four creatures use it, and its sole purpose is to select a random motion code whenever a contact situation calls for doing that. That phase concludes by pointing the creature to phase 2.

All four creatures also use the phase-2 operations shown in Fig. 15-2B. This one does the essential search ahead operation. And, if the path ahead is found to be clear, the creature being serviced at the moment is moved to its next position on the screen. But if the path ahead is not clear, one of two things can happen, depending on whether the creature being serviced is an Alpha or a Beta creature. If it is an Alpha, it is pointed to phase-5 operations, and that represents the Alpha version of a kill sequence. If the creature happens to be a Beta, the phase-2 operations fetch the relevant memory response and point the Beta to phase-3 operations.

Phases 3 and 4 are used only by the Beta creatures. Shown here in Figs. 15-2C and 15-2D, you will find they are virtually identical to killer Beta phases used in the programming for the dual Beta demonstration in Chapter 14. A Beta creature emerging from that set of operations will have committed itself to making a successful response, either to kill or a flight response. And it will remember that response for immediate application.

Phase-5 operations, flowcharted for you in Fig. 15-2E, are used only by the Alpha creatures. It amounts to selecting a random kill code. If it is a kill, the Alpha will attempt to make the kill and it is direct to phase-2 operations. But if the kill code turns out to represent a no-kill, or flight, response, the Alpha is directed back to phase-1 operations to pick a random motion code. In either case, the Alpha is committed to its fight-or-flight response when it leaves its phase-5 sequence of operations.

TRS-80 PROGRAMMING

The TRS-80 programming for this demonstration, ALPHA/BETA KILLER DEMO, is shown in Listing 15-1. As usual, the two common subroutines, BORDER and SEARCH AHEAD, can be loaded from tape or disk if you have saved some earlier Beta programs in that fashion. The mainline programming, BETA MAINLINE, V.6 must be typed in, however.

Listing 15-1. TRS-80 Programming for ALPHA/BETA KILLER DEMO.

```
10  REM    ALPHA/BETA KILLER DEMO
15  REM      TRS-80
20  REM
25  REM
100 REM ** BETA MAINLINE, V.6—TRS-80 **
105 CLS:PRINT "BETA MEMORIES ARE BEING CLEAR-
    ED"
110 DIM M(4,4,3,2):DIM CC(4,12)
115 FOR MI=0 TO 4:FOR MJ=0 TO 4:FOR KL=1 TO 3:FOR
    CN=1 TO 2
120 M(MI,MJ,KL,CN)=2:NEXT CN,KL,MJ,MI
125 CC(1,8)=66:CC(2,8)=66:CC(3,8)=65:CC(4,8)=65
130 CLS:GOSUB 1000
135 FOR CN=1 TO 4
140 CC(CN,2)=15360+RND(831):IF PEEK(CC(CN,2))<
    >32 THEN 140
145 POKE CC(CN,2),CC(CN,8)
150 FOR N=4 TO 5:CC(CN,N)=RND(5)−3:NEXT N
155 IF CC(CN,4)=0 AND CC(CN,5)=0 THEN 150
160 CC(CN,1)=1:CC(CN,9)=1:NEXT CN
165 REM **** MULTI-TASKING DRIVER ****
170 FOR CN=1 TO 4
175 S$=INKEY$:IF S$<>"K" THEN 185
180 FOR N=1 TO 2:CC(N,1)=1:NEXT N
185 IF CC(CN,9)=0 THEN 195
190 CN CC(CN,1) GOTO 200,220,285,370,395
195 NEXT CN:GOTO 170
200 REM **** PHASE-1 OPERATIONS ****
205 FOR N=4 TO 5:CC(CN,N)=RND(5)−3:NEXT N
210 IF CC(CN,4)=0 AND CC(CN,5)=0 THEN 205
215 CC(CN,1)=2:GOTO 195
220 REM **** PHASE-2 OPERATIONS ****
225 CP=CC(CN,2):CI=CC(CN,4):CJ=CC(CN,5)
230 GOSUB 2000
235 IF NOT(CX=32 AND CY=32) THEN 250
240 POKE CP,32:CP=NP:POKE CP,CC(CN,8)
```

191

```
245 CC(CN,1)=2:GOTO 280
250 IF CN>2 THEN CC(CN,1)=5:GOTO 280
255 CC(CN,10)=CC(CN,4)+2:CC(CN,11)=CC(CN,5)+2
260 CC(CN,4)=M(CC(CN,10),CC(CN,11),1,CN)
265 CC(CN,5)=M(CC(CN,10),CC(CN,11),2,CN)
270 CC(CN1,2)=M(CC(CN,10),CC(CN,11),3,CN)
275 CC(CN,1)=3
280 CC(CN,2)=CP:CC(CN,3)=NP:GOTO 195
285 REM **** PHASE-3 OPERATIONS ****
290 IF CC(CN,4)=2 AND CC(CN,5)=2 OR CC(CN,12)=2
    THEN CC(CN,1)=4:GOTO 195
295 IF CC(CN,12)=0 THEN 330
300 IF PEEK(CC(CN,3))<129 OR PEEK(CC(CN,3))>176
    THEN 310
305 POKE CC(CN,3),153:GOTO 330
310 POKE CC(CN,3),32
315 FOR N=1 TO 4
320 IF CC(CN,3)=CC(N,2) THEN CC(N,9)=0:GOTO 330
325 NEXT N
330 CP=CC(CN,2):CI=CC(CN,4)-2:CJ=CC(CN,5)-2
335 GOSUB 2000
340 CC(CN,3)=NP:CC(CN,4)=CI+2:CC(CN,5)=CJ+2
345 IF NOT(CX=32 AND CY=32) THEN CC(CN,1)= 4:
    GOTO 195
350 M(CC(CN,10),CC(CN,11),1,CN)=CC(CN,4)
355 M(CC(CN,10),CC(CN,11),2,CN)=CC(CN,5)
360 M(CC(CN,10),CC(CN,11),3,CN)=CC(CN,12)
365 CC(CN,4)=CC(CN,4)-2:CC(CN,5)=CC(CN,5)-2:CC
    (CN,1)=2:GOTO 195
370 REM **** PHASE-4 OPERATIONS ****
375 CC(CN,12)=RND(2)-1
380 IF CC(CN,12) THEN CC(CN,4)=CC(CN,10)
    :CC(CN,5)=CC(CN,11):GOTO 390
385 FOR N=4 TO 5:CC(CN,N)=RND(5)-1:NEXT N
390 CC(CN,1)=3:GOTO 195
395 REM **** PHASE-5 OPERATIONS ****
400 CC(CN,12)=RND(2)-1:IF  CC(CN,12)=0  THEN
    CC(CN,1)=1:GOTO 195
405 IF PEEK(CC(CN,3))<129 OR PEEK(CC(CN,3))>176
    THEN 415
410 POKE CC(CN,3),153:GOTO 425
```

```
 415 POKE CC(CN,3),32
 420 FOR N=1 TO 4
 425 IF PEEK(CC(CN,3))=CC(N,2) THEN CC(N,9)=0:GOTO
     435
 430 NEXT N
 435 CC(CN,1)=2:GOTO 195
 440 REM
 445 REM
1000 REM ** BORDER, V.1—TRS-80 **
1005 F0=15360:F1=15423:F2=16128:F3=16191
1010 FOR N=F0 TO F1:POKE N,176:NEXT N
1015 FOR N=F2 TO F3:POKE N,131:NEXT N
1020 FOR N=F0 TO F2 STEP 64:POKE N,170:NEXT
1025 FOR N=F1 TO F3 STEP 64:POKE N,149:NEXT
1030 POKE F0,160:POKE F1,144:POKE F2,130:POKE
     F3,129
1035 RETURN
1040 REM
1045 REM
2000 REM ** SEARCH AHEAD, V.2—TRS-80 **
2005 NP=CP:CX=32:CY=32
2010 SI=SGN(CI):SJ=SGN(CJ):AI=ABS(CI):AJ=ABS(CJ)
2015 IF AI=0 THEN 2030 ELSE AI=AI—1
2020 IF SI>0 THEN NP=NP+1 ELSE NP=NP—1
2025 CX=PEEK(NP)
2030 IF AJ=0 THEN 2045 ELSE AJ=AJ—1
2035 IF SJ>0 THEN NP=NP+64 ELSE NP=NP—64
2040 CY=PEEK(NP)
2045 IF NOT((CX=32 OR CX=TC) AND (CY=32 OR
     CY=TC)) THEN RETURN
2050 IF AI=0 AND AJ= 0 THEN RETURN ELSE GOTO 2015
2055 REM
2060 REM
```

When running the program as listed here, the two Alpha creatures appear as letter As, and the Betas are Bs. As suggested later, you can change their images to some more imaginative forms if you wish.

The program runs endlessly. So when there is just one creature left on the screen, you can terminate the program by striking the BREAK key. Of course you can end the program in that fashion anytime you want.

Theory of Operation

The variable listing for the program is shown in Table 15-1. Be sure you are fully acquainted with the definitions of the array variables before attempting to make any sense out of the program listing, itself.

Table 15-1. TRS-80 Variable List for ALPHA/BETA KILLER DEMO.

Arrays

M(MI,MJ,1,CN)	Memory CI for Beta creature CN
M(MI,MJ,2,CN)	Memory CJ for Beta creature CN
M(MI,MJ,3,CN)	Memory kill code for Beta creature CN
CC(CN,1)	Operating phase for creature CN
CC(CN,2)	CP for creature CN
CC(CN,3)	NP for creature CN
CC(CN,4)	CI for creature CN
CC(CN,5)	CJ for creature CN
CC(CN,6)*	CX for creature CN
CC(CN,7)*	CY for creature CN
CC(CN,8)	Character code for creature CN
CC(CN,9)	Dead-or-alive code for creature CN:
	0 for dead, 1 for alive
CC(CN,10)	Working MI for Beta creature CN
CC(CN,11)	Working MJ for Beta creature CN
CC(CN,12)	Working kill code for creature CN

*Array variable not used in the current program; reserved for future expansion.

Simple Variables

CP	Current creature's screen position
NP	Current creature's next screen position
CI	Horizontal component of motion code
CJ	Vertical component of motion code
CX	Horizontal component of contact code
CY	Vertical component of contact code
KL,N	General-purpose numeric variables
S$	General-purpose string variable
CN	Current creature number:
	1 and 2 for Beta creatures
	3 and 4 for Alpha creatures
MI	Beta memory version of current CI
MJ	Beta memory version of current CJ
SI	Sign value of CI
SJ	Sign value of CJ
AI	Absolute value of CI
AJ	Absolute value of CJ
TC	Trail graphic code number
F0	Upper-left corner of border figure
F1	Upper-right corner of border figure
F2	Lower-left corner of border figure
F3	Lower-right corner of border figure

The following discussion of the programming assumes you have already done your homework regarding earlier versions of multi-tasked Alpha and Beta creatures. If you become confused, you might do well to refer back to some of the more detailed discussions in earlier chapters.

Lines 105-120—Clear the Beta memories to the invalid response codes, and print a messsage to let you know the program is actually underway.

Line 125—Define the graphic codes for the four creatures.

Line 130—Clear the screen and draw the border figure.

Lines 135-160—Pick a random initial position for each creature, making sure it does not fall onto an element of the border figure or another creature. Draw the creature and assign it an initial motion code. Set it for phase-1 operations. Continue this sequence of operations until all four creatures are successfully initialized.

Lines 170-175—Scan the keyboard. If the K key is depressed, then set creatures 1 and 2 (the Beta creatures) for doing phase-1 operations again—picking up new motion codes.

Lines 180-195—If the creature being serviced is dead (CC(CN,9) is 0), skip the whole sequence and go on to the next creature. Otherwise point the creature to its current operating phase.

Lines 200-215—Phase-1 operations for all creatures. See Fig. 15-2A.

Lines 220-280—Phase-2 operations for all creatures. See Fig. 15-2B.

Lines 285-365—Phase-3 operations for the Beta creatures. See Fig. 15-2C.

Lines 370-390—Phase-4 operations for the Beta creatures. See Fig. 15-2D.

Lines 395-435—Phase-5 operations for the Alpha creatures. See Fig. 15-2E.

Lines 1000-1035—Border drawing subroutine.

Lines 2000-2050—Search ahead subroutine.

Some Possible Modifications

The creature images are defined in line 125. Those images are defined by the array variable CC(CN,8), where CN is the creature number. When CN is 1, it refers to Beta creature number 1. When CN is 2, it refers to Beta creature number 2. And when CN is equal to 3 or 4, it refers to Alpha creatures 1 and 2, respectively. Being aware of those facts, you can set the arrays equal to any alphanumeric, punctuation or graphic codes (excepting those in the range of 129 through 176) to give them any other appearance you like.

Fixed, killable obstacles can be inserted into the environment by adding an obstacle-drawing subroutine that begins at line 1500. Those routines appear in a number of previous program listings. Then to call that subroutine, insert this line into the programming:

132 GOSUB 1500

Including some killable obstacles in the community of creatures has some special significance for further experimentation with creature psychology and social behavior. Be sure to read about it in the closing section of this chapter.

The arena of combat can be made even more complicated and interesting by having the creatures leave behind footprints wherever they go—especially if those footprints are regarded as obstacles the creatures must contend with. Since array CC(CN,6) isn't used in the program, it can be assigned trail code numbers.

Leaving behind the same sort of trail figure for all four creatures is a rather straightforward procedure. Just insert this line:

137 CC(CN,6)=191

And then change line 240 to read:

240 POKE CP, CC(CN,6):CP=CN:POKE CP,CC(CN,8)

Doing that, all four creatures will leave behind a trail of graphic-191 figures. If you don't like the 191 figures, change the number to any other printable ASCII code number. Using code 46, for instance, will make the creatures leave a trail of dots—periods to be exact.

If you want the four creatures to leave behind trails that are different for each one, use the modified version of line 240 as just described, but do not use the added line 137. Instead, add this line:

127 CC(1,6)=34:CC(2,6)=39:CC(3,6)=43:CC(4,6)=58

Try it, and see what happens. You ought to be able to figure out how to assign trail codes of your own choosing.

APPLESOFT PROGRAMMING

The Applesoft programming for ALPHA/BETA KILLER DEMO is shown as Listing 15-2. As usual, the two commonly used subroutines, BORDER and SEARCH AHEAD, can be loaded from tape or disk if you have saved them from earlier Beta experiments.

Listing 15-2. Applesoft Programming for ALPHA/BETA KILLER DEMO.

```
 10 REM    ALPHA/BETA KILLER DEMO
 15 REM       APPLESOFT
 20 REM
 25 REM
100 REM ** BETA MAINLINE, V.6—APPLESOFT **
105 TEXT : HOME : PRINT "BETA MEMORIES ARE BEING
    CLEARED"
110 DIM M(4,4,3,2): DIM CC(4,14)
115 DEF FN R(R) = INT (5 * RND (1)) - 2
120 FOR MI = 0 TO 4: FOR MJ = 0 TO 4: FOR KL = 1 TO 2:
    FOR CN = 1 TO 2
125 M(MI,MJ,KL,CN) = 2: NEXT CN,KL,MJ,MI
130 CC(1,10) = 9:CC(2,10) = 9:CC(3,10) = 13:CC(4,10) =
    13
135 HOME : GR : GOSUB 1000
140 FOR CN = 1 TO 4
145 CC(CN,2) = INT (38 * RND (1)) + 1
150 CC(CN,3) = INT (35 * RND (1)) + 1
155 IF SCRN(CC(CN,2),CC(CN,3)) < > 0 THEN 145
160 COLOR= CC(CN,10): PLOT CC(CN,2),CC(CN,3)
165 FOR N = 6 TO 7:CC(CN,N) = FN R(0): NEXT N
170 IF CC(CN,6) = 0 AND CC(CN,7) = 0 THEN 165
175 CC(CN,1) = 1:CC(CN,11) = 1: NEXT CN
180 REM **** MULTI-TASKING DRIVER ****
185 FOR CN = 1 TO 4
190 S = PEEK (- 16384): POKE - 16368,0
195 IF S < > 203 THEN 205
200 FOR N = 1 TO 2:CC(N,1) = 1: NEXT N
205 IF CC(CN,11) = 0 THEN 215
210 ON CC(CN,1) GOTO 220,240,315,410,440
215 NEXT CN: GOTO 185
220 REM **** PHASE-1 OPERATIONS ****
225 FOR N = 6 TO 7:CC(CN,N) = FN R(0):NEXT N
230 IF CC(CN,6) = 0 AND CC(CN,7) = 0 THEN 225
235 CC(CN,1) =2: GOTO 215
240 REM **** PHASE-2 OPERATIONS ****
245 PX = CC(CN,2):PY = CC(CN,3):CI = CC(CN,6):CJ =
    CC(CN,7)
250 GOSUB 2000
255 IF NOT (CX = 0 AND CY = 0) THEN 275
260 COLOR= 0: PLOT PX,PY:PX = NX:PY = NY
```

```
265 COLOR= CC(CN,10): PLOT PX,PY
270 CC(CN,1) = 2: GOTO 305
275 IF CN > 2 THEN CC(CN,1) = 5: GOTO 305
280 CC(CN,12) = CC(CN,6) + 2:CC(CN,13) = CC(CN,7) + 2
285 CC(CN,6) = M(CC(CN,12),CC(CN,13),1,CN)
290 CC(CN,7) = M(CC(CN,12),CC(CN,13),2,CN)
295 CC(CN,14) = M(CC(CN,12),CC(CN,13),3,CN)
300 CC(CN,1) = 3
305 CC(CN,2) = PX:CC(CN,3) = PY:CC(CN,4) = NX:CC
    (CN,5) = NY
310 GOTO 215
315 REM **** PHASE-3 OPERATIONS ****
320 IF NOT (CC(CN,6) = 2 AND CC(CN,7) = 2 OR
    CC(CN,14) =2) THEN 330
325 CC(CN,1) = 4: GOTO 215
330 IF CC(CN,14) = 0 THEN 365
335 IF SCRN(CC(CN,4),CC(CN,5)) < 14 THEN 345
340 COLOR= 14: PLOT CC(CN,4),CC(CN,5):GOTO 365
345 COLOR= 0: PLOT CC(CN,4),CC(CN,5)
350 FOR N = 1 TO 4
355 IF CC(CN,4) = CC(N,2) AND CC(CN,5) = CC(N,3) THEN
    CC(N,11) = 0: GOTO 365
360 NEXT N
365 PX = CC(CN,2):PY = CC(CN,3):CI = CC(CN,6) − 2:CJ
    = CC(CN,7) −2
370 GOSUB 2000
375 CC(CN,4) = NX:CC(CN,5) = NY:CC(CN,6) = CI +
    2:CC(CN,7) = CJ + 2
380 IF NOT (CX = 0 AND CY = 0) THEN CC(CN,1) = 4:
    GOTO 215
385 M(CC(CN,12),CC(CN,13),1,CN) = CC(CN,6)
390 M(CC(CN,12),CC(CN,13),2,CN) = CC(CN,6)
395 M(CC(CN,12),CC(CN,13),3,CN) = CC(CN,14)
400 CC(CN,6) = CC(CN,6) − 2:CC(CN,7) = CC(CN,7) − 2
405 CC(CN,1) = 2: GOTO 215
410 REM **** PHASE-4 OPERATIONS ****
415 CC(CN,14) = INT (RND (1) + .5)
420 IF CC(CN,14) = 0 THEN 430
425 CC(CN,6) = CC(CN,12):CC(CN,7) = CC(CN,13):GOTO
    435
430 FOR N = 6 TO 7:CC(CN,N) = FN R(0) + 2: NEXT N
```

198

```
 435 CC(CN,1) = 3: GOTO 215
 440 REM **** PHASE-5 OPERATIONS ****
 445 CC(CN,14) = INT (RND (1) + .5)
 450 IF CC(CN,14) = 0 THEN CC(CN,1) = 1: GOTO 215
 455 IF SCRN(CC(CN,4),CC(CN,5)) < 14 THEN 465
 460 COLOR= 14: PLOT CC(CN,4),CC(CN,5): GOTO 485
 465 COLOR= 0: PLOT CC(CN,4),CC(CN,5)
 470 FOR N = 1 TO 4
 475 IF CC(CN,4) = CC(N,2) AND CC(CN,5) = CC(N,3) THEN
     CC(N,11) = 0: GOTO 485
 480 NEXT N
 485 CC(CN,1) = 2: GOTO 215
 490 REM
 495 REM
1000 REM ** BORDER,V.1—APPLESOFT **
1005 COLOR= 15
1010 HLIN 0,39 AT 0: HLIN 0,39 AT 36
1015 VLIN 0,36 AT 0: VLIN 0,36 AT 39
1020 RETURN
1025 REM
1030 REM
2000 REM ** SEARCH AHEAD, V.2—APPLESOFT **
2005 NX = PX:NY = PY:CX = 0:CY = 0
2010 SI = SGN (CI):SJ = SGN (CJ):AI = ABS (CI):AJ = ABS
     (CJ)
2015 IF AI = 0 THEN 2040
2020 AI = AI − 1
2025 IF SI > 0 THEN NX = NX + 1: GOTO 2035
2030 NX = NX − 1
2035 CX = SCRN(NX,NY)
2040 IF AJ = 0 THEN 2065
2045 AJ = AJ − 1
2050 IF SJ > 0 THEN NY = NY + 1: GOTO 2060
2055 NY = NY − 1
2060 CY = SCRN(NX,NY)
2065 IF NOT ((CX = 0 OR CX = TC) AND (CY = 0 OR CY =
     TC)) THEN RETURN
2070 IF AI = 0 AND AJ = 0 THEN RETURN
2075 GOTO 2015
2080 REM
```

BETA MAINLINE, V.6, however, has to be typed in from the keyboard.

When running the program as it is listed here, the two Alpha creatures are yellow and the Betas are bright orange. As suggested later, you can change the colors, giving all four a different color if you wish.

The program runs endlessly. So when there is just one live creature left on the screen, or when you want to terminate the program for any reason, just do a CTRL C operation from the keyboard.

Theory of Operation

The variable list for the program is shown in Table 15-2. Be sure you are fully acquainted with the definitions of the array variables before attempting to make any sense out of the program listing. The following discussion of the programming assumes you have already done your homework regarding earlier versions of multi-tasked Alpha and Beta programs. If you become lost in the details, you might do well to refer back to some of the more detailed explanations in earlier chapters.

Lines 105-115—Clear the screen, print a start-up message, dimension the arrays, and define the random motion code function.

Lines 120-125—Clear the two Beta memories to invalid memory codes.

Line 130—Define the color codes for the creatures.

Line 135—Clear the screen, set the graphics mode, and draw the border figure.

Lines 140-175—Initialize all four creatures in turn. Give them a random screen position where they do not overlap any part of the border figure or another creature, draw them, and give them a random motion code.

Lines 185-215—This is the main operating loop. See Fig. 15-1. If the K key is depressed, set the Betas (creatures 1 and 2) for phase-1 operations. If the creature is not alive, skip all further operations and select the next creature at line 215. If the creature being serviced is alive, point it to the appropriate operating phase.

Lines 220-235—Phase-1 operations for all creatures. See Fig. 15-2A.

Lines 240-310—Phase-2 operations for all creatures. See Fig. 15-2B.

Table 15-2. Applesoft Variable List for ALPHA/BETA KILLER DEMO.

Arrays

M(MI,MJ,1,CN)	Memory CI for Beta creature CN
M(MI,MJ,2,CN)	Memory CJ for Beta creature CN
M(MI,MJ,3,CN)	Memory kill code for Beta creature CN
CC(CN,1)	Operating phase for creature CN
CC(CN,2)	PX for creature CN
CC(CN,3)	PY for creature CN
CC(CN,4)	NX for creature CN
CC(CN,5)	NY for creature CN
CC(CN,6)	CI for creature CN
CC(CN,7)	CJ for creature CN
CC(CN,8)*	CX for creature CN
CC(CN,9)*	CY for creature CN
CC(CN,10)	Color code for creature CN
CC(CN,11)	Dead-or-alive code for creature CN:
	0 for dead, 1 for alive
CC(CN,12)	Working MI for Beta creature CN
CC(CN,13)	Working MJ for Beta creature CN
CC(CN,14)	Working kill code for Beta creature CN

*Array variable not used in the current program; reserved for future expansion.

Simple Variables

PX	Horizontal component of creature's screen position
PY	Vertical component of creature's screen position
NX	Horizontal component of next screen position
NY	Vertical component of next screen position
CI	Horizontal component of motion code
CJ	Vertical component of motion code
CX	Horizontal component of contact code
CY	Vertical component of contact code
KL,N,S	General-purpose numeric variables
CN	Current creature number:
	1 and 2 for Beta creatures
	3 and 4 for Alpha creatures
MI	Memory version of current CI
MJ	Memory version of current CJ
SI	Sign value of CI
SJ	Sign value of CJ
AI	Absolute value of CI
AJ	Absolute value of CJ
TC	Trail color code

Lines 315-405—Phase-3 operations for Beta creatures. See Fig. 15-2C.

Lines 410-435—Phase-4 operations for Beta creatures. See Fig. 15-2D.

Lines 440-485—Phase-5 operations for Alpha creatures.

Lines 1000-1020—Border drawing subroutine.

Lines 2000-2075—Search ahead subroutine.

Some Possible Modifications

The creature colors are defined in line 130. Those colors are carried by array CC(CN,10), where CN is the creature number. When CN is 1, it refers to Beta creature number 1. When CN is 2, it refers to Beta creature number 2. And when CN is equal to 3 or 4, it refers to Alpha creatures 1 and 2, respectively. Being aware of these facts, you can set the arrays for any color code except 14 and 15 (those are reserved for the border figure and "dents" in the border figure).

Fixed, killable obstacles can be inserted into the environment by adding an obstacle-drawing subroutine that can begin at line 1500. Those routines appear in a number of earlier projects, and can be transferred to this one by making appropriate changes in the line numbers. Then to call that obstacle-drawing subroutine, simply insert this line into the programming:

137 GOSUB 1500

Including some killable obstacles in the community of Alpha and Beta creatures has some special significance for further experiments with creature psychology and social behavior. Be sure to read about it in the next, and final, major section of this chapter.

The arena of combat can be made even more complex and interesting by having the creatures leave behind footprints wherever they go—especially if those footprints are regarded as obstacles to be contended with. Since array CC(CN,8) isn't used in the program, it can be assigned trail color codes.

Having all four creatures leave behind the same trail color is a rather straightforward procedure. Just insert this line:

142 CC(CN,8)=8

and then change line 26 to read:

260 COLOR=CC(CN,8):PLOT PX,PY:PX=NX:PY=NY

Doing that, all four creatures will leave behind a trail of brown. If you don't happen to like that particular color, equate the array in line 142 to any other color code but 14 or 15.

If you want the four creatures to leave behind trails that are different from one another, use the modified version of line 260, but do not use the added line 142. Instead, add this line:

132 CC(1,8)=1:CC(2,8)=5:CC(3,8)=6:CC(4,8)=7

Try it and see what happens. You ought to be able to figure out how to assign trail colors of your own choosing.

SUGGESTIONS FOR AN EXPERIMENT

There is good reason to believe that this program, as it is shown in Listing 15-1 and 15-2, favors the victory of Alpha creatures. That is not to say that one of the Alphas will always be the ultimate victor, but that, on the average, Alphas will tend to win more often.

That is a hypothesis that I have not yet tested. It takes a long time to run this program to its conclusion, and one would have to run it about 20 times or so in order to get a reliable average for the number of times an Alpha or Beta win. But here is why I think the results will show Alphas winning more often than Betas.

An Alpha creature has no memory of successful past experiences. Thus, each time it encounters a portion of the border figure or another creature, there is always a 50-50 chance that it will adopt a kill response. No matter how long that Alpha has been running, no matter what kind or how many responses it made in the past, it still has a 50-50 chance of picking a kill code when the opportunity arises.

Bearing that in mind, consider how the Beta creatures work under the same conditions. The programs, as shown in this chapter, do not insert any fixed, killable obstacles into the environment. That means the only encounters open to a Beta creature are those with elements of the border figure and other creatures. Now, encounters with the border figure must always result in the creature remembering a flight response—kill responses at the border figure never solve the situation. So the more often a Beta deals with the border figure, the more likely it is to adapt a more mild-mannered form of behavior. And when those remembered flight responses are used in a contact situation with another creature, the flight response will be the one that dominates the Beta's response. Using the programs as they are shown in this chapter, the only way a Beta will use and remember a kill response is if it comes about as a result of killing another creature.

There is a lot more border area than creature spaces on the screen, so the Betas take on few, if any, learned kill responses.

So the Betas tend to have very few kill responses in memory, but Alphas always have a 50-50 chance of picking a kill response. That is why I submit that, in the long run, the Alphas will tend to be the victors in this community more often than the Betas are. I haven't proven the idea by actual experimentation, so I will leave it up to you. Run the program to its conclusion some 20 times in succession, keeping track of which kind of creature, Alpha or Beta, turns out to be the ultimate victor more often.

Even if the results of that experiment show that the Alphas win more frequently than the Betas, the hypothesis is still a tenative one. The mechanism behind suggesting that result needs further testing.

To confirm the whole notion, try running the experiment about 20 more times, but inserting some fixed, killable obstacles into the environment; say, somewhere between 32 and 64 of them. I submit that the final results will be strikingly different—the Beta creatures will tend to win more often than the Alphas. Why? Because the Betas will have a chance to learn kill responses as they are forced to deal with all those obstacles. And when they do encounter another creature, those learned kill responses will be lurking there in memory, ready to strike out at anything that gets in the way.

In short, I suggest that raising a Beta creature in an obstacle cluttered environment encourages the development of some pretty mean Betas. The more cluttered the environment, the meaner they will be.

For the time being, I will leave the psychological and social implications to you.

Chapter 16
An Introduction
to Machine Psychology

The material offered in the preceding chapters is intended to acquaint you with the overall behavior of some simple Alpha and Beta machine creatures. This chapter opens a whole new phase of the work, treating those creatures as organisms worthy of serious study in a laboratory setting—in your own home laboratory, of course.

Generally, the experimental posture suggested here is that of experimental animal psychologists. Since experimental animal psychology isn't one of the ordinary career occupations, it calls for some definition at the outset.

A good many people tend to hold a one-sided view of psychology, thinking exclusively in terms of human clinical psychology. But that is just one part of a much larger field of study. Most psychologists are concerned with matters other than counseling people about their personal problems.

As a whole, psychology is concerned with the study of animal behavior in the broadest possible sense. Relatively few deal exclusively with human psychology, and even fewer are particularly interested in its clinical application. Most human psychologists work in a laboratory setting, investigating the ways we perceive the world and respond to it.

Animal psychology—the study of the behavior of lower animals—is closer to the sort of work suggested through the remainder of this book. But again, we aren't concerned with any sort of clinical applications, and that leads us to the matter of laboratory experiments with animals—experimental animal psychology.

Experimental animal psychologists are concerned with laboratory experiments aimed at generating and proving theories of animal behavior. Once we paint a picture of matters that concern experimental animal psychologists and the way they work, we can use it as a model for directing similar experiments with Alpha and Beta machine creatures.

THE METHODS OF EXPERIMENTAL ANIMAL PSYCHOLOGY

The proper subject of experimental animal psychology is the behavior of all sorts of animals; from simple, one-celled creatures to sophisticated apes and dolphins. The purpose of the experiment that is being conducted usually dictates the sort of animal that is used. The animals are nurtured in a controlled environment and then subjected to carefully controlled environmental manipulations that are aimed at enhancing the form of behavior being studied.

Observe any sort of animal for a while—even a household dog, cat, or even a tropical fish—and you will notice a form of behavior that brings up some questions. Why do guppies tend to spend part of their day in one part of the aquarium and the remainder of the day in another part? How long does it take a cat to learn to respond to the sound of a can opener running in the kitchen? Why does the dog jerk its face and legs while it sleeps?

Simple observation leads to questions, and questions lead to possible answers. The purpose of experimental psychology is to test the answers, either proving or disproving them. The experiments themselves, whether they prove the point or not, generally lead to further questions; and of course further questions lead to further answers that require experimental verification. What often begins as a simple question thus turns out to involve a lifetime of work for an experimental psychologist. A creative experimental psychologist never runs short of things to do.

Observation, question, suggested answer (*hypothesis*); those things lead to an experiment. You probably can appreciate how critical the design of the experiment can be.

Psychologists do not normally study animal behavior by dissecting the creature; that's the proper study of an animal psysiologist. One doesn't answer the questions about a cat's response to the sound of a can opener by tearing the cat to pieces.

Rather, psychologists perform their experiments by manipulating the animal's environment. Except for some very special kinds of studies, there is no need for considering the internal physical workings of the subject—everything can be studied in a more overt fashion. Experimental psychologists are far more concerned with the behavior of living things.

Suppose you are dealing with the question of why guppies spend more time in one part of the aquarium than another. Your hypotheses might run along these lines. It's because they have learned to move to the top of the aquarium for feeding purposes; it's because the water temperature changes through the day and they prefer certain temperatures; it's because they like a certain light level, and the light level changes with the time of day. Those are just a few—maybe obvious—hypotheses. The next step is to design a series of experiments aimed at proving one of them.

In the first case, it might appear that the fish have learned your feeding schedule. So alter the feeding schedule and note whether or not their behavior changes. If temperature is a determining factor in their behavior, rig an experiment that lets you control the temperature at fixed places in the aquarium. Or if the observed behavior is dictated by regularly changing light levels, devise an experiment that lets you control the lighting intensity and schedule.

The experiment should be devised so that it "homes in" on the form of behavior in question and manipulates the creatures' environment in a manner dictated by the hypothesis. What's more, it is sound experimental practice to gather observed data from two sources; from a *control* group and from an *experimental* group. In the case of the control group, you gather the data without making any of the changes in the environment that are set up to test the hypothesis. You note where the fish are and when they are there under normal conditions. Then you gather the same data, but while manipulating the environment according to the hypothesis—that data is coming from the experimental group. The comparison of the two sets of data, from the control and experimental groups, determines what ought to be done next.

The comparison of data from the control and experimental groups will verify your hypothesis, work contrary to your hypothesis, or turn out to be entirely inconclusive. In any event, there is a lot more work to be done.

Suppose you find that the data supports your hypothesis; you find, for instance, that altering the feeding schedule of the fish does indeed change their behavior. Things shouldn't end there on a note of victory. If everything is properly handled, the experiment should be verifiable any number of times in the future and in any similar experimental setting anywhere else in the world. Bearing that in mind, an experimenter is not too quick to celebrate his or her newly found place in the annals of science. A supporting experiment is in order. The idea is to devise a different sort of experiment that will hopefully verify the same hypothesis from a different angle.

Experimental psychology, you see, is made especially challenging by the number of environmental conditions that are easy to overlook. Those overlooked conditions might play a powerful role in the form of behavior being studied, but they might become apparent when testing the same hypothesis from a different viewpoint; using a different method.

So when a carefully conducted experiment appears to support hypothesis, it is important to do two further things; run the same experiment a large number of times, and devise at least one more experiment aimed at testing the same hypothesis in an entirely different fashion.

But what if the results of the initial experiment turn up some data that contradict your hypothesis being tested? Don't be too quick to throw out the hypothesis—some of those overlooked variables might be messing up the results. Either search out some of those overlooked controlling variables in the environment, or devise another experiment to test the hypothesis. It is just as important to prove that your hypothesis is wrong as it is to prove it is correct. And finding it is wrong, discovering the reason can lead to as much knowledge and further experiments as anything else can. There is no such thing as total defeat in science.

Finally, there are situations where the results of a series of experiments can appear inconclusive. Sometimes the data supports the hypothesis and sometimes it does not. A lot of modern science is in that condition right now, and that is why so many honest experimenters are reluctant to advertise their hypotheses in public— the public, the popular media, is very anxious for clear-cut answers to questions that are answered in an inconclusive fashion.

There are a couple of ways to deal with inconclusive results. One is to conduct the experiment a great many times, keeping track of the data and finally treating all that data in a statistical fashion. With enough data to work from, it is often possible to spot subtle trends that have some bearing on the conclusion. But how subtle can a statistical trend be and still considered conclusive? That question can be answered only on a case-by-case basis. One's own sense of honesty and conscience enter the picture at that point.

A better way to handle inconclusive results is by redesigning the experiment from scratch, perhaps regarding the results of the original experiment as contrary to the hypothesis.

No matter how an experiment is set up, and no matter what the results might be, gathering data is a vital part of the whole procedure. Data is the structure that supports experimental psychology.

THE METHODS OF EXPERIMENTAL MACHINE PSYCHOLOGY

The notion that a machine can be the proper study of experimental psychology will seem far-fetched, and maybe irresponsible, to most people. But since we have defined animal psychology as the study of behavior, there's little difficulty in extending the idea to machines; especially to machines that can behave in a complex fashion.

The problem stems from the fact that the machine age grew up on the philosophical notion that the universe and everything in it works according to a precise clockwork mechanism. The universe was put together before man began studying it, so we have been forced to analyze things of nature from the outside in. We study the behavior of animals from the outside, so to speak, and try to unravel the inner workings in a indirect fashion.

But when the machine age was born, we had the advantage of being the creators. Machines are built from the bottom up—from the inside out. Knowing the function of every cog and screw, we can eventually predict the operation of any machine.

It is the disparity of these two viewpoints—studying animals from the outside in, and machines from the inside out—that makes it seem silly to study the two on the same terms. But wait! Is it so silly? Haven't a lot of serious scientists been trying to understand animals in terms of machines for a long time now? Haven't there been shelves of books written that attempt to explain animal behavior in terms of machines? Just look at all the books and magazine articles that compare human brains with the workings of computers. It is a viable and exciting topic.

What I am suggesting is that the time is right for adding a new point of view; studying the behavior of complex machines as we study animal behavior. I'm certainly not going to bother with the notion of studying the psychology of the clock hanging on the wall; that particular machine is too simple to justify such a notion. But those little Alpha and Beta creatures demonstrated in earlier chapters of this book certainly lend themselves to the methods of experimental psychology.

An important principle—a critical one at this point—is to regard those Alpha and Beta creatures as creatures that must be observed from the outside in. You have already seen that they can exhibit seemingly rational behavior, even though they aren't consciously programmed to exhibit anything of the sort. For our present purposes, the exact cog and screw, mechanistic view of the Alpha and Beta programming is irrelevant. It is the observation of their outward behavior that is all important.

Step 1: Observation. You've had a chance to observe Alpha and Beta creatures under a number of different circumstances suggested in earlier chapters.

Step 2: Ask a question. Your observations ought to form the basis for some questions about the creatures' behavior. For instance, do Beta creatures adapt to a changing environment any sooner than Alpha creatures do?

Step 3: Form an hypothesis. Take at least an educated guess, based on your observations in the past, and state it as a formal hypothesis. If you haven't made enough observations or you think you might have overlooked something, take some time to set up the program and observe the creature more carefully.

Step 4: Design an experiment to test the hypothesis. That means starting with the basic Alpha or Beta mechanisms used in earlier chapters, combining them with some control programming aimed at gathering relevant data and manipulating the environment in a relevant fashion. Do not, however, tamper with the basic Alpha and Beta mechanisms.

Step 5: Conduct the experiment and gather the data. That is the main topic of most of the remaining discussions in this book.

Step 6: Form a conclusion. Does the data support the hypothesis?

Step 7: Run further experiments.

THE PRIMITIVE CHARACTER OF THE CREATURES

The fundamental Alpha and Beta mechanisms as treated here are admittedly quite primitive in nature. They represent only the first steps in the evolution of machine creatures. And as primitive creatures, there are just so many meaningful psychological experiments that can be performed with them.

That is not to suggest, however, that the range of possible experiments is too small to be of any significance. Quite the contrary. We are cast into the unusual role of both creator and studier, and it appears at the present time that the only way to encourage the evolution of more sophisticated machine creatures is by studying the character and limitations of the current versions.

Chapter 17
Gathering Data for Alpha Creatures

Gathering data is an essential part of most experimental procedures; and quite often, the ultimate success or failure of a project depends on how well the data is selected and gathered. The purpose of the present discussion is to illustrate some techniques for gathering data that seems to be relevant to most Alpha experiments.

Two of the most important data elements for studies with Alpha creatures are the number of times the creature has encountered an obstacle in its path, and the number of times it picks a response that successfully gets it away from those obstacles. Those data elements can be called the *contact score* and the *good moves score,* respectively.

The computer program, itself, can be responsible for totalling those scores as the experiment progresses. The program can increment the contact-score counter every time the creature encounters an obstacle in its path, and it can increment the good-moves counter when the creature subsequently finds its way out of a contact situation. The contact score ought to be programmed such that it counts the number of unworkable responses, regarding those unworkable responses as additional contacts. Doing that, it becomes possible to devise an *overall scoring* figure that indicates how well the creature deals with its environment. That can be a simple matter of dividing the good moves score by the contact score.

These scoring routines can be inserted into a standard Alpha creature program, but they must be inserted in such a way that they do not disrupt the basic flow of operations for the Alpha behavior. There is little gained by using methods of measurement that disrupt the activity to be measured.

Figure 17-1 is a flowchart for an Alpha scoring scheme. It runs the Alpha creature in the usual fashion, but also keeps a running tally of the contact, good moves and overall scoring figures. Those figures are conveniently displayed along the bottom of the crt display.

The flowchart begins with a series of initialization routines. The only routine that is different from any others described thus far is INITIALIZE THE SCORING. That routine, of course, zeros the CONTACT and GOOD moves counters.

Once the Alpha portion of the program is underway, it does the SEARCH AHEAD routine. If the path ahead is found to be clear, the creature is moved to its next position on the screen—a position determined by the current motion code. And immediately after that, the program loops back to do another SEARCH AHEAD. The system runs that particular loop until the creature encounters an obstacle, including elements of the border figure.

If it is ever deemed necessary to keep track of the total number of moves the creature makes, the search ahead and move loop can be expanded to include an operation that increments a total move counter. That scoring operation could be inserted immediately after MOVE THE CREATURE. Such a score is not really important to the current series of Alpha experiments, so it is not used here.

The second major portion of the flowchart is executed only while the creature is dealing with an obstacle it has encountered in its path. The first operation in that loop is to INCREMENT CONTACT SCORE; that signifies a contact situation. Then, in keeping with the nature of Alpha behavior, the program does a FETCH RANDOM MOTION CODE, and then it tests the workability of the new motion code by doing a SEARCH AHEAD and testing the path. If the path is not clear, the system loops back to the beginning of the contact sequence, incrementing the contact score again, fetching another random motion code, and searching ahead once more. The system remains in that particular loop—incrementing the CONTACT score and trying new motion codes—until it comes up with a motion code that gets it away from the obstacle (or obstacles) in its path.

Once the creature finds a workable motion code, the system does the INCREMENT GOOD SCORE operation, updates the scoring and the scoring display on the screen, and returns to the main running loop to resume its free-running motion. Aside from updating the CONTACT and GOOD moves scoring on the screen, the UPDATE SCORE DISPLAY also calculates the overall

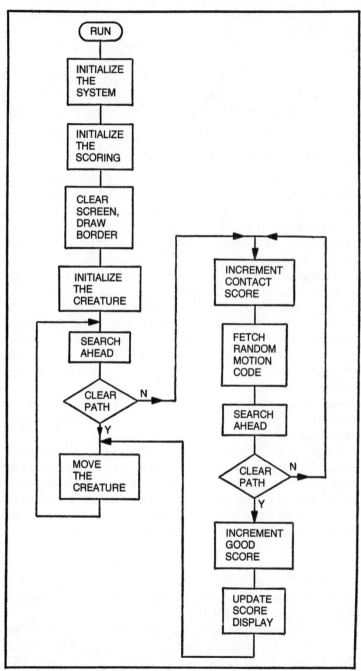

Fig. 17-1. Flowchart for Alpha creatures with scoring.

SCORE—GOOD divided by CONTACT— and displays it with the two elements of raw data.

As shown in this flowchart, the program runs endlessly. It tallies the scores for an indefinite period of time.

Variations of the flowchart and/or the programming it engenders can lead to a wide range of useful data-gathering experiments for Alpha creatures. The remainder of this chapter demonstrates some of those variations.

FUNDAMENTAL ALPHA WITH SCORING

The program listing in this section is a straightforward implementation of the flowchart just described. In addition to demonstrating how the scoring can be done, it leads to a useful piece of experimental information; how well a simple Alpha creature deals with contacts at the simple border figure. That project, itself, can serve as an important control for further studies.

Load the listing into your computer and run it for a while. Upon making its first contact with an element of the border figure, the Alpha's scoring will appear along the bottom of the screen. CONTACT will indicate the total number of contacts, GOOD will indicate the number of successful choices of motion codes, and SCORE will indicate the ratio of GOOD to CONTACT. So if the creature happens to pick a good response on the first encounter, the scores will be 1. But the creature will inevitably make a bad choice for a response in a short time, so the SCORE figure will begin falling below 1 (a SCORE of 1 indicates that the creature is not picking any unworkable motion codes).

The SCORE figure varies a great deal through the first 30 contacts or so, but it eventually settles down to a fairly constant figure. After about 1000 contacts, the TRS-80 version begins showing an average SCORE of 0.47, and the Apple version shows about 0.5. The significance is that the Alpha creature selects a workable response about half the time it is called upon to do so.

TRS-80 Version

Table 17-1 defines the variables that are used in the TRS-80 version of this ALPHA WITH SCORING program. The program, itself, is shown as Listing 17-1.

The program uses subroutines BORDER V.1 and SEARCH AHEAD V.1 as described in earlier projects. ALPHA PSYCH MAINLINE V.1 is structured to execute the flowchart in Fig. 17-1, and a new subroutine, SCORING ROUTINES V.1, is used for

Table 17-1. TRS-80 Variable List for ALPHA WITH SCORING.

CP	Current creature position
NP	Next creature position
CI	Horizontal component of motion code
CJ	Vertical component of motion code
CX	Horizontal component of contact code
CY	Vertical component of contact code
SI	Sign value of CI
SJ	Sign value of CJ
AI	Absolute value of CI
AJ	Absolute value of CJ
CS	Contact score
GS	Good-move score
AS	Average response score
F$	Field specifier for printing AS
S$	General-purpose string variable
N	General-purpose numeric variable
F0	Upper-left corner of border figure
F1	Upper-right corner of border figure
F2	Lower-left corner of border figure
F3	Lower-right corner of border figure

displaying the scores and calculating the current value of the Alpha's overall SCORE.

Listing 17-1. TRS-80 Programming for ALPHA WITH SCORING.

```
 10 REM   ALPHA WITH SCORING
 15 REM      TRS-80
 20 REM
 25 REM
100 REM ** ALPHA PSYCH MAINLINE, V.1—TRS-80 **
105 CLEAR 128:F$="#.##"
110 CLS:Print STRING$(6,26):PRINT TAB(25);"ALPHA
    WITH SCORING"
115 PRINT STRING$(4,26);"STRIKE 'ENTER' TO START
    . . ."
120 S$=INKEY$:IF S$="" THEN N=RND(1000):GOTO 120
125 CS=0:GS=0
130 CLS:GOSUB 1000
135 CP=15776+RND(5)−3+64*(RND(5)−3)
140 CI=RND(5)−3:CJ=RND(5)−3:IF CI=0 AND CJ=0
    THEN 140
145 GOSUB 2000
150 IF NOT (CX=32 AND CY=32) THEN 160
155 POKE CP,32:CP=NP:POKE CP,42:GOTO 145
```

```
 160 CS=CS+1
 165 CI=RND(5)−3:CJ=RND(5)−3:IF CI=0 AND CJ=0
     THEN 165
 170 GOSUB 2000
 175 IF NOT(CX=32 AND CY=32) THEN 160
 180 GS=GS+1:GOSUB 3000
 185 GOTO 155
 190 REM
 195 REM
1000 REM ** BORDER, V.1—TRS-80**
1005 F0=15360:F1=15423:F2=16128:F3=16191
1010 FOR N=F0 TO F1:POKE N,176:NEXT N
1015 FOR N=F2 TO F3:POKE N,131:NEXT N
1020 FOR N=F0 TO F2 STEP 64:POKE N,170:NEXT N
1025 FOR N=F1 TO F3 STEP 64:POKE N,149:NEXT N
1030 POKE F0,160:POKE F1,144:POKE F2,130:POKE
     F3,129
1035 RETURN
1040 REM
1045 REM
2000 REM ** SEARCH AHEAD, V.1—TRS-80 **
2005 NP=CP:CX=32:CY=32
2010 SI=SGN(CI):SJ=SGN(CJ):AI=ABS(CI):AJ=ABS(CJ)
2015 IF AI=0 THEN 2030 ELSE AI=AI−1
2020 IF SI>0 THEN NP=NP+1 ELSE NP=NP−1
2025 CX=PEEK(NP)
2030 IF AJ=0 THEN 2045 ELSE AJ=AJ−1
2035 IF SJ>0 THEN NP=NP+64 ELSE NP=NP−64
2040 CY=PEEK(NP)
2045 IF NOT(CX=32 AND CY=32) THEN RETURN
2050 IF AI=0 AND AJ=0 THEN RETURN ELSE GOTO 2015
2055 REM
2060 REM
3000 REM ** SCORING ROUTINES,V.1—TRS-80 **
3005 AS=GS/CS
3010 PRINT@832, "CONTACTS","GOOD  MOVES",
     "SCORE"
3015 PRINT @ 896,STRING$(64,32);
3020 PRINT @ 896,CS,GS;:PRINT @ 928,USING F$;AS;
3025 RETURN
3030 REM
3035 REM
```

The analysis of the mainline looks like this:

Line 105—Clear 128 bytes for string information and define a field specifier for printing the SCORE figure to 2 decimal places.

Lines 110-120—Display an opening title message and run the TRS-80's random generator an indefinite number of times. The title message is really unimportant; it is simply used to cover a far more important operation; running that random number generator. When a TRS-80 is first turned on, some models select the same random number in its random number generator; and that means the Alpha creature will always behave the same way every time the computer is turned on and loaded with the program. Getting around that undesirable situation is a matter of cycling the computer's random number generator an indefinite number of times—continuously using it for no real purpose until the user strikes the ENTER key. See the statements in Line 120.

Line 125—Initialize the scoring.

Line 130—Clear the screen and draw the standard, rectangular border figure.

Lines 135-140—Initialize the creature's screen position and motion code.

Lines 145-155—Do the SEARCH AHEAD routine. If the path ahead is not clear, jump down to line 160; otherwise move the creature and loop back to do the SEARCH AHEAD routine again.

Line 160—Increment the CONTACT score. The program reaches this point only when the creature is dealing with an obstacle in its path.

Line 165—Fetch a valid random motion code.

Line 170—Do the SEARCH AHEAD routine to test the workability of the new motion code.

Line 175—Test the workability of the new motion code. If it doesn't lead to a clear path ahead, loop back to increment the CONTACT score, pick another motion code, and so on.

Lines 180-185—When a workable motion code is found, increment the GOOD score, update the display by executing the SCORING subroutine that begins at line 3000, and then return to the main operating loop where the creature is moved to its next position on the screen.

The SCORING routine is a rather simple one. It is called as a subroutine at line 3000. From that point, it calculates the overall SCORE (line 3005), prints the scoring titles (line 3010), erases the old scoring figures (line 3015), and prints the updated version of them (line 3020). The field specifier is used in line 3020 to keep the overall SCORE figure short and simple—there is no need for 6-place precision.

Apple II Version

Table 17-2 defines the variables that are used in the Apple version of this program, ALPHA WITH SCORING. The program is shown here as Listing 17-2.

Table 17-2. Applesoft Variable List for ALPHA WITH SCORING.

FN R(0)	Random function for values between −2 and 2
PX	Horizontal component of current creature position
PY	Vertical component of current creature position
NX	Horizontal component of next creature position
NY	Vertical component of next creature position
CX	Horizontal component of contact code
CY	Vertical component of contact code
SI	Sign value of CI
SJ	Sign value of CJ
AI	Absolute value of CI
AJ	Absolute value of CJ
CS	CONTACT score
GS	GOOD-moves score
AS	Average response SCORE
N	General-purpose numeric variable

Listing 17-2. Applesoft Programming for ALPHA WITH SCORING.

```
10 REM   ALPHA WITH SCORING
15 REM      APPLESOFT
20 REM
25 REM
100 REM ** ALPHA PSYCH MAINLINE, V.1—APPLESOFT
    **
105 DEF FN R(R) = INT (5 * RND (1)) − 2
110 TEXT : HOME : VTAB (8): PRINT TAB(12)"ALPHA WITH
    SCORING"
115 VTAB (15):PRINT "STRIKE 'RETURN' TO START . . ."
120 N = FN R(0):N = PEEK ( − 16384): POKE − 16368,0
125 IF N < > 141 THEN 120
130 CS = 0:GS = 0
135 HOME : GR : GOSUB 1000
```

```
 140  PX = 20 + FN R(0):PY = 20 + FN R(0)
 145  CI = FN R(0):CJ = FN R(0): IF CI = 0 AND CJ= 0 THEN
      145
 150  GOSUB 2000
 155  IF NOT (CX = 0 AND CY = 0) THEN 175
 160  COLOR= 0: PLOT PX,PY
 165  PX = NX:PY = NY
 170  COLOR= 9: PLOT PX,PY: GOTO 150
 175  CS = CS + 1
 180  CI = FN R(0):CJ = FN R(0): IF CI = 0 AND CJ = 0 THEN
      180
 185  GOSUB 2000
 190  IF NOT (CX = 0 AND CY = 0) THEN 175
 195  GS = GS + 1: GOSUB 3000
 200  GOTO 160
 205  REM
 210  REM
1000  REM ** BORDER, V.1—APPLESOFT **
1005  COLOR= 15
1010  HLIN 0,39 AT 0: HLIN 0,39 AT 36
1015  VLIN 0,36 AT 0: VLIN 0,36 AT 39
1020  RETURN
1025  REM
1030  REM
2000  REM ** SEARCH AHEAD, V.1—APPLESOFT **
2005  NX = PX:NY = PY:CX = 0:CY = 0
2010  SI = SGN (CI):SJ = SGN (CJ):AI = ABS (CI):AJ = ABS
      (CJ)
2015  IF AI = 0 THEN 2040
2020  AI = AI − 1
2025  IF SI > 0 THEN NX = NX + 1: GOTO 2035
2030  NX = NX − 1
2035  CX = SCRN(NX,NY)
2040  IF AJ = 0 THEN 2065
2045  AJ = AJ − 1
2050  IF SJ > 0 THEN NY = NY + 1: GOTO 2060
2055  NY = NY − 1
2060  CY = SCRN(NX,NY)
2065  IF NOT (CX = 0 AND CY = 0) THEN RETURN
2070  IF AI = 0 AND AJ = 0 THEN RETURN
2075  GOTO 2015
2080  REM
```

```
2085 REM
3000 REM ** SCORING ROUTINES, V.1—APPLESOFT **
3005 ASD = INT ((GS / CS) * 1000) / 1000
3010 HOME : PRINT "CONTACTS", "GOOD", "SCORE"
3015 PRINT CS,GS,AS
3020 RETURN
3025 REM
3030 REM
```

The program uses subroutines BORDER V.1 and SEARCH AHEAD V.1 as in many earlier projects. The mainline and an additional subroutine, SCORING ROUTINES V.1, have to be added in from scratch. The mainline portion of the listing is built around the operational flowchart shown in Fig. 17-1; and the purpose of the SCORING subroutine is to calculate the average response SCORE and display the scoring data along the bottom of the screen.

An analysis of the mainline looks like this:

Line 105—Define the random code function.

Lines 110-125—This group of program statements obstensibly print out a simple title message; but there's more to them than that. The whole purpose of the series of operations is to make certain that the Apple's random number generator is not beginning the experiment with a random number that might have been used at the beginning of a previous experiment. The operation is especially critical when running the program, just having applied power to the computer. (Some BASIC monitors initialize their random number generators with the same value.)

Line 130—Initialize the scoring.

Line 135—Clear the screen, set the graphics mode, and draw the usual, rectangular border figure.

Lines 140-145—Initialize the creature's screen position and motion code.

Line 150—Execute the SEARCH AHEAD routine.

Line 155—If the path ahead is *not* clear, jump down to program line 175; otherwise move the creature.

Lines 160-170—Move the creature to its next position on the screen and loop back to do the SEARCH AHEAD operation again.

Line 175—Increment the CONTACT counter.

Line 180—Pick a valid, random motion code.

Line 185—Test the workability of the new motion code by
executing the SEARCH AHEAD routine.

Line 190—If the new motion code is *not* a workable one, go
back to increment the CONTACT counter, pick another
motion code, do the SEARCH AHEAD, and so on.

Line 195—Upon finding a workable solution to the present
contact situation (the new motion code points to a clear
path ahead), increment the GOOD counter, update the
scoring display on the screen, and return to the main
running loop at the point where the creature is moved to
its next position on the screen.

The SCORING subroutine, beginning at program line 3000,
calculates the SCORE average and adjusts it for an adequate 3-place
precision (line 3005). Line 3010 then clears the previous scoring
information and reprints the names of the scoring elements. Line
3015 then prints the scores.

ALPHA WITH SCORING AND RANDOM OBSTACLES

The programs just described show that the average SCORE
eventually works its way to approximately 0.5; usually a bit less
than that. The implication is that an Alpha creature is correct about
half the time when it comes to selecting a random motion code that
will extracate it from a contact situation. The contact situations
available with the usual rectangular border figure are quite limited,
however, and one must wonder how changing the nature of the
creatures environment—especially making it more complex—will
affect the scoring. The suggested program in this section can lead
you to the answer.

Observation: Using a clean, rectangular border figure of
generous proportions, an Alpha creature picks a correct response to
a contact about half the time.

Question: Would environments or borders of different sizes
and/or configurations change the scoring?

One might suggest an hypothesis at this point, and then devise
a formal experiment to test it. I would suggest some further observations, or tests of a less formal nature, first.

Test: Prepare an Alpha program with scoring that lets you
specify any number of randomly distributed obstacles within the
creature's environment. Run the program for a while, until it appears that the SCORE figure is settling down. Record the figure and
number of selected obstacles. Then repeat the experiment any
number of times, using more and more obstacles. Somewhere along

the line, you ought to notice a dramatic reduction in the scores. Plot a graph shown the number of obstacles along the horizontal axis and the "settled-down" SCORE along the vertical axis.

Where on the graph does the decline in scoring begin? More importantly, why does it decline at all?

The experiment, as described here, really proves nothing. It is a preliminary experiment—a series of directed observations intended to engender questions rather than answer them. Those questions form the basis for formal experiments in the future.

Upon running the program, you will see a title message and a request to strike the ENTER key (TRS-80) or RETURN key (Apple) to get the program running. As before, the real purpose of this phase is to cycle the computer's random number generator an indefinite number of times, thereby reducing the chances of running exactly the same patterns of motion through an extended series of tests.

The program then requests the number of obstacles you want distributed about the environment. Select any number you want. I suggest you begin with 0 obstacles—that would be your control experiment. Then use maybe 16 of them the next time, then 32, then 64. Increase the number of obstacles until you see a dramatic change in the SCORE figure after a hundred contacts or more. (I know where that decline begins, but I'm not telling. That would spoil your fun).

A flowchart of the program is not necessary, because there is just some simple modifications from the one shown in Fig. 17-1. All that is new is a short subroutine for entering the number of obstacles, OBSTACLES V.2 at line 1500, and a couple of extra lines in the mainline programming for drawing the obstacles on the screen. The whole obstacle portion of the program can be considered part of an initialization operation in the original flowchart.

TRS-80 Version

The definitions of variables and programming for ALPHA WITH SCORING AND RANDOM OBSTACLES appear in Table 17-3 and Listing 17-3, respectively.

Lines 105-120—Initialize the system by clearing some string space, defining the field specifier F$, and running the random-generator function until the user strikes the ENTER key.

Line 125—Go to subroutine 1500 to pick up the desired number of obstacles to be drawn in the environment.

222

Table 17-3. TRS-80 Variable List for ALPHA WITH SCORING AND RANDOM OBSTACLES.

CP	Current creature position
NP	Next creature position
CI	Horizontal component of motion code
CJ	Vertical component of motion code
CX	Horizontal component of contact code
CY	Vertical component of contact code
TP	Position of an obstacle
SI	Sign value of CI
SJ	Sign value of CJ
AI	Absolute value of CI
AJ	Absolute value of CJ
CS	Contact score
GS	Good-move score
AS	Average response score
F$	Field specifier for printing AS
S$	General-purpose string variable
N	General-purpose numeric variable
NT%,NT	Number of obstacles to be plotted
F0	Upper-left corner of border figure
F1	Upper-right corner of border figure
F2	Lower-left corner of border figure
F3	Lower-right corner of border figure

Listing 17-3. TRS-80 Programming for
ALPHA WITH SCORING AND RANDOM OBSTACLES.

```
 10 REM    ALPHA WITH SCORING
 15 REM    AND RANDOM OBSTACLES
 20 REM      TRS-80
 25 REM
 30 REM
100 REM ** ALPHA PSYCH MAINLINE, V.2—TRS-80 **
105 CLEAR 128:F$="#.##"
110 CLS:PRINT STRING$(6,26):PRINT TAB(25); "ALPHA
    WITH SCORING"
115 PRINT TAB(24) "AND RANDOM OBSTACLES":
    PRINT:PRINT "STRIKE 'ENTER' TO START . . ."
120 S$=INKEY$:IF S$="" THEN N=RND(1000):GOTO 120
125 GOSUB 1500
130 CS=0:GS=0
135 CLS:GOSUB 1000
140 IF NT=0 THEN 165
145 FOR N=1 TO NT
150 TP=15360+RND(831):IF PEEK(TP)<>32 THEN 150
155 POKE TP,191
```

223

```
160  NEXT N
165  CP=15776+RND(5)−3+64*(RND(5)−3):IF
     PEEK(CP)<>32 THEN 165
170  CI=RND(5)−3:CJ=RND(5)−3:IF CI=0 AND CJ=0
     THEN 170
175  GOSUB 2000
180  IF NOT(CX=32 AND CY=32) THEN 190
185  POKE CP,32:CP=NP:POKE CP,42:GOTO 175
190  CS=CS+1
195  CI=RND(5)−3:CJ=RND(5)−3:IF CI=0 AND CJ=0
     THEN 195
200  GOSUB 2000
205  IF NOT(CX=32 AND CY=32) THEN 190
210  GS=GS+1:GOSUB 3000
215  GOTO 185
220  REM
225  REM
1000 REM ** BORDER, V.1—TRS-80 **
1005 F0=15360:F1=15423:F2=16128:F3=16191
1010 FOR N=F0 TO F1:POKE N,176:NEXT N
1015 FOR N=F2 TO F3:POKE N,131:NEXT N
1020 FOR N=F0 TO F2 STEP 64:POKE N,170:NEXT N
1025 FOR N=F1 TO F3 STEP 64:POKE N,149:NEXT N
1030 POKE F0,160:POKE F1,144:POKE F2,130:POKE
     F3,129
1035 RETURN
1040 REM
1045 REM
1500 REM ** OBSTACLES, V.2—TRS-80 **
1505 CLS:INPUT "HOW MANY OBSTACLES";NT%
1510 NT=NT%:IF NT<0 THEN 1505
1515 RETURN
1520 REM
1525 REM
2000 REM ** SEARCH AHEAD, V.1—TRS-80 **
2005 NP=CP:CX=32:CY=32
2010 SI=SGN(CI):SJ=SGN(CJ):AI=ABS(CI):AJ=ABS(CJ)
2015 IF AI=0 THEN 2030 ELSE AI=AI−1
2020 IF SI>0 THEN NP=NP+1 ELSE NP=NP−1
2025 CX=PEEK(NP)
2030 IF AJ=0 THEN 2045 ELSE AJ=AJ−1
2035 IF SJ>0 THEN NP=NP+64 ELSE NP=NP−64
```

```
2040  CY=PEEK(NP)
2045  IF NOT(CX=32 AND CY=32) THEN RETURN
2050  IF AI=0 AND AJ=0 THEN RETURN ELSE GOTO 2015
2055  REM
2060  REM
3000  REM ** SCORING ROUTINES, V.1—TRS-80**
3005  AS=GS/CS
3010  PRINT @ 832, "CONTACTS", "GOOD MOVES",
      SCORE
3015  PRINT @ 896,STRING$(64,32);
3020  PRINT @ 896,CS,GS;:PRINT @ 928,USING F$;AS;
3025  RETURN
3030  REM
3035  REM
```

Lines 130-135—Initialize the scoring, clear the screen, and draw the border figure.

Lines 140-160—Draw the selected number of obstacles at random positions, but in such a way that none overlaps.

Lines 165-170—Initialize the creature's position and motion code.

Lines 175-205—Search the path ahead. If it is not clear, jump down to get a new motion code; otherwise, move the creature and search ahead again.

Lines 210-215—Increment the CONTACT score, fetch a new random motion code, test its workability. If it doesn't work, start the sequence all over again; otherwise increment the GOOD score and return to the main running loop.

Apple II Version

The variables for this program are defined for you in Table 17-4, and the programming is shown in Listing 17-4.

Lines 105-135—Define functions for random motion codes and random obstacle positions, and cycle the random number generator until the user strikes the RETURN key.

Line 140—Go to the subroutine at line 1500 to pick up the number of obstacles to be plotted on the screen.

Lines 145-150—Initialize the scoring, clear the screen, set the graphics mode, and draw the border figure.

Lines 155-180—If no obstacles are to be drawn, skip over this series of statements. Otherwise draw the specified

Table 17-4. Applesoft Variable List for
ALPHA WITH SCORING AND RANDOM OBSTACLES.

FN R(0)	Random function for motion codes, −2 through 2
FN T(T)	Random function for placing obstacles
PX	Horizontal component of current creature position
PY	Vertical component of current creature position
NX	Horizontal component of next creature position
NY	Vertical component of next creature position
CI	Horizontal component of motion code
CJ	Vertical component of motion code
CX	Horizontal component of contact code
CY	Vertical component of contact code
SI	Sign value of CI
SJ	Sign value of CJ
AI	Absolute value of CI
AJ	Absolute value of CJ
CS	Contact score
GS	Good-move score
AS	Average response score
NT%,NT	Number of obstacles to be plotted
TX	Horizontal component of an obstacle position
TY	Vertical component of an obstacle position
N	General-purpose numeric variable

Listing 17-4. Applesoft Programming for
ALPHA WITH SCORING AND RANDOM OBSTACLES.

```
 10 REM     ALPHA WITH SCORING
 15 REM   AND RANDOM OBSTACLES
 20 REM
 25 REM
 30 REM
100 REM ** ALPHA PSYCH MAINLINE, V.2—APPLESOFT
    **
105 DEF FN R(R) = INT (5 * RND (1)) − 2
110 DEF FN T(T) = INT (T * RND (1)) + 1
115 TEXT : HOME : PRINT TAB(12)"ALPHA WITH SCOR-
    ING"
120 PRINT TAB(11)"AND RANDOM OBSTACLES"
125 VTAB (15): PRINT "STRIKE 'RETURN' TO START . . ."
130 N = FN R(0):N = PEEK ( − 16384): POKE − 16368,0
135 IF N < > 141 THEN 130
140 GOSUB 1500
145 CS = 0:GS = 0
150 HOME : GR : GOSUB 1000
155 IF NT = 0 THEN 185
160 COLOR= 13
```

```
 165 FOR N = 1 TO NT
 170 TX = FN T(38):TY = FN T(35):IF SCRN(TX,TY) < > 0
     THEN 170
 175 PLOT TX,TY
 180 NEXT N
 185 PX = 20 + FN R(0):PY = 20 + FN R(0): IF SCRN(PX,PY)
     < > 0 THEN   185
 190 CI = FN R(0):CJ = FN R(0):IF CI = 0 AND CJ = 0 THEN
     190
 195 GOSUB 2000
 200 IF NOT (CX = 0 AND CY = 0) THEN 220
 205 COLOR= 0: PLOT PX,PY
 210 PX = NX:PY = NY
 215 COLOR=9: PLOT PX,PY: GOTO 195
 220 CS = CS + 1
 225 CI = FN R(0):CJ = FN R(0): IF CI = 0 AND CJ = 0 THEN
     225
 230 GOSUB 2000
 235 IF NOT (CX = 0 AND CY = 0) THEN 220
 240 GS = GS + 1: GOSUB 3000
 245 GOTO 205
 250 REM
 255 REM
1000 REM ** BORDER, V.1—APPLESOFT **
1005 COLOR= 15
1010 HLIN 0,39 AT 0: HLIN 0,39 AT 36
1015 VLIN 0,36 AT 0: VLIN 0,36 AT 39
1020 RETURN
1025 REM
1030 REM
1500 REM ** OBSTACLES, V.2—APPLESOFT **
1505 TEXT : HOME : INPUT "HOW MANY OBSTACLES?";
     NT%
1510 NT = NT%:IF NT< 0 THEN 1505
1515 RETURN
1520 REM
1525 REM
2000 REM ** SEARCH AHEAD, V.1—APPLESOFT **
2005 NX = PX:NY = PY:CX =0CY =0
2010 SI = SGN(CI):SJ = SGN (CJ):AI = ABS (CI):AJ = ABS
     (CJ)
2015 IF AI = 0 THEN 2040
```

```
2020 AI = AI − 1
2025 IF SI > 0 THEN NX = NX + 1: GOTO 2035
2030 NX = NX − 1
2035 CX = SCRN(NX,NY)
2040 IF AJ = 0 THEN 2065
2045 AJ = AJ − 1
2050 IF SJ > 0 THEN NY = NY + 1: GOTO 2060
2055 NY = NY − 1
2060 CY = SCRN(NX,NY)
2065 IF NOT (CX = 0 AND CY = 0) THEN RETURN
2070 IF AI = 0 AND AJ = 0 THEN RETURN
2075 GOTO 2015
2080 REM
2085 REM
3000 REM ** SCORING ROUTINES, V.1—APPLESOFT **
3005 AS = INT ((GS / CS) * 1000) / 1000
3010 HOME : PRINT "CONTACTS","GOOD","SCORE"
3015 PRINT CS,GS,AS
3020 RETURN
3025 REM
3030 REM
```

number of obstacles at random, non-overlapping positions on the screen.

Lines 185-190—Initialize the creature's screen position and motion code, making sure the creature isn't plotted on top of an obstacle.

Lines 195-215—Search the path ahead. If it is not clear, jump down to get a new motion code; otherwise move the creature and repeat the entire sequence.

Lines 220-245—Increment the CONTACT score, fetch a new random motion code, test the workability of the new code. If it doesn't work, repeat this sequence; otherwise, increment the GOOD score, update the score display, and return to the main running loop.

ALPHA WITH SCORING AND CUSTOM BORDER

The creatures' primary mode of behavior is to move in a straight line and at a constant speed across the screen. The most desirable condition is thus one where no obstacles lie in the path ahead. But of course obstacles do intervene, making it necessary for the creatures to adjust their behavior to find a new path that is clear.

Alphas accomplish the adjustment by selecting random motion codes until they stumble across one that works. Betas first refer to their memory of past experiences, and if a workable response worked under similar contact conditions in the past, that response is tried. But if there is no memory of a similar experience, or if the remembered response no longer works for some reason, the Betas resort to purely Alpha-like random behavior.

In any event, the geometry of the contact situation influences the chances of picking a workable motion code, and that influences the SCORE data generated through the experiments described in this chapter. Discussions in Chapter 2 describe the geometry of motion codes in great detail; 24 valid motion codes and 16 possible angles of motion. Upon making contact with an obstacle, however, not all possible motion codes are workable ones and that means the chances of picking a workable motion code on the first try are certainly less than perfect.

When running into a long, straight line obstacle, for example, the chances of selecting a workable motion code are 18 of 24, or 3:4. Those aren't bad odds, and an experimenter could expect to see SCORE values running in the neighborhood of 0.75—if there were nothing but long straight lines as obstacles. Clearly that is not possible. There have to be some corners in the confining field of play. The standard rectangular border figure, for example, has 4 90-degree corners and 90-degree inside corners offer 10 out of 24, or 5:12, chances of picking a workable motion code the first time. The scoring, as defined in this chapter, is thus pulled down a significant amount each time the creature has to deal with a contact situation near the corners of the border figure.

Following this line of reasoning, it figures that contacts with inside corners less than 90 degrees will produce increasingly smaller odds of selecting a workable response on the first try, while contacts with large outside angles that are greater than 180 degrees will yield scores that are better than 3:4.

Testing this idea is a matter of confining the creatures within border figures of shapes other than rectangular. How well does an Alpha score within a circular border? A border shaped like a 5-pointed star? The answer to such questions is found by devising custom border figures for the creatures—and that is the purpose of these programs.

ALPHA WITH SCORING AND CUSTOM BORDER allows you to draw a border figure of any desired size and geometric configuration. Once it is drawn during the initial part of the experiment, the Alpha creature is allowed to roam around within your border figure, dealing with the various angles of contact in its own random fashion. The scoring is tallied as in the experiments offered earlier in this chapter.

The mechanism for drawing the free-hand border figure differs for the TRS-80 and Apple II machines. The techniques will be described separately at a later time. The experiments conducted with custom border figures are rather meaningless, however, unless you devise a way for documenting the exact geometry of them. One practical technique is to overlay the screen with a clean sheet of tracing paper, then simply trace the custom border figure. That tracing, along with the scoring results, have some particular meaning for future experiments—experiments dealing with the relationships between the creatures' modes of sensing and responding to the geometry of their environment.

TRS-80 Version

The TRS-80 version of ALPHA WITH SCORING AND CUSTOM BORDER follows the flowchart in Fig. 17-1 fairly well. The only difference is that the present program includes a special border-drawing subroutine, CUSTOM BORDER, V.1. But even so, that routine can be considered part of the initialization phase of the experiment—nothing with regard to the Alpha behavior is changed.

When the program is begun, you will see the usual opening message and it still plays the role of a simple technique for occupying the user's mind while the random number generator is cycling some indefinite number of times. What comes after that, however, is the unique feature of the project.

You will see the screen clear and a rendition of the Alpha creature in its initial position on the screen. There is also a drawing cursor—a little square of light—located in the upper left-hand quadrant of the screen. The position of that drawing cursor can be controlled by manipulating the TRS-80's arrow keys. Depressing the up-arrow key makes that cursor move upward, depressing the down-arrow key makes it move downward, depressing the right-arrow key makes it move to the right, and so on. Depressing meaningful combinations of keys causes compound motions. Depressing the up and right keys, for instance, makes that little drawing cursor move at an angle, up and to the right. The motion created by depressing the keys continues until the keys are released; or, saying the same thing in a different way, the motion continues only as long as the direction keys are depressed.

It is probably a good idea to play with those direction controls until you become used to how they work. Notice that the cursor cannot be driven off the screen nor more than four lines from the bottom.

Now, suppose you want to draw something with that drawing cursor. Simply strike the *P* key to make it "plot" on the screen. Everywhere your controls take that cursor, it leaves behind a trail of light. That is the main drawing mode for this custom-border project. And whenever you want to discontinue the line or use the cursor to "erase" any portion of a line, strike the *E* key. So the arrow keys determine the distance and direction of motion for the drawing cursor, the *P* and *E* keys determine whether the cursor is to leave a trail of light or move without leaving a trail of light (and erasing any previously drawn segments as it passes through them).

When the drawing is done, striking the *A* key "aborts" the drawing phase and sends the program directly to the creature-running phase of the experiment. Here is a summary of the key controls for the drawing phase:

Up-arrow—Move the drawing cursor upward as long as the key is depressed.

Down-arrow—Move the drawing cursor downward as long as the key is depressed.

Left-arrow—Move the drawing cursor to the left as long as the key is depressed.

Right-arrow—Move the drawing cursor to the right as long as the key is depressed.

P key—Plot border elements after striking this key.

E key—Erase or move the cursor without drawing.

A key—End the plotting phase and begin the main creature-operating mode.

If you are totally unhappy with the appearance of the custom border you have drawn, and you figure it isn't worth patching with the Plot and Erase modes, simply strike the BREAK key and RUN the program from the start.

The creature, incidentally, is shown at the beginning of the border-drawing phase so that you know where it will be sitting when the running phase begins. With this information at hand, you are in a better position to draw a border figure that will encompass the creature. Indeed, it would be pointless to draw a nice border figure, only to discover later that the creature is running outside it.

The border figure you draw ought to be continuous; that is, there should be no gaps where the creature can escape from it.

Believe me, an Alpha can eventually find such a hole. But if you should accidentally leave a hole, the program won't bomb when the creature escapes. The program draws the standard rectangular border around your own version.

The variables for ALPHA WITH SCORING AND CUSTOM BORDER are defined for you in Table 17-5, and the programming is shown as Listing 17-5.

Lines 105-125—Initialize the system, cycling the random number generator until the ENTER key is operated.

Lines 130-140—Initialize the creature, clear the screen, draw the creature figure, and call the CUSTOM BORDER subroutine.

Line 145—Draw the standard border figure (around the custom border).

Lines 150-155—Do the SEARCH AHEAD routine. If the path ahead is clear, jump down to move the creature; otherwise, get a new random motion code, etc.

Line 160—Move the creature and jump back to SEARCH AHEAD for the next move.

Table 17-5. TRS-80 Variable List for ALPHA WITH SCORING AND CUSTOM BORDER.

CP	Current creature position
NP	Next creature position
CI	Horizontal component of motion code
CJ	Vertical component of motion code
CX	Horizontal component of contact code
CY	Vertical component of contact code
SI	Sign value of CI
SJ	Sign value of CJ
AI	Absolute value of CI
AJ	Absolute value of CJ
CS	CONTACT score
GS	GOOD-moves score
AS	Average response SCORE
F$	Field specifier for printing AS
FX	Horizontal component of drawing-cursor position
FY	Vertical component of drawing-cursor position
FM	Drawing flag—1 for plot, 0 for erase
DX	Horizontal motion vector for cursor
DY	Vertical motion vector for cursor
FC	Keyboard code for drawing vectors
S$	General-purpose string variable
N	General-purpose numeric variable
F0	Upper-left corner of standard border figure
F1	Upper-right corner of standard border figure
F2	Lower-left corner of standard border figure
F3	Lower-right corner of standard border figure

```
10 REM  ALPHA WITH SCORING
15 REM  AND CUSTOM BORDER
20 REM  TRS-80
25 REM
30 REM
100 REM ** ALPHA PSYCH MAINLINE, V.3—TRS-80 **
105 CLEAR 128:F$="#.##"
110 CLS:PRINT STRING$(6,26):PRINT TAB(25);"ALPHA
    WITH SCORING"
115 PRINT TAB(25)"AND CUSTOM BORDER"
120 PRINT: PRINT "STRIKE 'ENTER' TO DRAW BOR-
    DER..."
125 S$=INKEY$:IF S$="" THEN N=RND(1000):GOTO 125
130 CP=15776+RND(5)−3+64*(RND(5)−3)
135 CI=RND(5)−3:CJ=RND(5)−3:IF CI=0 AND CJ=0
    THEN 135
140 CLS:POKE CP,42:GOSUB 1500
145 GOSUB 1000
150 GOSUB 2000
155 IF NOT(CX=32 AND CY=32) THEN 165
160 POKE CP,32:CP=NP:POKE NP,42:GOTO 150
165 CS=CS+1
170 CI=RND(5)−3:CJ=RND(5)−3:IF CI=0 AND CJ=0
    THEN 170
175 GOSUB 2000
180 IF NOT(CX=32 AND CY=32) THEN 165
185 GS=GS+1:GOSUB 3000
190 GOTO 155
195 REM
200 REM
1000 REM ** BORDER, V.1—TRS-80 **
1005 F0=15360:F1=15423:F2=16128:F3=16191
1010 FOR N=F0 TO F1:POKE N,176:NEXT N
1015 FOR N=F2 TO F3:POKE N,131:NEXT N
1020 FOR N=F0 TO F2 STEP 64:POKE N,170:NEXT N
1025 FOR N=F1 TO F3 STEP 64:POKE N,149:NEXT N
1030 POKE F0,160:POKE F1,144:POKE F2,130:POKE
     F3,129
1035 RETURN
1040 REM
```

```
1045 REM
1500 REM ** CUSTOM BORDER, V.1—TRS-80 **
1505 FX=10:FY=10:FM=0
1510 RESET(FX,FY):SET(FX,FY)
1515 IF PEEK(14337)=2 THEN RETURN
1520 IF PEEK(14340)=1 THEN FM=1
1525 IF PEEK(14337)=32 THEN FM=0
1530 DX=0:DY=0:FC=PEEK(14400)
1535 IF FC=8 THEN DX=0:DY=-1
1540 IF FC=16 THEN DX=0:DY=1
1545 IF FC=32 THEN DX=-1:DY=0
1550 IF FC=40 THEN DX=-1:DY=-1
1555 IF FC=48 THEN DX=-1:DY=1
1560 IF FC=64 THEN DX=1:DY=0
1565 IF FC=72 THEN DX=1:DY=-1
1570 IF FC=80 THEN DX=1:DY=1
1575 IF FX+DX<0 OR FX+DX>127 THEN 1510
1580 IF FY+DY<0 OR FY+DY>35 THEN 1510
1585 IF FM=0 THEN RESET(FX,FY)ELSE SET(FX,FY)
1590 FX=FX+DX:FY=FY+DY:GOTO 1510
1595 REM
1600 REM
2000 REM ** SEARCH AHEAD, V.1—TRS-80 **
2005 NP=CP:CX=32:CY=32
2010 SI=SGN(CI):SJ=SGN(CJ):AI=ABS(CI):AJ=ABS(CJ)
2015 IF AI=0 THEN 2030 ELSE AI=AI-1
2020 IF SI>0 THEN NP=NP+1 ELSE NP=NP-1
2025 CX=PEEK(NP)
2030 IF AJ=0 THEN 2045 ELSE AJ=AJ-1
2035 IF SJ>0 THEN NP=NP+64 ELSE NP=NP-64
2040 CY=PEEK(NP)
2045 IF NOT(CX=32 AND CY=32) THEN RETURN
2050 IF AI=0 AND AJ=0 THEN RETURN ELSE GOTO 2015
2055 REM
2060 REM
3000 REM ** SCORING ROUTINES, V.1—TRS-80 **
3005 AS=GS/CS
3010 PRINT @ 832 ,"CONTACTS","GOOD        MOVE-
     S","SCORE"
3015 PRINT @ 896,STRING $(64,32);
3020 PRINT @ (896,CS,GS; :PRINT@ 928,USING F$; AS;
3025 RETURN
```

3030 REM
3035 REM

Lines 165-180—Increment the CONTACT counter, fetch a
   valid random motion code, try the new code by doing a
   SEARCH AHEAD routine. If the new code is not workable, recycle this routine; otherwise wrap it up.

Lines 185-190—Increment the GOOD score, update the scoring display and return to the main running routines.

Lines 1000-1035—The standard border drawing subroutine.

Lines 1500-1590—The special, custom border drawing subroutine. Basically, it initializes the position of the drawing cursor (line 1505), blinks it (line (1010), then scans
   the keyboard for instructions (lines 1515-1525). The
   remaining portion of the subroutine decodes the
   direction-control key depressions and carries out the
   appropriate cursor moves.

Lines 2000-2050—The standard SEARCH AHEAD subroutine.

Lines 3000-3035—Score updating and display subroutine.

Apple II Version

This version calls for adding the special, custom-border drawing subroutine. See lines 1500-1535 in Listing 17-6. Generally
speaking, however, the overall programming follows the Alpha
scoring flowchart in Fig. 17-1.

When the program is started, you will see the usual opening
message; and it still plays the role of a technique for cycling the
random number generator an indefinite number of times. The border drawing routine is begun immediately after that.

When the custom border routine begins, you will first see the
creature plotted somewhere near the middle of the screen. That
represents the Alpha creature's initial position when the experiment is continued later on. You will also see a drawing cursor
located in the upper left-hand quadrant of the screen. The drawing
cursor can be moved by manipulating the Apple II paddle controls;
one moves the cursor in a horizontal direction, and the other moves
it in the vertical directions. The drawing cursor can thus be located
anywhere in the graphics portion of the screen.

Whenever you want to draw a segment of your custom border
figure, simply depress the pushbutton on either of the paddle control units. As long as that button is depressed, the cursor leaves
behind a trail of light that represents a segment of your custom

border figure. Releasing the pushbutton lets you move the drawing cursor without leaving behind a trail of light and, incidentally, lets you erase through undesired portions of previously drawn border segments.

When you are satisfied with the custom border figure, strike any key to resume normal program operation.

It is a good idea to draw the custom border in such a way that it surrounds the orange creature figure and has no gaps in it. An Alpha creature is fully capable of finding a gap in the border and escaping from it. But to be on the safe side, the program surrounds your custom border with the usual rectangular border when you return to the normal program operations. Return by striking any key.

If you are completely dissatisfied with the appearance of your custom border figure, and you deem it impractical to attempt repairing it with the available drawing and erasing modes, simply break out of the program by doing a CTRL C, and then RUN the whole thing from the beginning.

The program variables are defined in Table 17-6, and the programming itself is shown as Listing 17-6.

Line 105—Define the function for generating random numbers between −2 and 2.

Lines 110-135—Cycle the random number generator until the user strikes the RETURN key.

Lines 140-145—Initialize the creature's screen position and motion code.

Table 17-6. Applesoft Variable List for ALPHA WITH SCORING AND CUSTOM BORDER.

FN R(0)	Random function for values between −2 and 2
PX	Horizontal component of current creature position
PY	Vertical component of current creature position
NX	Horizontal component of next creature position
NY	Vertical component of next creature position
CX	Horizontal component of contact code
CY	Vertical component of contact code
CI	Horizontal component of motion code
CJ	Vertical component of motion code
SI	Sign value of CI
SJ	Sign value of CJ
AI	Absolute value of CI
AJ	Absolute value of CJ
CS	CONTACT score
GS	GOOD-move score
AS	Average response SCORE
FX	Horizontal component of custom border cursor
FY	Vertical component of custom border cursor
N	General-purpose numeric variable

```
10  REM   ALPHA WITH SCORING AND
15  REM      CUSTOM BORDER
20  REM
25  REM
30  REM
100 REM ** ALPHA PSYCH MAINLINE, V.3—APPLE
    SOFT **
105 DEF FN R(R) = INT (5 * RND (1)) − 2
110 TEXT : HOME : PRINT TAB(12)"ALPHA WITH SCOR-
    ING"
115 PRINT TAB(12)"AND CUSTOM BORDER"
120 VTAB (15): PRINT "STRIKE 'RETURN' TO DRAW
    BORDER . . ."
125 N = FN R(0):N = PEEK ( − 16384): POKE − 16368,0
130 IF N < > 141 THEN 125
135 CS = 0:GS = 0
140 PX = 20 + FN R(0):PY = 20 + FN R(0)
145 CI = FN R(0):CJ = FN R(0): IF CI = 0 AND CJ = 0 THEN
    145
150 HOME : GR : COLOR= 9: PLOT PX,PY
155 GOSUB 1500
160 GOSUB 1000
165 GOSUB 2000
170 IF NOT (CX = 0 AND CY = 0) THEN 190
175 COLOR= 0: PLOT PX,PY
180 PX = NX:PY = NY
185 COLOR= 9: PLOT PX,PY: GOTO 165
190 CX = CS + 1
195 CI = FN R(0):CJ = FN R(0): IF CI = 0 AND CJ = 0 THEN
    195
200 GOSUB 2000
205 IF NOT (CX = 0 AND CY = 0) THEN 190
210 GS = GS + 1: GOSUB 3000
215 GOTO 165
220 REM
225 REM
1000 REM ** BORDER, V.1—APPLESOFT **
1005 COLOR= 15
1010 HLIN 0,39 AT 0: HLIN 0,39 AT 36
```

```
1015  VLIN 0,36 AT 0: VLIN 0,36 AT 39
1020  RETURN
1025  REM
1030  REM
1500  REM ** CUSTOM BORDER,V.1—APPLESOFT **
1505  FX = PDL (0) / 6.54:FY = PDL (1) / 7.1
1510  COLOR= 7: PLOT FX,FY
1515  IF PEEK ( − 16384) > 127 THEN COLOR= 0: PLOT
      FX,FY: RETURN
1520  IF PEEK ( − 16286) > 127 THEN COLOR= 13
1525  IF PEEK ( − 16287) > 127 THEN COLOR= 13: GOTO
      1535
1530  COLOR= 0
1535  PLOT FX,FY: GOTO 1505
1540  REM
1545  REM
2000  REM ** SEARCH AHEAD, V.1—APPLESOFT **
2005  NX = PX:NY = PY:CX = 0:CY = 0
2010  SI = SGN (CI):SJ = SGN (CJ):AI = ABS (CI):AJ = ABS
      (CJ)
2015  IF AI = 0 THEN 2040
2020  AI = AI − 1
2025  IF SI > 0 THEN NX = NX + 1: GOTO 2035
2030  NX = NX − 1
2035  CX = SCRN(NX,NY)
2040  IF AJ = 0 THEN 2065
2045  AJ = AJ − 1
2050  IF SJ > 0 THEN NY = NY + 1: GOTO 2060
2055  NY = NY − 1
2060  CY = SCRN(NX,NY)
2065  IF NOT (CX = 0 AND CY = 0) THEN RETURN
2070  IF AI = 0 AND AJ = 0 THEN RETURN
2075  GOTO 2015
2080  REM
2085  REM
3000  REM ** SCORING ROUTINES,V.1—APPLESOFT **
3005  AS = INT ((GS / CS) * 1000) / 1000
3010  HOME : PRINT "CONTACTS","GOOD","SCORE"
3015  PRINT CS,GS,AS
3020  RETURN
3025  REM
3030  REM
```

Lines 150-155—Clear the screen, set the graphics mode, plot the creature in its initial position, and call the custom border routine.

Line 160—Draw the usual border figure.

Lines 165-170—Do the SEARCH AHEAD routine. If the path ahead is clear, jump down to move the creature to its next position; otherwise, check out a new motion code.

Lines 175-185—Move the creature to its next position on the screen, then jump back to search the next position.

Lines 190-205—Increment the CONTACT score, pick a new valid motion code, check its workability by doing the SEARCH AHEAD subroutine. If the path ahead is *not* clear (new motion code is not workable), loop back to do this sequence all over again.

Lines 210-215—Increment the GOOD score, update the scoring and score display, then jump back to resume normal running.

Lines 1000-1020—The usual border drawing subroutine.

Line 1500-1535—The custom border drawing subroutine.

Lines 2000-2075—SEARCH AHEAD subroutine.

Lines 3000-3020—Score updating subroutine.

Chapter 18
Compiling Data for Alpha Studies

Running two or three Alphas with scoring might provide some insight into the nature of those creatures, but it does not provide adequate data for drawing firm conclusions. Rather, such conclusions ought to be based upon data that is gathered from a large number of observations under the same conditions.

Alpha creatures behave in a statistical fashion. Their behavior is fairly predictable in an overall sense, but there is no telling exactly how a given Alpha creature will behave—exactly what motion code it will use—under a certain contact situation. And there is no telling exactly how well a given Alpha will be scoring at any particular time in its life; especially through the first 50 contacts or so. Run the program FUNDAMENTAL ALPHA WITH SCORING, from the previous chapter about four times, and you will end up with four different sets of scoring data. Figure 18-1 is a graph that resulted from running that scoring program four different times. The SCORE figure was reckoned at the conclusion of every 10 CONTACTS for each creature. That was done for 100 contacts per creature. Then the results were plotted on the graph.

It was mentioned earlier that the Alphas tend to show scores just a bit below 0.5; but that is only a tendency. The actual SCORE figures for the creatures bounce around between 0.3 and 0.55—sometimes more than that. Notice that there is more disparity in the scoring through the first 50 contacts than through the final 50. Is that a significant fact? Or is it a statistical glitch that stems more from

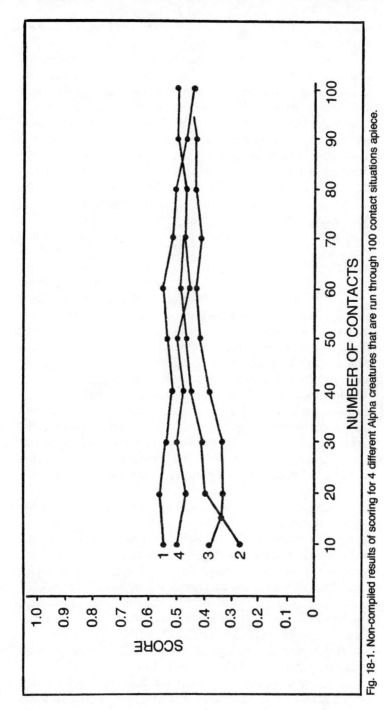

Fig. 18-1. Non-compiled results of scoring for 4 different Alpha creatures that are run through 100 contact situations apiece.

the design of the data-gathering operation than from the nature of Alpha creatures?

One way to answer those questions is to average the scores, coming up with a set of data that draws a line along the middle of the individual plots. But even then there is going to be some changes in the slope of the line. The problem is that the graph is based on an insufficient number of creature tests. Things might be more meaningful if we could average the results of a hundred or more such tests. Then, if the line is perfectly straight, we can conclude that the disparity of the individual plots is a simple statistical glitch that disappears when a sufficient number of creatures is studied. On the other hand, the averaged result of a hundred different tests might show a graph that is not very nearly horizontal; and that would at least indicate that there is some relationship between the Alpha's SCORE and the number of CONTACTs it makes with its environment.

Knowing whether or not there is any predictable relationship between the SCORE and number of CONTACTS for an Alpha creature forms the basis for a great deal of further studies in the psychological behavior of these little critters. It doesn't seem that there should be any change in the SCORE as a function of the number of CONTACT situations; but dealing with "what seems" and "what is" is part of the excitement of science.

Running a hundred or more Alphas through 100 consecutive contacts, and keeping track of their scores all along the way, can be a tedious and time-consuming task. So why not take advantage of the fact that you have a nice computer sitting in front of you? Why not let the computer do all the data-gathering operations and compile the final results for you? That's the purpose of the programs featured in this chapter.

The programs, generally speaking, allow you to specify the number of creatures to participate in the experiment, and the number of contacts each is to make before it is "killed" and replaced with the next creature. Once that preliminary information is entered into the system, the computer runs the entire experiment for you. The final result—the data necessary for plotting the SCORE vs. CONTACT graph—is tabulated at the end of the experiment. You have to draw the graph yourself, but you won't have to hang around for hours while the experiment is running.

A flowchart that is applicable to all variations of this data-compiling experiment is shown in Fig. 18-2.

The first two basic steps in the flowchart are to initialize the system and set up the experiment. The information entered at those

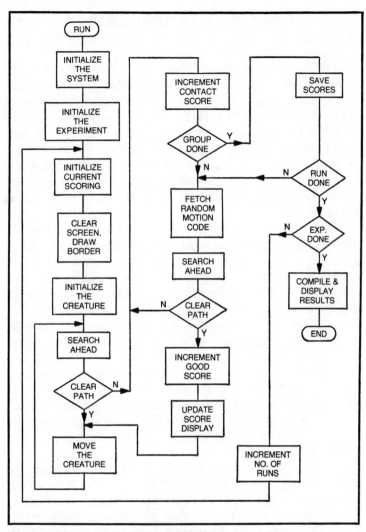

Fig. 18-2. General flowchart for compiling Alpha creature scores.

points refer to the entire experiment. The third step, INITIALIZE CURRENT SCORING, refers to the Alpha creature to be run at one particular time; its scores are set to zero. After that, the system draws the border figure, gives the current creature its initial screen position and motion code, and then it enters the standard Alpha motion sequence.

SEARCH AHEAD looks to the next position on the screen. If that position is clear, the program moves the creature to that new position and loops back to do a SEARCH AHEAD at the next one. That loop is executed as long as the creature is running freely across the screen.

When SEARCH AHEAD finds that the path is *not* clear, the flowchart enters a whole different phase. That phase begins with INCREMENT CONTACT SCORE—an operation that increases the CONTACT count by 1. Then the system encounters a GROUP DONE conditional operation. In the context of the present programming, a group refers to a number of contacts that is a multiple of 10. Looking at the graph in Fig. 18-1, you can see that it is sufficient to plot at intervals of 10 contacts. GROUP DONE merely determines whether or not the current contact figure is one of those multiples of 10.

If it isn't, the system is mainly concerned with getting the Alpha out of its present contact situation. It fetches a random motion code, does a SEARCH AHEAD to test the workability of that new motion code, and then takes action determined by CLEAR PATH. If the path is *not* clear—if the new motion code doesn't resolve the present contact situation—the system loops back up to INCREMENT CONTACT SCORE, and from there, the system tests the contact number for a multiple of 10, picks a new random motion code, and checks its workability. The system continues in that particular loop until one of two things happen; either the CONTACT score reaches a multiple of 10 (at the GROUP DONE conditional), or the Alpha finds a CLEAR PATH ahead. In the latter case, the system executes INCREMENT GOOD SCORE, updates the score display on the screen, and then returns to the main running loop to MOVE THE CREATURE.

Now suppose that a contact has just occured. Suppose the system has just executed the INCREMENT CONTACT SCORE operation and GROUP DONE shows that the number of contacts is a multiple of 10. That being the case, the flowchart shows a SAVE SCORES operation. That operation saves the number of GOOD moves for that particular group and creature. That is the raw information that is used at the conclusion of the experiment.

After saving that scoring data, the system encounters a RUN DONE conditional. The question is this: Has the program run the full number of contacts the experimenter specified in the initial phase of the project? If not, the system returns to FETCH RANDOM MOTION CODE: otherwise, it checks to see whether or not the entire experiment is done. See the conditional, EXP. DONE.

EXP. DONE answers this question: Have all the creatures specified in the initial part of the experiment been run? If so, the system compiles and displays the final results. Otherwise, the system sets itself for killing off the present creature and initializing a new one at INITIALIZE CURRENT SCORING.

Basically, the program begins by letting you enter the number of creatures to be run and the number of contacts each is to experience. It ends by showing the average SCORE at increments of 10 contacts. The results can be a powerful tool for devising future experiments.

As shown throughout this chapter, the same flowchart can apply to several interesting variations of the basic data-gathering program. By showing these few examples, you should be getting some ideas about how you can use the technique for customized experiments with Alpha creatures, including killers and multiple-Alpha communities.

ALPHA WITH COMPILED SCORING

The program described here runs any chosen number of Alpha creatures through a selected number of contact situations, and then it compiles the average scores at increments of 10 contacts. Used as shown here, the program can serve as a control experiment for a variety of different creature studies; but more importantly, it can serve as a basic framework for structuring custom experiments that require compiling of scores.

The program begins with the title message which, again, really acts as a mechanism for running the random number generator an indefinite number of times. After that, the program requests the number of contacts each creature is to experience. If you reckon that most Alphas show rather steady scoring after a hundred contacts, you might respond to ENTER NUMBER OF CONTACTS PER CREATURE RUN by entering 100. That entry, incidentally, must be a multiple of 10; entering figures such as 25 or 52 will cause the program to repeat the request. This is done simply to make sure that the averages carry equal weight throughout the experiment.

After setting the number of contacts per creature run, the program requests the number of creatures to participate in the experiment. Generally speaking, the larger the number of creatures to be run, the more reliable the statistical results will be. But of course you shouldn't get carried away. I think most people will agree that a hundred creatures is more than adequate. Running a thousand of them is pointless; it takes a lot of time and maybe more memory than your system has available.

Once the number of contacts per creature and the number of creatures are entered into the system, it shows a summary of your figures. That is the time to change your mind, answering the OK? query with an *N*. Assuming you are satisfied with the parameters you have entered, striking the ENTER key gets the experiment underway.

The program runs the Alpha creatures through their paces one at a time. Each creature survives until it has encountered the designated number of contacts. At that time, the screen is cleared and a new creature is initialized and run through its paces. The experiment runs in that fashion until the designated number of creatures have done their part.

Incidentally, there is a new label, CREAT, printed near the lower left-hand corner of the screen. That figure shows which creature is being run. The idea is to give you some idea of how well the experiment is progressing.

The program concludes when all Alphas have been run. The results are tabulated for you at intervals of 10 contacts. You might see something like this:

CONTACT	SCORE
10	.47
20	.48
30	.47
40	.47
50	.48

That would indicate a fairly even scoring through 50 consecutive contact situtations. A graph of that data would look much like the one described in the early part of this chapter.

TRS-80 Version

The variable list for ALPHA WITH COMPILED SCORING is shown as Table 18-1, and the programming is shown here as Listing 18-1. The BORDER, SEARCH AHEAD, and SCORING ROUTINES subroutines can be entered from CSAVED versions of earlier programs; although you will notice some changes in the SCORING ROUTINES section.

Lines 105-125—Initialize the system and run the random number generator until the user strikers the ENTER key.

Table 18-1. TRS-80 Variable List for ALPHA WITH COMPILED SCORING.

F$	Field specifier for printing average SCORE values
S$	General-purpose string variable
N,M	General-purpose numeric variables
RN	Number of contacts per creature
CE,CE%	Number of creatures to be run
GS(a,b)	GOOD score at multiples of 10 contacts, a, for creature number b
AS(a)	Average SCORE at intervals of 10 contacts for all creatures that have been run
CS	Number of contacts for creature being run at the time
GS	GOOD score for the creature being run
AS	Average SCORE for the creature being run
CP	Current screen position for the creature
NP	Next screen position for the creature
CI	Horizontal component of creature motion code
CJ	Vertical component of creature motion code
CX	Horizontal component of creature contact code
CY	Vertical component of creature contact code
CN	Current creature number
SI	Sign value of CI
SJ	Sign value of CJ
AI	Absolute value of CI
AJ	Absolute value of CJ
SM	Sum of GOOD scores at a given multiple-of-10 contact point
F0	Upper left corner of border figure
F1	Upper right corner of border figure
F2	Lower left corner of border figure
F3	Lower right corner of border figure

Listing 18-1. TRS-80 Version of ALPHA WITH COMPILED SCORING.

```
10 REM   ALPHA WITH COMPILED SCORING
15 REM      TRS-80
20 REM
25 REM
100 REM ** ALPHA PSYCH MAINLINE, V.4—TRS-80 **
105 CLEAR 128:F$="#.##"
110 CLS:PRINT STRING$(6,26):PRINT TAB(18);
115 PRINT "ALPHA WITH COMPILED SCORING"
120 PRINT:PRINT "STRIKE 'ENTER' TO START . . ."
125 S$=INKEY$:IF S$="" THEN N=RND(1000):GOTO 125
130 CLS:PRINT "ENTER NUMBER OF CONTACTS PER
    CREATURE RUN"
135 PRINT "(MUST BE A MULTIPLE OF 10)":INPUT RN
140 IF RN/10<>INT(RN/10) THEN 135
145 PRINT:PRINT "ENTER NUMBER OF CREATURES TO
    BE RUN"
```

```
150  INPUT CE%:CE=CE%
155  CLS:PRINT "SUMMARY OF INFORMATION:":PRINT
160  PRINT TAB(5);"NUMBER OF CONTACTS PER RUN—
     "RN
165  PRINT TAB(5);"NUMBER OF CREATURES TO BE
     RUN—"CE
170  PRINT:PRINT:INPUT "OK (Y/N)":S$:IF S$="N" THEN
     130
175  DIM GS(RN/10,CE):DIM AS(RN):CN=1
180  CS=0:GS=0
185  CLS:GOSUB 1000
190  CP=15776+RND(5)-3+64*(RND(5)-3)
195  CI=RND(5)-3:CJ=RND(5)-3:IF CI=0 AND CJ=0
     THEN 195
200  GOSUB 2000
205  IF NOT(CX=32 AND CY=32) THEN 215
210  POKE CP,32:CP=NP:POKE CP,42:GOTO 200
215  CS=CS+1
220  IF CS/10=INT(CS/10) THEN 250
225  CI=RND(5)-3:CJ=RND(5)-3:IF CI=0 AND CJ=0
     THEN 225
230  GOSUB 2000
235  IF NOT(CX=32 AND CY=32) THEN 215
240  GS=GS+1:GOSUB 3000
245  GOTO 210
250  GS(CS/10,CN)=GS
255  IF CS<RN THEN 225
260  IF CN<CE THEN CN=CN+1:GOTO 180
265  GOSUB 3100
270  REM
275  REM
1000 REM ** BORDER, V.1—TRS-80 **
1005 F0=15360:F1=15423:F2=16128:F3=16191
1010 FOR N=F0 TO F1:POKE N,176:NEXT N
1015 FOR N=F2 TO F3:POKE N,131:NEXT N
1020 FOR N=F0 TO F2 STEP 64:POKE N,170:NEXT N
1025 FOR N=F1 TO F3 STEP 64:POKE N,149:NEXT N
1030 POKE F0,160:POKE F1,144:POKE F2,130:POKE
     F3,129
1035 RETURN
1040 REM
1045 REM
```

```
2000  REM ** SEARCH AHEAD, V.1—TRS-80 **
2005  NP=CP:CX=32:CY=32
2010  SI=SGN(CI):SJ=SGN(CJ):AI=ABS(CI):AJ=ABS(CJ)
2015  IF AI=0 THEN 2030 ELSE AI=AI−1
2020  IF SI>0 THEN NP=NP+1 ELSE NP=NP−1
2025  CX=PEEK(NP)
2030  IF AJ=0 THEN 2045 ELSE AJ=AJ−1
2035  IF SJ>0 THEN NP=NP+64 ELSE NP=NP−64
2040  CY=PEEK(NP)
2045  IF NOT(CX=32 AND CY=32) THEN RETURN
2050  IF AI=0 AND AJ=0 THEN RETURN ELSE GOTO 2015
2055  REM
2060  REM
3000  REM ** SCORING ROUTINES, V.2—TRS-80 **
3005  AS=GS/CS
3010  PRINT 832, "CONTACTS" , "GOOD MOVES",
      "SCORE","CREATURE"
3015  PRINT     896,STRING$(64,32);
3020  PRINT 896,CS/GS;:PRINT 928,USING F$;AS,:
      PRINT, CN;
3025  RETURN
3030  REM
3035  REM
3100  FOR N=1 TO RN/10
3105  SM=0
3110  FOR M=1 TO CN
3115  SM=SM+GS(N,M)
3120  NEXT M
3125  AS(N)=SM/(10*N*CN)
3130  NEXT N
3135  CLS:PRINT "FINAL DATA":PRINT
3140  PRINT TAB(5);"CONTACT","SCORE":PRINT
3145  FOR N=1 TO RUN/10
3150  PRINT TAB(5);N*10;:PRINT USING F$;AS(N)
3155  NEXT N
3160  END
```

Lines 130-140—Allow the experimenter to enter the desired
    number of contacts per creature; it is a figure that must
    be a multiple of 10.
Lines 145-150—Allow the experimenter to enter the number
    of creatures to participate in the experiment; it must be
    an integer value.

Lines 155-170—Display the information entered thus far. If it is not OK, then jump back to start all over. Otherwise continue from line 175.

Line 175—Dimension the arrays for keeping track of the GOOD scores at intervals of 10 and the average SCORE at intervals of 10. Set the current creature number to 1.

Line 180—Zero the current scoring figures.

Line 185—Clear the screen and draw the standard border figure.

Lines 190-195—Initialize the current creature's screen position and motion code. Both are randomly selected parameters.

Lines 200-210—This is the main running loop. Do the SEARCH AHEAD routine and if the path ahead is clear, move the creature (line 210) and run the loop again. If the path ahead is *not* clear, break out of the main running loop, going to line 215.

Line 215—Increment the current CONTACT score.

Line 220—If the current contact score is a multiple of 10, it is time to save some results by jumping down to line 250.

Lines 225—235—Fetch a valid random motion code (line 225), then check to see whether or not it gets the creature out of the contact situation (lines 230 and 235). If not, go back to line 215 to cycle the contact situation again.

Lines 240-245—At this point, the creature has found its way out of a contact situation. Increment the GOOD score and display the overall scoring (line 240), and then jump back into the main running loop to set the creature onto its new path.

Line 250—Save the current GOOD score for the present multiple-of-10 contact and creature.

Line 255—If the number of contacts is less than the number specified for each creature, jump back to line 225 to continue the run.

Line 260—If the number of creatures that has been run is less than the number specified for the experiment, increment the creature number and jump back to begin running a new one.

Line 265—Go to the final scoring routine to conclude the experiment.

Lines 1000-1035—BORDER drawing subroutine.

Lines 2000-2050—SEARCH AHEAD subroutine.

Lines 3000-3025—Update and display the scoring for the current Alpha creature.

Lines 3100-3160—Compile and display the final results; end the experiment.

The program is written in such a way that you can do a BREAK at any point during its execution, and yet recover the results that have been accumulated to that time. After doing the BREAK, simply enter GOTO 3100. The program will tabulate the results based on the information that is available. It is better, however, to let the program run to its conclusion.

Apple Version

The variable list for ALPHA WITH COMPILED SCORING is shown as Table 18-2, and the programming is shown here as Listing 18-2. The BORDER, SEARCH AHEAD and SCORING ROUTINES can be entered from SAVEd versions of earlier programs; although it is necessary to modify SCORING ROUTINES a little bit.

Line 105—Define the random function for generating integers between −2 and 2.

Lines 110-130—Print the title message and cycle the random number generator until the user strikes the RETURN key.

Lines 135-150—Allow the experimenter to enter the desired number of contacts per creature as a multiple of 10.

Lines 155-160—Allow the experimenter to designate the number of Alpha creatures to participate in the experiment; make sure it is an integer value.

Lines 165-185—Display the information entered thus far, and give the experimenter a chance to change it.

Line 190—Dimension the arrays for keeping track of the GOOD scores at intervals of 10 contacts and the average SCORE at intervals of 10 contacts. Set the current creature number to 1.

Line 195—Zero the scoring figures for the current creature.

Line 200—Clear the screen, set the graphics mode, and draw the standard BORDER figure.

Lines 205—210—Initialize the current creature's screen position and motion code.

Lines 215-240—Search the path ahead (line 215). If it is not clear (line 220), jump out of this main running loop.

Table 18-2. Apple Variable List for ALPHA WITH COMPILED SCORING.

FN R(R)	Random number function for integers −2 to 2
N,M	General-purpose numeric variables
RN	Number of contacts per creature
CE, CE%	Number of creatures to be run
S$	General-purpose string variable
GS(a,b)	GOOD score at multiples of 10 contacts, a, for creature number b
AS(a)	Average SCORE at intervals of 10 contacts for all creatures that have been run
CS	Number of contacts for the creature being run
GS	GOOD score for the creature being run
AS	Average SCORE for the creature being run
PX	Horizontal component of current creature position
PY	Vertical component of current creature position
CI	Horizontal component of current motion code
CJ	Vertical component of current motion code
CX	Horizontal component of current contact code
CY	Vertical component of current contact code
SI	Sign value of CI
SJ	Sign value of CJ
AI	Absolute value of CI
AJ	Absolute value of CJ
NX	Horizontal component of next creature position
NY	Vertical component of next creature position
SM	Sum of GOOD scores at a given multiple-of-10 contact point

Listing 18-2. Apple Version of ALPHA WITH COMPILED SCORING.

```
10 REM   ALPHA WITH COMPILED SCORING
15 REM      APPLE II
20 REM
25 REM
100 REM ** ALPHA PSYCH MAINLINE,V.4—APPLESOFT **
105 DEF FN R(R) = INT (5 * RND (1)) − 2
110 TEXT : HOME : VTAB (10)
115 PRINT TAB(8)"ALPHA WITH COMPILED SCORING"
120 VTAB (20): PRINT "STRIKE 'RETURN' TO START . . ."
125 N = FN R(0):N = PEEK ( − 16384): POKE − 16368,0
130 IF N < > 141 THEN 125
135 HOME : VTAB (5): PRINT "ENTER NUMBER OF CON-
    TACTS"
140 PRINT "PER CREATURE": PRINT
145 PRINT "(MUST BE A MULTIPLE OF 10)"
150 INPUT RN: IF RN < = 0 OR RN/ 10 < > INT (RN/ 10)
    THEN 145
```

```
155 HOME : VTAB (5): PRINT "ENTER NUMBER OF CREA-
    TURES TO BE  RUN"
160 INPUT CE%:CE = CE%
165 HOME : PRINT : PRINT "SUMMARY OF INFORMA-
    TION:": PRINT
170 PRINT TAB(5)"CONTACTS PER RUN: "RN
175 PRINT TAB(5)"CREATURES TO BE RUN:"CE
180 VTAB (20): PRINT "OK (Y/N);: INPUT S$
185 IF S$ = "N" THEN 135
190 DIM GS(RN / 10,CE),AS(RN):CN = 1
195 CS = 0:GS = 0
200 HOME : GR : GOSUB 1000
205 PX = 20 + FN R(0):PY = 20 + FN R(0)
210 CI = FN R(0):CJ = FN R(0): IF CI = 0 AND CJ = 0 THEN
    210
215 GOSUB 2000
220 IF NOT (CX = 0 AND CY = 0) THEN 245
225 COLOR= 0: PLOT PX,PY
230 PX = NX:PY = NY
235 COLOR= 9: PLOT PX,PY
240 GOTO 215
245 CS = CS + 1
250 IF CS / 10 = INT (CS / 10) THEN 280
255 CI = FN R(0):CJ = FN R(0): IF CI = 0 AND CJ = 0 THEN
    255
260 GOSUB 2000
265 IF NOT (CX = 0 AND CY = 0) THEN 245
270 GS = GS + 1: GOSUB 3000
275 GOTO 225
280 GS(CS / 10,CN) = GS
285 IF CS < RN THEN 255
290 IF CN < CE THEN CN = CN + 1: GOTO 195
295 GOSUB 3100
300 REM
305 REM
1000 REM ** BORDER, V.1—APPLESOFT **
1005 COLOR= 15
1010 HLIN 0,39 AT 0: HLIN 0,39 AT 36
1015 VLIN 0,36 AT 0: VLIN 0,36 AT 39
1020 RETURN
1025 REM
```

```
1030 REM
2000 REM ** SEARCH AHEAD, V.1—APPLESOFT **
2005 NX = PX:NY = PY:CX = 0:CY = 0
2010 SI = SGN (CI):SJ = SGN (CJ):AI = ABS (CI):AJ = ABS
     (CJ)
2015 IF AI = 0 THEN 2040
2020 AI = AI − 1
2025 IF SI > 0 THEN NX = NX + 1: GOTO 2035
2030 NX = NX − 1
2035 CX = SCRN(NX,NY)
2040 IF AJ = 0 THEN 2065
2045 AJ = AJ − 1
2050 IF SJ > THEN NY = NY + 1: GOTO 2060
2055 NY = NY − 1
2060 CY = SCRN(NX,NY)
2065 IF NOT (CX = 0 AND CY = 0) THEN RETURN
2070 IF AI = 0 AND AJ = 0 THEN RETURN
2075 GOTO 2015
2080 REM
2085 REM
3000 REM ** SCORING ROUTINES, V.2—APPLESOFT **
3005 AS = INT ((GS / CS) * 1000) / 1000
3010 HOME : PRINT "CONT" SPC(4)"GOOD"SPC(4)
     SCORE" SPC(4)"CREAT"
3015 PRINT CS; TAB(9)GS; TAB(18)AS; TAB(27)CN
3020 RETURN
3025 REM
3030 REM
3100 FOR N = 1 TO RN / 10
3105 SM = 0
3110 FOR M = 1 TO CN
3115 SM = SM + GS(N,M)
3120 NEXT M
3125 AS(N) = INT (100 * SM / (10 * N * CN)) / 100
3130 NEXT N
3135 TEXT : HOME : PRINT "FINAL DATA:": PRINT
3140 PRINT "CONT" SPC(4)"SCORE" SPC(8)"CONT"
     SPC(4)"SCORE"
3145 FOR N = 1 TO RN / 10
3150 IF N / 2 = INT (N / 2) THEN 3160
3155 PRINT N * 10 TAB(10)AS(N);: GOTO 3165
```

```
3160  PRINT TAB(22)N * 10 TAB(30)AS(N)
3165  NEXT N
3170  END
```

Otherwise move the creature and run the loop again
(lines 225-240).

Lines 245-250—Increment the current CONTACT score. If
this new score is a multiple of 10, jump down to line 280.

Lines 255-265—Fetch a random motion code and check it out.
If it gets the creature out of the current contact situation,
jump down to line 270. Otherwise continue looping from
line 245.

Lines 270-275—Increment the GOOD score for the current
creature, then jump back into the main running loop to
set the creature onto its new path.

Line 280—Save the current GOOD score for the present
multiple-of-10 contacts and current creature.

Line 285—If the number of contacts is less than the number
specified for each creature, jump back to line 255 to
continue the run.

Line 290—If the number of creatures that has been run is less
than the number specified for the experiment, increment
the creature number and jump back to start running a new
one.

Line 295—Go to the final scoring routine to conclude the
experiment.

Lines 1000-1020—BORDER drawing subroutine.

Lines 2000-2075—SEARCH AHEAD subroutine.

Lines 3000-3020—Update and display the current scoring.

Lines 3100-3170—Compile and display the final results; END
the experiment.

COMPILING WITH RANDOM OBSTACLES

How does the complexity of an environment affect a creature's
ability to perform within it? That is a complicated question, but only
because its terms require careful definition. Once the terms are
clearly understood, the answer—or at least the road to the
answer—becomes more apparent.

We hear from modern animal psychology, for instance, that
animals growing up in a rich and active environment tend to perform
better (lead "happier" lives) in later life. Animals raised in a plain

and uninteresting environment, on the other hand, seem unable to cope with "real" life later on.

Given that notion from animal psychology, we ought to infer that our machine creatures will behave in a similar fashion. Those raised in a complex environment will perform better than those raised in a spartian one. This experiment, however, does not support that inference. In fact, it indicates that things work to the contrary. Alphas operating in a very complex environment tend to show lower performance scores than those running in a plain environment.

What is the problem here? Is there some chance that this whole business of machine psychology is a lot of nonsense?

While I think it is important to leave some of the more subtle considerations to you and your own experiments, it is important to point out the fallacy in the foregoing discussion. Indeed, there is a positive relationship between an enriching environment and the performance of animals raised in it. And, indeed, there is a negative relationship between the number of obstacles tossed into the environment and the performance of Alpha creatures. The discrepancy is one of definition, however. Tossing a lot of obstacles into a machine-creature's environment does not constitute an *enriching* environment; rather, it is a *restrictive* one. These obstacles tend to confine a creature's motion code options, making it increasingly difficult to find workable motion codes.

The following programs compile performance data for creatures living in this restrictive environment. While it merely supports what ought to be intuitively obvious at this time, the project can be a meaningful one. First, it is meaningful because it is always necessary to support even the most obvious notions with experimental data, and second, the results can serve as a control experiment for other kinds of studies in machine psychology.

Like the previous program, the experiment runs a designated number of Alpha creatures through a designated number of contact situations. The scores are gathered at intervals of 10 contacts and compiled into a set of average scoring figures at the conclusion of the run. Here, however, the experimenter can designate the number of obstacles to be randomly distributed within the environment. At the conclusion of each run, it is possible to run the same number of creatures in an environment having a different number of obstacles in it.

The program is thus designed to generate a set of scoring curves, where each performance curve represents the creature activity in environments having different numbers of obstacles. Suppose you wish to base the entire experiment on 50 Alpha creatures undergoing 100 contact situations. The program requests that information at its beginning. Then the programs asks for the number of obstacles to be placed in the environment. For the sake of running a control experiment, you might specify no obstacles at first. That being the case, the program runs those 50 Alphas through 100 contact situations, and then displays the compiled results.

When that is done, striking the ENTER or RETURN key brings up the request for a number of obstacles again. The assumption is that you will still want to work with 50 Alphas at 100 contacts apiece. So if you respond to the request by entering 64 obstacles, the same experiment will be run with an environment sprinkled with 64 randomly distributed obstacles in the environment. And, of course, the run concludes by showing the compiled scoring results.

The idea of the experiment is to run it with an increasing number of obstacles. Just where you end the project is up to you. The final results ought to show a scoring curve that is somewhat lower for every increase in the number of obstacles.

TRS-80 Version

The variable list and programming for ALPHA WITH COM-PILED SCORING AND RANDOM OBSTACLES are shown in Table 18-3 and Listing 18-3, respectively.

Lines 105-125—Initialize the system, printing the title message and cycling the random number generator until the user strikes the ENTER key.

Lines 130-140—Enter the number of contacts per creature as a multiple of 10.

Lines 145-150—Enter the number of creatures to be run with a given number of obstacles in the environment. It must be an integer value.

Lines 155-170—Show the data entered thus far, and give the user an opportunity to change that data.

Line 175—Dimension the necessary arrays.

Line 180—Call the subroutine for setting the number of obstacles to be placed into the environment. Set the creature number to 1.

Line 185—Zero the scoring for the current creature.

Line 190—Draw the border figure and call the subroutine that plots the designated number of obstacles.

Table 18-3. TRS-80 Variable List for
ALPHA WITH COMPILED SCORING AND RANDOM OBSTACLES.

F$	Field specifier for printing SCORE values
M,N	General-purpose numeric variables
S$	General-purpose string variable
RN	Number of contacts specified for each creature
CE,CE%	Number of creatures to be run in each obstacle format
GS(a,b)	GOOD score for a multiple-of-10 contacts for creature number b
AS(a)	Average score for multiple-of-10 contacts, a
CS	Current CONTACT score
GS	Current GOOD score
AS	Current SCORE
CP	Current creature screen position
NP	Next screen position for the current creature
CI	Horizontal component of motion code
CJ	Vertical component of motion code
CX	Horizontal component of contact code
CY	Vertical component of contact code
SI	Sign value of CI
SJ	Sign value of CJ
AI	Absolute value of CI
AJ	Absolute value of CJ
NT,NT%	Number of obstacles to be plotted in the environment
TP	Screen position of an obstacle
SM	Sum of a multiple-of-10 GOOD score values for CN creatures
F0	Upper left corner of the border figure
F1	Upper right corner of the border figure
F2	Lower left corner of the border figure
F3	Lower right corner of the border figure

Listing 18-3. TRS-80 Version of ALPHA
WITH COMPILED SCORING AND RANDOM OBSTACLES.

```
10 REM   ALPHA WITH COMPILED SCORING
15 REM   AND RANDOM OBSTACLES
20 REM      TRS-80
25 REM
30 REM
100 REM ** ALPHA PSYCH MAINLINE, V.5—TRS-80 **
105 CLEAR 128:F$="#.##"
110 CLS:PRINT STRING$(6,26):PRINT TAB(18);
115 PRINT "ALPHA WITH COMPILED SCORING":PRINT
    TAB(22);"AND RANDOM OBSTACLES"
120 PRINT:PRINT "STRIKE 'ENTER' TO START . . ."
125 S$=INKEY$:IF S$="" THEN N=RND(1000):GOTO 125
130 CLS:PRINT "ENTER NUMBER OF CONTACTS PER
    CREATURE RUN"
```

```
135 PRINT "(MUST BE A MULTIPLE OF 10)":INPUT RN
140 IF RN/10<>INT(RN/10) THEN 135
145 PRINT:PRINT "ENTER NUMBER OF CREATURES TO
    BE RUN"
150 PRINT "(PER OBSTACLE FORMAT)":INPUT
    CE%:CE=CE%
155 CLS:PRINT "SUMMARY OF INFORMATION:":PRINT
160 PRINT TAB(5);"NUMBER OF CONTACTS PER RUN—
    "RN
165 PRINT TAB(5);"NUMBER OF CREATURES TO BE
    RUN—"CE
170 PRINT:PRINT:INPUT "OK (Y/N)";S$:IF S$="N" THEN
    130
175 DIM GS(RN/10,CE):DIM AS(RN)
180 GOSUB 1500:CN=1
185 CS=0:GS=0
190 CLS:GOSUB 1000:GOSUB 1550
195 CP=15773+RND(5)+64*(RND(5)−3):IF
    PEEK(CP)<>32 THEN 195
200 CI=RND(5)−3:CJ=RND(5)−3:IF CI=0 AND CJ=0
    THEN 200
205 GOSUB 2000
210 IF NOT(CX=32 AND CY=32) THEN 220
215 POKE CP,32:CP=NP:POKE CP,42:GOTO 205
220 CS=CS+1
225 IF CS/10=INT(CS/10) THEN 255
230 CI=RND(5)−3:CJ=RND(5)−3:IF CI=0 AND CJ=0
    THEN 230
235 GOSUB 2000
240 IF NOT(CX=32 AND CY=32) THEN 220
245 GS=GS+1:GOSUB 3000
250 GOTO 215
255 GS(CS/10,CN)=GS
260 IF CS<RN THEN 230
265 IF CN<CE THEN CN=CN+1:GOTO 185
270 GOSUB 3100
275 GOTO 180
280 REM
285 REM
1000 REM ** BORDER, V.1—TRS-80 **
1005 F0=15360:F1=15423:F2=16128:F3=16191
1010 FOR N=F0 TO F1:POKE N,176:NEXT N
```

259

```
1015 FOR N=F2 TO F3:POKE N,131:NEXT N
1020 FOR N=F0 TO F2 STEP 64:POKE N,170:NEXT N
1025 FOR N=F1 TO F3 STEP 64:POKE N,149:NEXT N
1030 POKE F0,160:POKE F1,144:POKE F2,130:POKE
     F3,129
1035 RETURN
1040 REM
1045 REM
1500 REM ** OBSTACLES, V.3—TRS-80 **
1505 CLS:PRINT STRING$(4,13);
1510 PRINT "HOW MANY OBSTACLES";
1515 INPUT NT%:NT=NT%:IF NT<0 THEN 1515
1520 RETURN
1525 REM
1530 REM
1550 IF NT=0 THEN RETURN
1555 FOR N=1 TO NT
1560 TP=15360+RND(831):IF PEEK(TP)<>32 THEN 1560
1565 POKE TP,191
1570 NEXT N
1575 RETURN
1580 REM
1585 REM
2000 REM ** SEARCH AHEAD, V.1—TRS-80 **
2005 NP=CP:CX=32:CY=32
2010 SI=SGN(CI):SJ=SGN(CJ):AI=ABS(CI):AJ=ABS(CJ)
2015 IF AI=0 THEN 2030 ELSE AI=AI−1
2020 IF SI>0 THEN NP=NP+1 ELSE NP=NP−1
2025 CX=PEEK(NP)
2030 IF AJ=0 THEN 2045 ELSE AJ=AJ−1
2035 IF SJ>0 THEN NP=NP+64 ELSE NP=NP−64
2040 CY=PEEK(NP)
2045 IF NOT(CX=32 AND CY=32) THEN RETURN
2050 IF AI=0 AND AJ=0 THEN RETURN ELSE GOTO 2015
2055 REM
2060 REM
3000 REM ** SCORING ROUTINES, V.3—TRS-80 **
3005 AS=GS/CS
3010 PRINT 832, "CONTACTS" , "GOOD MOVES",
     "SCORE","CREATURE"
3015 PRINT 896,STRING $(64,32)
3020 PRINT 896,CS,GS,;:PRINT 928,USING F$;AS, :PRINT,
     CN;
```

```
3025 RETURN
3030 REM
3035 REM
3100 FOR N=1 TO RN/10
3105 SM=0
3110 FOR M=1 TO CN
3115 SM=SM+GS(N,M)
3120 NEXT M
3125 AS(N)=SM/(10*N*CN)
3130 NEXT N
3135 CLS:PRINT "EXPERIMENTAL DATA:":PRINT
3140 PRINT TAB(5)NT "OBSTACLES"
3145 PRINT TAB(5)CE "CREATURES PER RUN"
3150 PRINT TAB(5)RN "CONTACTS PER CREATURE"
3155 PRINT:PRINT:PRINT "STRIKE 'ENTER' TO SEE THE
     DATA":INPUT S$
3160 CLS:PRINT "TEST DATA:":PRINT
3165 PRINT "CONT";TAB(10);"SCORE;TAB(30);
     "CONT";TAB(40);"SCORE"
3170 FOR N=1 TO RN/10
3175 IF N/2=INT(N/2) THEN 3185
3180 PRINT N*10;:PRINT TAB(10) USING F$;AS(N);:GOTO
     3190
3185 PRINT TAB(30);N*10;:PRINT TAB(40) USING F$;AS(N)
3190 NEXT N
3195 INPUT S$:CLS:PRINT "ANY MORE OBSTACLE FOR-
     MATS (Y/N)";
3200 INPUT S$
3205 IF S$="N" THEN END
3210 RETURN
3215 REM
```

Lines 195-200—Initialize the creature's screen position and
     motion code.
Lines 205-215—Do the SEARCH AHEAD routine. If the path
     ahead is clear, then move the creature. Otherwise jump
     to line 220 to begin resolving the contact situation.
Line 220—Increment the CONTACT score.
Line 225—If the current CONTACT score is a multiple of 10,
     jump down to save the scoring.
Lines 230-240—Find a motion code that resolves the current
     contact situation.

Lines 245-250—Increment the GOOD score and jump back into the main running loop.

Line 255—Save the current GOOD score as a 2 dimensional variable that specifies the multiple-of-10 contact and current creature number.

Line 260—If the number of contacts is less than the number specified for each creature, continue the run.

Line 265—If the number of creatures that has been run is less than the number specified for the experiment, increment the current creature number and start a new creature.

Lines 270-275—Go to a subroutine that prints out the data for the current experiment, then jump back to give the user a chance to specify a different number of obstacles in the environment for the next set of Alpha creatures.

Lines 1000-1035—BORDER drawing subroutine.

Lines 1500-1520—Subroutine for specifying the number of obstacles to be included in the environment.

Lines 1550-1575—Subroutine for drawing the specified number of obstacles at randomly selected places in the environment.

Lines 2000-2050—SEARCH AHEAD subroutine.

Lines 3000-3025—Subroutine for displaying the current scoring and creature number.

Lines 3100-3210—Subroutine for displaying the compiled results and requesting a different number of obstacles for the next series of runs.

Apple II Version

The variable list and programming for ALPHA WITH COMPILED SCORING AND RANDOM OBSTACLES are shown as Table 18-4 and Listing 18-4, respectively.

Lines 105-110—Define the functions for generating random motion codes and random screen positions for the obstacles.

Lines 115-140—Initialize the system by printing the title message and cycling the random number generator until the user strikes the RETURN key.

Lines 145-155—Enter the number of contacts per creature as a multiple of 10.

Lines 160-170—Enter the number of creatures to be run in a given obstacle format. It must be an integer value that is greater than zero.

Table 18-4. Apple Variable list for
ALPHA WITH COMPILED SCORING AND RANDOM OBSTACLES.

APPLE II VERSION	
FN R(R)	Function for generating motion codes, −2 to 2
FN T(T)	Function for generating random screen positions for obstacle figures
N,M	General-purpose numeric variables
S$	General-purpose string variable
RN	Specified number of contacts per creature
CE,CE%	Specified number of creatures to be run in a given obstacle format
GS(a,b)	GOOD score for a multiple-of-10 contacts and creature number b
AS(a)	Average GOOD score at a multiple-of-10 contacts
CS	Current CONTACT score
GS	Current GOOD score
AS	Current SCORE figure
CN	Current creature number
PX	Horizontal component of creature position
PY	Vertical component of creature position
NX	Horizontal component of next creature position
NY	Vertical component of next creature position
CI	Horizontal component of motion code
CJ	Vertical component of motion code
SI	Sign value of CI
SJ	Sign value of CJ
AI	Absolute value of CI
AJ	Absolute value of CJ
NT,NT%	Number of obstacles to be plotted
TX	Horizontal component of an obstacle position
TY	Vertical component of an obstacle position
SM	Sum of all multiple-of-10 GOOD scores

Listing 18-4. Apple Version of ALPHA
WITH COMPILED SCORING AND RANDOM OBSTACLES.

```
10 REM  ALPHA WITH COMPILED SCORING
15 REM  AND RANDOM OBSTACLES
20 REM    APPLE II
25 REM
30 REM
100 REM ** ALPHA PSYCH MAINLINE, V.5—APPLESOFT
    **
105 DEF FN R(R) = INT (5 * RND (1)) − 2
110 DEF FN T(T) = INT (T * RND (1)) + 1
115 TEXT : HOME : VTAB (10)
120 PRINT TAB(8)"ALPHA WITH COMPILED SCORING"
125 PRINT TAB(12)"AND RANDOM OBSTACLES"
130 VTAB(15):PRINT "STRIKE 'RETURN' TO START . . ."
```

```
135  N = FN R(0):N = PEEK ( - 16384): POKE - 16368,0
140  IF N < > 141 THEN 135
145  HOME : VTAB (5): PRINT "ENTER NUMBER OF
     CONTACTS PER CREATURE"
150  PRINT "(MUST BE A MULTIPLE OF 10)"
155  PRINT : INPUT RN: IF RN / 10 < > INT (RN /10)
     OR RN > = 0 THEN 150
160  HOME : VTAB (5): PRINT "ENTER NUMBER OF
     CREATURES TO BE RUN"
165  PRINT "(PER OBSTACLE FORMAT)"
170  PRINT : INPUT CE%:CE = CE%:IF CE < = 0 THEN 160
175  HOME : VTAB (3): PRINT "SUMMARY:"
180  HTAB (5):PRINT "CONTACTS PER CREATURE—"RN
185  HTAB (5):PRINT "CREATURES PER RUN—"CE
190  VTAB (15): PRINT "OK (Y/N)";
195  INPUT S$: IF S$ = "N" THEN 145
200  DIM GS(RN / 10,CE),AS(RN)
205  GOSUB 1500:CN = 1
210  CS = 0:GS = 0
215  HOME : GR : GOSUB 1000: GOSUB 1550
220  PX = 20 + FN R(0):PY = 20 + FN R(0): IF SCRN(PX,PY)
     < > 0 THEN 220
225  CI = FN R(0):CJ = FN R(0): IF CI = 0 AND CJ = 0 THEN
     225
230  GOSUB 2000
235  IF NOT (CX = 0 AND CY = 0) THEN 260
240  COLOR= 0: PLOT PX,PY
245  PX = NX:PY = NY
250  COLOR= 9: PLOT PX,PY
255  GOTO 230
260  CS = CS + 1
265  IF CS / 10 = INT (CS / 10) THEN 295
270  CI = FN R(0):CJ = FN R(0): IF CI = 0 AND CJ = 0 THEN
     270
275  GOSUB 2000
280  IF NOT (CX = 0 AND CY = 0) THEN 260
285  GS = GS + 1: GOSUB 3000
290  GOTO 240
295  GS(CS / 10,CN) = GS
300  IF CS < RN THEN 270
305  IF CN < CE THEN CN = CN + 1: GOTO 210
310  GOSUB 3100
```

```
 315 GOTO 205
 320 REM
 325 REM
1000 REM ** BORDER, V.1—APPLESOFT **
1005 COLOR= 15
1010 HLIN 0,39 AT 0: HLIN 0,39 AT 36
1015 VLIN 0,36 AT 0: VLIN 0,36 AT 39
1025 REM
1030 REM
1500 REM ** OBSTACLES, V.3—APPLESOFT **
1505 HOME : TEXT : VTAB (8)
1510 PRINT "HOW MANY OBSTACLES";
1515 INPUT NT%:NT = NT%: IF NT < 0 THEN 1515
1520 RETURN
1525 REM
1530 REM
1550 COLOR= 13: IF NT = 0 THEN RETURN
1555 FOR N = 1 TO NT
1560 TX = FN T(38):TY = FN T(35): IF SCRN(TX,TY) < > 0
     THEN 1560
1565 PLOT TX,TY
1570 NEXT N
1575 RETURN
1580 REM
1585 REM
2000 REM ** SEARCH AHEAD, V.1—APPLESOFT **
2005 NX = PX:NY = PY:CX = 0:CY = 0
2010 SI = SGN (CI):SJ = SGN (CJ):AI = ABS (CI):AJ = ABS
     (CJ)
2015 IF AI = 0 THEN 2040
2020 AI = AI − 1
2025 IF SI > 0 THEN NX = NX + 1: GOTO 2035
2030 NX = NX − 1
2035 CX = SCRN(NX,NY)
2040 IF AJ = 0 THEN 2065
2045 AJ = AJ − 1
2050 IF SJ > 0 THEN NY = NY + 1: GOTO 2060
2055 NY = NY − 1
2060 CY = SCRN(NX,NY)
2065 IF NOT (CX = 0 AND CY = 0) THEN RETURN
2070 IF AI = 0 AND AJ = 0 THEN RETURN
2075 GOTO 2015
```

```
2080 REM
2085 REM
3000 REM ** SCORING ROUTINES, V.3—APPLESOFT **
3005 AS = INT ((GS / CS) * 1000) / 1000
3010 HOME : PRINT "CONT" SPC(4)"GOOD"
     SPC(4)"SCORE" SPC(4)"CREAT
3015 PRINT CS: TAB(9)GS; TAB(18)AS: TAB(27)CN
3020 RETURN
3025 REM
3030 REM
3100 FOR N = 1 TO RN / 10
3105 SM = 0
3110 FOR M = 1 TO CN
3115 SM = SM + GS(N,M)
3120 NEXT M
3125 AS(N) = INT (100 * SM / (10 * N * CN)) / 100
3130 NEXT N
3135 TEXT : HOME : VTAB (3): PRINT "EXPERIMENTAL
     DATA:": PRINT
3140 PRINT TAB( 5)NT"OBSTACLES"
3145 PRINT TAB( 5)CE "CREATURES PER RUN"
3150 PRINT TAB( 5)RN"CONTACTS PER CREATURE"
3155 VTAB (15): PRINT "STRIKE 'RETURN' TO SEE THE
     DATA": INPUT S$
3160 HOME : PRINT "TEST DATA:": PRINT
3165 PRINT "CONT" SPC(4)"SCORE" SPC(8)"CONT"
     SPC(4)"SCORE"
3170 FOR N = 1 TO RN / 10
3175 IF N / 2 = INT (N / 2) THEN 3185
3180 PRINT N * 10 TAB(10)AS(N);: GOTO 3190
3185 PRINT TAB(22)N * 10 TAB(30)AS(N)
3190 NEXT N
3195 INPUT S$
3200 HOME : VTAB (5): PRINT "ANY MORE OBSTACLE
     FORMATS (Y/N)";
3205 INPUT S$
3210 IF S$ = "N" THEN END
3215 RETURN
```

Lines 175-195—Summarize the information entered thus far,
  giving the user a chance to change it.
Line 200—Dimension the necessary array variables.
Line 205—Call the subroutine that lets the user specify the

number of obstacles to be included in the environment. Set the current creature number to 1.

Line 210—Initialize the scoring for the current creature.

Line 215—Clear the screen, set the graphics mode, draw the standard border figure, and call a subroutine that plots the specified number of obstacles.

Lines 220-225—Initialize the current creature's screen position and motion code.

Lines 230-255—Do the SEARCH AHEAD routine. If the path ahead is clear, then move the creature to its next position. Otherwise drop down to begin dealing with the contact situation at line 260.

Lines 260-265—Increment the CONTACT score. If it is now a multiple of 10, jump down to save the current scoring.

Lines 270-280—Find a workable motion code—one that resolves the current contact situation.

Lines 285-290—Increment the GOOD score, update the score display, and jump back to the main running loop.

Line 295—Save the current GOOD score as a 2 dimensional array variable that specifies the multiple-of-10 CONTACT score and the current creature number.

Line 300—If the CONTACT score is less than the number of contacts originally specified for each creature, continue the run.

Line 305—If the number of creatures that has been run is less than the number of specified for the experiment, increment the current creature number and start a new creature.

Lines 310-315—Go to a subroutine that brings out the data for the current experiment, then jump back to give the user a chance to specify a different number of obstacles in the environment for the next set of Alpha creatures.

Lines 1000-1020—BORDER drawing subroutine.

Lines 1500-1520—Subroutine for specifying the number of obstacles to be included in the environemnt.

Lines 1550-1575—Subroutine for drawing the specified number of obstacles at random, non-overlapping positions on the screen.

Lines 2000-2075—SEARCH AHEAD subroutine.

Lines 3000-3020—Subroutine for displaying the current scoring.

Lines 3100-3215—Subroutine for compiling and displaying the results of the current experiment.

Chapter 19

Gathering Data for Beta Creatures

Beta creatures differ from their Alpha counterparts in that the more sophisticated Betas can remember workable responses from the past, then use them whenever a similar situation arises in the future. The responses saved in Beta memory are originally found through Alpha-like, random responses. Once a workable one is found, it is saved in the Beta memory. In that sense, Beta creatures are self-programming creatures.

An immediate consequence of using Beta programming is that the creatures gradually develop a habit pattern of motion—the creature finds a "comfortable" set of motion codes that move it around the screen in a fashion that guarantees a good move every time. If necessary, you can review the details in Chapter 10.

Observation: Beta creatures gradually develop a habit pattern of motion.

Hypothesis: Beta creatures should score no better than the Alphas do at first, but gradually show scores approaching 1.0.

Experiment: Develop a Beta-oriented program that displays the same scoring used for the earlier Alpha projects.

Basis for Confirmation: A scoring curve that resembles that in Fig. 19-1—a *learning curve*, if you will.

FUNDAMENTAL BETA WITH SCORING

The flowchart in Fig. 19-2 represents a general program for displaying the following information about a "live" Beta creature:

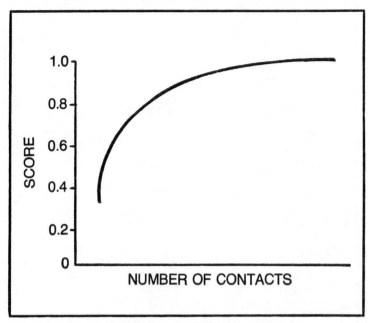

Fig. 19-1. An hypothetical learning curve for Beta creatures.

CONTACTS—The accumulated number of contacts with an obstacle in the creature's path.

GOOD MOVES—The accumulated number of responses to a contact situation that frees the creature from that contact.

SCORE—A running score of the creature's performance; GOOD MOVES divided by CONTACTS.

Referring to the flowchart, the program first initializes the system, and then it initializes the Beta memory by loading the stop code (CI=2 and CJ=2) into the Beta memory locations. (Recall that motion code responses as saved in Beta memory as values between 0 and 4; that makes 2 a stop code.)

The initialization phase is completed by initializing the creature's screen position and motion code, zeroing the scoring, clearing the screen, and drawing the standard border figure.

The main running loop consists of operations SEARCH AHEAD, CLEAR PATH, and MOVE THE CREATURE. The system searches the path ahead, and, if it is clear, moves the creature to its next position on the screen. After making the move, the system loops back to SEARCH AHEAD again. The creature breaks out of this loop only upon finding that the path ahead is no longer clear.

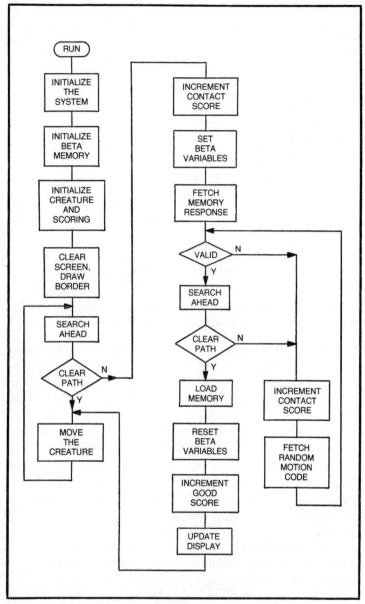

Fig. 19-2. Flowchart for FUNDAMENTAL BETA WITH SCORING.

Upon finding that the path ahead is not clear (that it is making contact with an obstacle), the flowchart shows INCREMENT CONTACT SCORE. Immediately after that, the current motion code is used as an index for fetching a possible response from Beta memory. SET BETA VARIABLES sets up the memory index, and FETCH MEMORY RESPONSE pulls the response from Beta memory.

The VALID conditional operation checks to see whether or not the creature has ever encountered the current contact situation before. It looks to the response data. If it is a pair of 2's (as set in the INITIALIZE BETA MEMORY operation) the creature apparently has not encountered the situation before. But if something other than the stop-code combination is pulled from Beta memory, the assumption is that the creature has dealt with that particular situation before.

Suppose that VALID conditional is *not* statisfied—the creature has not yet encountered the present contact situation in the past. That being the case, the creature resorts to a purely Alpha-like response by incrementing the contact score and fetching a random motion code response. The response is tested for workability by looping back through VALID, SEARCH AHEAD and CLEAR PATH. If the response doesn't work, the CLEAR PATH conditional fails, and the creature has to pick another random response. The system remains in that loop until a workable response is found.

Now, back up to the FETCH MEMORY RESPONSE operation, and suppose that the stored response is valid. That would indicate that the creature has encountered and resolved the present contact situation at some time in the past. Even so, it is doublechecked by the SEARCH AHEAD and CLEAR PATH operations. If, for some reason, the response doesn't work this time, the creature enters the FETCH RANDOM MOTION CODE loop until it comes up with a response that does work. But if the fetched Beta response is a good one, if the CLEAR PATH conditional is satisfied, the creature goes through a set of memory and scoring operations.

By the time the program reaches the LOAD MEMORY operation, the creature is working with a good response to the current contact situation. It makes no difference whether that response originally came from Beta memory or was derived from a series of Alpha-like fetches of random responses. The good response is saved in Beta memory for future use.

RESET BETA VARIABLES adjusts the motion code response to the normal range of −2 to 2, INCREMENT GOOD SCORE increments the GOOD score display, and UPDATE DISPLAY both calculates the SCORE value and displays the scoring figures along the bottom of the screen.

Having found a workable response, the creature finally re-enters the main running loop at MOVE THE CREATURE; and normal, straight-line motion continues until the next contact situation arises.

The longer the creature runs, the less Alpha behavior it exhibits, and once the habit pattern of motion is established, the creature is running in a purely Beta mode, making no references at all to the fetching of random motion codes, every response comes from Beta memory.

Run the program as listed here, and you will see the Beta begin with scores on the order of 0.3 or 0.4. As the habit pattern of motion develops and the creature begins relying more on its Beta memory, you will see SCORE rise gradually into the 0.9 region.

TRS-80 Version

The variable list and programming for FUNDAMENTAL BETA WITH SCORING are shown in Table 19-1 and Listing 19-1, respectively.

Lines 105-130—Initialize the system, including running the random number generator until the user strikes the ENTER key.

Lines 135-140—Initialize the Beta memory, setting its contents to motion code 2s.

Lines 145-155—Initialize the creature's screen position and motion code; zero the scoring.

Line 160—Clear the screen and draw the border figure.

Lines 165-180—This is the main running loop. Do the SEARCH AHEAD routine; if the path ahead is *not* clear, break out of the loop to line 185; otherwise move the creature and loop back to the beginning of this running loop.

Line 185—Increment the CONTACT score.

Line 190—Set Beta variables.

Line 195—Fetch the Beta memory response.

Line 200—If the Beta response is *not* a pair of 2s, it is a VALID response. In that case, jump down to line 220 to search ahead.

Lines 205-215—Increment the CONTACT score again, fetch a random motion code, and jump back to the VALID test.

Line 220—Adjust the motion code variables to make them compatible with the SEARCH AHEAD routine, do the SEARCH AHEAD, and re-adjust the variables again.

Table 19-1. TRS-80 Variable List for FUNDAMENTAL BETA WITH SCORING.

F$	Field specifier for printing SCORE
S$	General-purpose string variable
M(m,n,k)	Beta memory variable; m is CI of current motion code, n is CJ of current motion code, k is response motion-code selector—1 for CI, 2 for CJ
MI	CI of current motion code
MJ	CJ of current motion code
KL	Response select, 1 or 2
CP	Next creature screen position
CI	Horizontal component of motion code
CJ	Vertical component of motion code
CX	Horizontal component of contact code
CY	Vertical component of contact code
CS	CONTACT score
GS	GOOD score
AS	Overall SCORE
SI	Sign value of CI
SJ	Sign value of CJ
AI	Absolute value of CI
AJ	Absolute value of CJ
F0	Upper left of border figure
F1	Upper right of border figure
F2	Lower left of border figure
F3	Lower right of border figure

Listing 19-1. TRS-80 Program Listing for FUNDAMENTAL BETA WITH SCORING.

```
10 REM   FUNDAMENTAL BETA
15 REM   WITH SCORING
20 REM      TRS-80
25 REM
100 REM ** BETA PSYCH MAINLINE, V.1—TRS-80 **
105 CLEAR 128:F$="#.##"
110 CLS:PRINT STRING$(6,26):PRINT TAB(18);
115 PRINT "FUNDAMENTAL BETA WITH SCORING"
120 PRINT:PRINT "STRIKE 'ENTER' TO START . . ."
125 S$=INKEY$:IF S$="" THEN N=RND(1000):GOTO 125
130 CLS:DIM M(4,4,2)
135 FOR MI=0 TO 4:FOR MJ=0 TO 4:FOR KL=1 TO 2
140 M(MI,MJ,KL)=2:NEXT KL,MJ,MI
145 CP= 15773+RND(5)+64*(RND(5)−3)
150 CI=RND(5)−3:CJ=RND(5)−3:IF  CI=0  AND  CJ=0
    THEN 150
155 CS=0:GS=0
```

```
160  CLS:GOSUB 1000:POKE CP,42
165  GOSUB 2000
170  IF NOT(CX=32 AND CY=32) THEN 185
175  POKE CP,32:CP=NP:POKE CP,42
180  GOTO 165
185  CS=CS+1
190  MI=CI+2:MJ=CJ+2
195  CI=M(MI,MJ,1):CJ=M(MI,MJ,2)
200  IF NOT(CI=2 AND CJ=2) THEN 220
205  CS=CS+1
210  CI=RND(5)-1:CJ=RND(5)-1:IF CI=2 AND CJ=2
     THEN 210
215  GOTO 200
220  CI=CI-2:CJ=CJ-2:GOSUB 2000:CI=CI+2:CJ=CJ+2
225  IF NOT(CX=32 AND CY=32) THEN 205
230  M(MI,MJ,1)=CI:M(MI,MJ,2)=CJ
235  CI=CI-2:CJ=CJ-2
240  GS=GS+1:GOSUB 3000
245  GOTO 175
250  REM
255  REM
1000 REM ** BORDER, V.1—TRS-80 **
1005 F0=15360:F1=15423:F2=16128:F3=16191
1010 FOR N=F0 TO F1:POKE N,176:NEXT N
1015 FOR N=F2 TO F3:POKE N,131:NEXT N
1020 FOR N=F0 TO F2 STEP 64:POKE N,170:NEXT N
1025 FOR N=F1 TO F3 STEP 64:POKE N,149:NEXT N
1030 POKE F0,160:POKE F1,144:POKE F2,130:POKE
     F3,129
1035 RETURN
1040 REM
1045 REM
2000 REM ** SEARCH AHEAD, V.1—TRS-80 **
2005 NP=CP:CX=32:CY=32
2010 SI=SGN(CI):SJ=SGN(CJ):AI=ABS(CI):AJ=ABS(CJ)
2015 IF AI=0 THEN 2030 ELSE AI=AI-1
2020 IF SI >0 THEN NP=NP+1 ELSE NP=NP-1
2025 CX=PEEK(NP)
2030 IF AJ=0 THEN 2045 ELSE AJ=AJ-1
2035 IF SJ >0 THEN NP=NP+64 ELSE NP=NP-64
2040 CY=PEEK(NP)
2045 IF NOT(CX=32 AND CY=32) THEN RETURN
```

274

```
2050  IF AI=0 AND AJ= 0 THEN RETURN ELSE GOTO 2015
2055  REM
2060  REM
3000  REM ** SCORING ROUTINES, V.1—TRS-80 **
3005  AS=GS/CS
3010  PRINT @ 832,"CONTACTS","GOOD   MOVES",
      "SCORE"
3015  PRINT @ 896,STRING$(64,32);
3020  PRINT @ 896,CS,GS;:PRINT @ 928,USING F$;AS;
3025  RETURN
3030  REM
3035  REM
```

Line 225—If the path ahead is *not* clear under the given motion
    code, then loop back to line 205 to get another motion
    code.
Lines 230-245—Save the workable motion code in Beta mem-
    ory (line 230), adjust the motion code to the normal
    running range of −2 to 2 (line 235), increment the GOOD
    score, display the scoring, and jump back into the main
    running loop at line 175.
Lines 1000-1035—BORDER drawing subroutine.
Lines 2000-2050—SEARCH AHEAD subroutine.
Lines 3000-3025—SCORING subroutine.

Apple II Version

The variable list and programming for FUNDAMENTAL
BETA WITH SCORING are shown in Table 19-2 and Listing 19-2,
respectively.

Listing 19-2. Apple II Program Listing for FUNDAMENTAL BETA WITH SCORING.

```
 10  REM   FUNDAMENTAL BETA WITH SCORING
 15  REM       APPLESOFT
 20  REM
 25  REM
100  REM ** BETA PSYCH MAINLINE, V.1—APPLESOFT **
105  DEF FN R(R) = INT (5 * RND (1)) − 2
110  TEXT : HOME : VTAB (8): PRINT TAB(12)"BETA WITH
     SCORING"
115  VTAB(15):PRINT "STRIKE 'RETURN' TO START . . ."
120  N = FN R(0):N = PEEK ( − 16384): POKE − 16368,0
```

Table 19-2. Apple II Variable List for FUNDAMENTAL BETA WITH SCORING.

FN R(R)	Random function for motion codes, −2 to 2
N,M	General-purpose numeric variables
M(m,n,k)	Beta memory variables; m is CI of current motion code, n is CJ of current motion code, k is the response motion-code selector— 1 for CI, 2 for CJ
KL	Memory response select; 1 for CI, 2 for CJ
PX	Horizontal component of creature's current screen position
PY	Vertical component of creature's current screen position
NX	Horizontal component of creature's next screen position
NY	Vertical component of creature's next screen position
CI	Horizontal component of motion code
CJ	Vertical component of motion code
CX	Horizontal component of contact code
CY	Vertical component of contact code
CS	CONTACT score
GS	GOOD score
AS	Overall SCORE
SI	Sign value of CI
SJ	Sign value of CJ
AI	Absolute value of CI
AJ	Absolute value of CJ

```
125 IF N < > 141 THEN 120
130 HOME : DIM M(4,4,2)
135 FOR M = 0 TO 4: FOR N = 0 TO 4: FOR KL = 1 TO 2
140 M(M,N,KL) = 2: NEXT KL,N,M
145 PX = 20 + FN R(0):PY = 20 + FN R(0)
150 CI = FN R(0):CJ = FN R(0): IF CI = 0 AND CJ = 0 THEN
    150
155 CS = 0:GS = 0
160 HOME : GR : GOSUB 1000
165 GOSUB 2000
170 IF NOT (CX = 0 AND CY = 0) THEN 195
175 COLOR= 0: PLOT PX,PY
180 PX = NX:PY = NY
185 COLOR= 9: PLOT PX,PY
190 GOTO 165
195 CS = CS + 1
200 MI = CI + 2:MJ = CJ + 2
205 CI = M(MI,MJ,1):CJ = M(MI,MJ,2)
210 IF NOT (CI = 2 AND CJ = 2) THEN 230
```

```
215  CS = CS + 1
220  CI = FN R(0) + 2:CJ = FN R(0) + 2: IF CI = 2 AND CJ = 2
     THEN 220
225  GOTO 210
230  CI = CI - 2:CJ = CJ - 2: GOSUB 2000:CI = CI + 2:CJ +
     2
235  IF NOT (CX = 0 AND CY = 0) THEN 215
240  M(MI,MJ,1) = CI:M(MI,MJ,2) = CJ
245  CI = CI - 2:CJ = CJ - 2
250  GS = GS + 1: GOSUB 3000
255  GOTO 175
260  REM
265  REM
1000 REM ** BORDER, V.1—APPLESOFT **
1005 COLOR= 15
1010 HLIN 0,39 AT 0: HLIN 0,39 AT 36
1015 VLIN 0,36 AT 0: VLIN 0,36 AT 39
1020 RETURN
1025 REM
1030 REM
2000 REM ** SEARCH AHEAD, V.1—APPLESOFT **
2005 NX = PX:NY = PY:CX = 0:CY = 0
2010 SI = SGN (CI):SJ = SGN (CJ):AI = ABS (CI):AJ = ABS
     (CJ)
2015 IF AI = 0 THEN 2040
2020 AI = AI - 1
2025 IF SI > 0 THEN NX = NX + 1: GOTO 2035
2030 NX = NX - 1
2035 CX = SCRN(NX,NY)
2040 IF AJ = 0 THEN 2065
2045 AJ = AJ - 1
2050 IF SJ > 0 THEN NY = NY + 1: GOTO 2060
2055 NY = NY - 1
2060 CY = SCRN(NX,NY)
2065 IF NOT (CX = 0 AND CY = 0) THEN RETURN
2070 IF AI = 0 AND AJ = 0 THEN RETURN
2075 GOTO 2015
2080 REM
2085 REM
3000 REM ** SCORING ROUTINES, V.1—APPLESOFT **
3005 AS = INT ((GS / CS) * 1000) / 1000
3010 HOME : PRINT "CONTACTS","GOOD","SCORE"
```

```
3015  PRINT CS,GS,AS
3020  RETURN
3025  REM
3030  REM
```

Lines 105-130—Initialize the system, including a continuous running of the random number generator until the user strikes the RETURN key.

Lines 135-140—Initialize the Beta memory, setting all contents to motion code 2s.

Lines 145-155—Initialize the creature's screen position and motion code; zero the scoring.

Line 160—Clear the screen, set the graphics mode, and draw the border figure.

Lines 165-190—This is the main running loop. Do the SEARCH AHEAD routine; if the path ahead is *not* clear, jump out of the loop to line 195; otherwise move the creature and go back to the beginning of the loop.

Line 195—Increment the CONTACT score.

Line 200—Set the Beta variables.

Line 205—Fetch the Beta memory response.

Line 210—Do the VALID check. If the response is valid, jump to line 230 to test its workability.

Lines 215-225—Increment the CONTACT score, fetch a random motion code, and jump back to the VALID check at line 210.

Line 230—Adjust the motion code variables to make them compatible with the SEARCH AHEAD routine, do the SEARCH AHEAD routine, re-adjust the motion code variables for further Beta-memory operations.

Line 235—If the path ahead is *not* clear, jump back to get another motion code.

Lines 240-255—Save the working response in Beta memory, adjust the motion codes for normal running, increment the GOOD score and display the scoring, and jump back into the main running loop at line 175.

Lines 1000-1020—BORDER drawing subroutine.

Lines 2000-2075—SEARCH AHEAD subroutine.

Lines 3000-3020—SCORING subroutine.

BETA WITH SCORING AND MEMORY DISPLAY

While it is "against the rules" of experimental machine psychology to dig into the inner workings of the creatures, it is tempting to watch the Beta memory at work in a detailed fashion. During the initial Beta learning phase, its memory is a dynamic thing—it is something that is continuously changing and adjusting itself to the creature's first-hand experiences with its environment.

The program offered in this section allows you to observe the workings of the Beta memory on the CRT. The memory is scanned in a systematic fashion, and a representation of it is displayed and updated at the same time the scores are. In the TRS-80 version, a set of 50 little graphic symbols appear along the bottom of the border figure. The Apple version shortens the border figure a little bit, and displays the Beta memory contents as colored squares along the right-hand side of the screen.

You will be able to see the Beta memory starting as a complete blank. The creature's first encounter with an element of the border figure will alter the Beta memory a little bit. And as the creature develops a habit pattern of motion, its displayed memory cells will likewise develop a more or less complicated pattern of symbols.

The purpose of the whole thing is to observe the working of the Beta memory. Attempting to interpret the exact meaning of the cells is probably a hopeless task. But it is fun to watch.

The programming is a simple variation of the flowchart already described in connection with Fig. 19-2. Aside from running a little subroutine that displays the Beta memory cells, the program also lets you blank the Beta memory by simply striking the ENTER (TRS-80) or RETURN (Apple II) key. The latter feature lets you wipe out all previously learned responses, and you will see the memory display cleared out and the creature beginning its learning cycle from scratch. Of course the scoring is also reset to zero.

TRS-80 Version

The variable list and programming for FUNDAMENTAL BETA WITH SCORING AND MEMORY DISPLAY are shown in Table 19-3 and Listing 19-3. Remember that you can wipe out the Beta memory, effectively starting a new creature, by striking the ENTER key any time you choose. Watch the creature develop its habit pattern of motion, and then zing its memory to start it all over again. The chances of seeing identical habit patterns of motion are just about nil.

Since the programming is practically identical to that described in the previous section, the following analysis of the program listing is rather brief. Refer to the analysis of Listing 19-1 for more details.

F$	Field specifier for printing SCORE
S$	General-purpose string variable
M,N	General-purpose numeric variables
M(m,n,k)	Beta memory variables; m is CI of current motion code, n is CJ of current motion code, k is the response motion-code selector—1 for CI, 2 for CJ
MI	Memory version of current CI
MJ	Memory version of current CJ
KL	Memory response select; 1 for CI, 2 for CJ
CP	Creature's current screen position
NP	Creature's next screen position
CI	Horizontal component of motion code
CJ	Vertical component of motion code
CX	Horizontal component of contact code
CY	Vertical component of contact code
CS	CONTACT score
GS	GOOD score
AS	Overall SCORE
W	Screen position specifier for showing Beta memory
SI	Sign value of CI
SJ	Sign value of CJ
AI	Absolute value of CI
AJ	Absolute value of CJ
F0	Upper left of border figure
F1	Upper right of border figure
F2	Lower left of border figure
F3	Lower right of border figure

**Listing 19-3. TRS-80 Program Listing for
FUNDAMENTAL BETA WITH SCORING AND MEMORY DISPLAY.**

```
10 REM   FUNDAMENTAL BETA WITH
15 REM   SCORING AND MEMORY DISPLAY
20 REM      TRS-80
25 REM
30 REM
100 REM ** BETA PSYCH MAINLINE, V.2—TRS-80 **
105 CLEAR 128:F$="#.##"
110 CLS:PRINT STRING$(6,26):PRINT TAB(18);
115 PRINT "FUNDAMENTAL BETA WITH SCORING"
120 PRINT:PRINT "STRIKE 'ENTER' TO START . . ."
125 S$=INKEY$:IF S$="" THEN N=RND(1000):GOTO 125
130 CLS:DIM M(4,4,2)
135 FOR MI=0 TO 4:FOR MJ=0 TO 4:FOR KL=1 TO 2
140 M(MI,MJ,KL)=2:NEXT KL,MJ,MI
145 CP=15773+RND(5)+64*(RND(5)−3)
```

```
150 CI=RND(5)-3:CJ=RND(5)-3:IF CI=0 AND CJ=0
    THEN 150
155 CS=0:GS=0
160 CLS:GOSUB 1000:POKE CP,42
165 GOSUB 2000
170 IF NOT(CX=32 AND CY=32) THEN 185
175 POKE CP,32:CP=NP:POKE CP,42
180 S$=INKEY$:IF S ="" THEN 165   ELSE 135
185 CS=CS+1
190 MI=CI+2:MJ=CJ+2
195 CI=M(MI,MJ,2)
200 IF NOT(CI=2 AND CJ=2) THEN 220
205 CS=CS+1
210 CI=RND(5)-1:CJ=RND(5)-1:IF CI=2 AND CJ=2
    THEN 210
215 GOTO 200
220 CI=CI-2:CJ=CJ-2:GOSUB 2000:CI=CI+2:CJ=CJ+2
225 IF NOT(CX=32 AND CY=32) THEN 205
230 M(MI,MJ,1)=CI:M(MI,MJ,2)=CJ
235 CI=CI-2:CJ=CJ-2
240 GS=GS+1:GOSUB 3000:GOSUB 3500
245 GOTO 175
250 REM
255 REM
1000 REM ** BORDER, V.1—TRS-80 **
1005 F0=15360:F1=15423:F2=16128:F3=16191
1010 FOR N=F0 TO F1:POKE N,176:NEXT N
1015 FOR N=F2 TO F3:POKE N,131:NEXT N
1020 FOR N=F0 TO F2 STEP 64:POKE N,170:NEXT N
1025 FOR N=F1 TO F3 STEP 64:POKE N,149:NEXT N
1030 POKE F0,160:POKE F1,144:POKE F2,130:POKE
     F3,129
1035 RETURN
1040 REM
1045 REM
2000 REM ** SEARCH AHEAD, V.1—TRS-80 **
2005 NP=CP:CX=32:CY=32
2010 SI=SGN(CI):SJ=SGN(CJ):AI=ABS(CI):AJ=ABS(CJ)
2015 IF AI=0 THEN 2030 ELSE AI=AI-1
2020 IF SI >0 THEN NP=NP+1 ELSE NP=NP-1
2025 CX=PEEK(NP)
2030 IF AJ=0 THEN 2045 ELSE AJ= AJ-1
```

```
2035  IF SJ >0 THEN NP=NP+64 ELSE NP=NP-64
2040  CY=PEEK(NP)
2045  IF NOT(CX=32 AND CY=32) THEN RETURN
2050  IF AI=0 AND AJ=0 THEN RETURN ELSE GOTO 2015
2055  REM
2060  REM
3000  REM ** SCORING ROUTINES, V.1—TRS-80 **
3005  AS=GS/CS
3010  PRINT @ 832,"CONTACTS","GOOD
      "SCORE"
3015  PRINT @ 896,STRING$(64,32);
3020  PRINT @ 896,CS,GS;:PRINT @ 928,USING F$;AS;
3025  RETURN
3030  REM
3035  REM
3500  REM ** SHOW BETA MEMORY, V.1—TRS-80 **
3505  W=0
3510  FOR M=0 TO 4:FOR N=0 TO 4:FOR KL=1 TO 2
3515  PRINT @ 966+W,CHR$(M(M,N,KL)+130);
3520  W=W+1
3525  NEXT KL,N,M
3530  RETURN
3535  REM
3540  REM
```

Lines 105-130—Initialize the system.

Lines 135-140—Initialize the Beta memory.

Lines 145-155—Initialize the creature and scoring.

Line 160—Clear the screen and draw the border figure.

Lines 165-180—Main running loop. If any key, including the RETURN key, is depressed at line 180, the system will start a new creature from line 135.

Lines 185-195—Increment CONTACT score, set Beta variables, and fetch the Beta memory response for the contact situation at hand.

Line 200—Response VALID check.

Lines 205-215—Increment the CONTACT score and fetch a random motion code.

Lines 220-225—Search the path ahead and respond according to whether the path is clear or not.

Lines 230-235—Load the working response to Beta memory, and reset the motion code variables.

Line 240—Increment the GOOD score, update the scoring display, and call subroutine 3500 to display the Beta memory cells.

Line 245—Loop back to the main running loop.

Lines 1000-1035—BORDER drawing subroutine.

Lines 2000-2050—SEARCH AHEAD subroutine.

Lines 3000-3025—SCORING display subroutine.

Lines 3500-3530—Beta memory-cell display subroutine.

Apple II Version

The variable list and programming for FUNDAMENTAL BETA WITH SCORING AND MEMORY DISPLAY are shown as Table 19-4 and Listing 19-4. Take special note of the fact that the BORDER subroutine has to be modified in order to accommodate the memory-cell display.

Remember that you can wipe out the Beta memory at any time by striking the RETURN key. Watch the creature develop its habit pattern of motion, and then zing its memory to make it start all over again. The chances of seeing identical habit patterns of motion are just about nil.

The programming is nearly identical to that used in the previous section, so it is possible to offer an abbreviated version of its line-by-line analysis. Refer to the analysis of Listing 19-2 if you need more detail.

Lines 105-130—Initialize the system.

Lines 135-140—Initialize the Beta memory.

Lines 145-155—Initialize the creature and scoring.

Line 160—Clear the screen, set the graphics mode, and draw the revised border figure.

Lines 165-195—This is the main running loop. If any key, including the RETURN key, is depressed at line 190, then start a new memory.

Lines 200-210—Increment the CONTACT score, set the Beta variables, and fetch the Beta response.

Line 215—Do the VALID check and respond accordingly.

Lines 220-230—Increment the CONTACT score again, and fetch a random response, and jump back to the VALID check.

Lines 235-240—Do the SEARCH AHEAD routine and respond according to the condition of the path ahead.

**Table 19-4. Apple II Variable List for
FUNDAMENTAL BETA WITH SCORING AND MEMORY DISPLAY.**

```
APPLESOFT VERSION

FN R(R)     Random function for motion codes, −2 to 2
M,N         General-purpose numeric variables
M(m,n,k)    Beta memory variables; m is CI of current motion
            code, n is CJ of current motion code, k is the
            response motion-code selector—1 for CI, 2 for CJ
MI          Memory version of current CI
MJ          Memory version of current CJ
KL          Memory response select; 1 for CI, 2 for CJ
WX          Horizontal component of memory display
WY          Vertical component of memory display
PX          Horizontal component of creature's current screen position
PY          Vertical component of creature's current screen position
NX          Horizontal component of creature's next screen position
NY          Vertical component of creature's next screen position
CI          Horizontal component of motion code
CJ          Vertical component of motion code
CX          Horizontal component of contact code
CY          Vertical component of contact code
SI          Sign value of CI
SJ          Sign value of CJ
AI          Absolute value of CI
AJ          Absolute value of CJ
```

**Listing 19-4. Apple II Program Listing for
FUNDAMENTAL BETA WITH SCORING AND MEMORY DISPLAY**

```
10  REM   FUNDAMENTAL BETA WITH
15  REM   SCORING AND MEMORY DISPLAY
20  REM      APPLESOFT
25  REM
30  REM
100 REM ** BETA PSYCH MAINLINE, V.2—APPLESOFT **
105 DEF FN R(R) = INT (5 * RND (1)) − 2
110 TEXT : HOME : VTAB (8): PRINT TAB(12)"BETA WITH
    SCORING"
115 VTAB (15):PRINT "STRIKE 'RETURN' TO START . . ."
120 N = FN R(0):N = PEEK ( − 16384): POKE − 16368,0
125 IF N < > 141 THEN 120
130 HOME : DIM M(4,4,2)
135 FOR M = 0 TO 4: FOR N = 0 TO 4: FOR KL = 1 TO 2
140 M(M,N,KL) = 2: NEXT KL,N,M
145 PX = 20 + FN R(0):PY = 20 + FN R(0)
150 CI = FN R(0):CJ = FN R(0): IF CI = 0 AND CJ = 0 THEN
    150
```

```
 155 CS = 0:GS = 0
 160 HOME : GR : GOSUB 1000
 165 GOSUB 2000
 170 IF NOT (CX = 0 AND CY = 0) THEN 200
 175 COLOR= 0: PLOT PX,PY
 180 PX = NX:PY = NY
 185 COLOR= 9: PLOT PX,PY
 190 N = PEEK ( − 16384): POKE − 16368,0: IF N = 141
     THEN 135
 195 GOTO 165
 200 CS = CS + 1
 205 MI = CI + 2:MJ = CJ + 2
 210 CI = M(MI,MJ,1):CJ = M(MI,MJ,2)
 215 IF NOT (CI = 2 AND CJ = 2) THEN 235
 220 CS = CS + 1
 225 CI = FN R(0) + 2:CJ = FN R(0) + 2: IF CI = 2 AND CJ = 2
     THEN 225
 230 GOTO 215
 235 CI = CI − 2:CJ = CJ − 2: GOSUB 2000:CI = CI + 2:CJ =
     CJ  + 2
 240 IF NOT (CX = 0 AND CY = 0) THEN 220
 245 M(MI,MJ,1) = CI:M(MI,MJ,2) = CJ
 250 CI = CI − 2:CJ = CJ − 2
 255 GS = GS + 1: GOSUB 3000: GOSUB 3500
 260 GOTO 175
 265 REM
 270 REM
1000 REM ** BORDER, V.2—APPLESOFT **
1005 COLOR= 15
1010 HLIN 0,37 AT 0: HLIN 0,37 AT 36
1015 VLIN 0,36 AT 0: VLIN 0,36 AT 37
1020 RETURN
1025 REM
1030 REM
2000 REM ** SEARCH AHEAD, V.1—APPLESOFT **
2005 NX = PX:NY = PY:CX = 0:CY = 0
2010 SI = SGN (CI):SJ = SGN (CJ):AI = ABS (CI):AJ = ABS
     (CJ)
2015 IF AI = 0 THEN 2040
2020 AI = AI − 1
2025 IF SI > THEN NX = NX + 1: GOTO 2035
2030 NX = NX − 1
```

```
2035  CX = SCRN(NX,NY)
2040  IF AJ = 0 THEN 2065
2045  AJ = AJ – 1
2050  IF SJ > 0 THEN NY = NY + 1: GOTO 2060
2055  NY = NY – 1
2060  CY = SCRN(NX,NY)
2065  IF NOT (CX = 0 AND CY = 0) THEN RETURN
2070  IF AI = 0 AND AJ = 0 THEN RETURN
2075  GOTO 2015
2080  REM
2085  REM
3000  REM ** SCORING ROUTINES, V.1—APPLESOFT **
3005  AS = INT ((GS / CS) * 1000) / 1000
3010  HOME : PRINT "CONTACTS","GOOD","SCORE"
3015  PRINT CS,GS,AS
3020  RETURN
3025  REM
3030  REM
3500  REM ** SHOW BETA MEMORY, V.1—APPLESOFT **
3505  WX = 38:WY = 0
3510  FOR M = 0 TO 4: FOR N = 0 TO 4: FOR KL = 1 TO 2
3515  COLOR= M(M,N,KL) + 6
3520  PLOT WX,WY:WY = WY + 1
3525  IF WY > 24 THEN WX = 39:WY = 0
3530  NEXT KL,N,M
3535  RETURN
3540  REM
3545  REM
```

Lines 245-250—Load the working response into Beta memory, and reset the Beta variables.

Line 255—Increment the GOOD score, update and display the scoring, and go to subroutine 3500 to display the Beta memory cells.

Line 260—Jump back into the main running loop.

Lines 1000-1020—Draw the *revised* BORDER figure.

Lines 2000-2075—SEARCH AHEAD subroutine.

Lines 3000-3020—SCORING display subroutine.

Lines 3500-3535—Beta memory-cell display subroutine.

BETA WITH SCORING AND LEARNING DETECTION

An important psychological question at this time ought to be along this line: How many encounters with the environment are necessary to complete the learning phase for a Beta creature? How well a Beta learns—how effectively it develops a habit pattern of motion—is really more important than the scoring figures.

Casual observations based on the two previous programs in this chapter will show that some Betas establish their habit patterns in something less than 50 contacts, while others might require 100 contacts or more. Certainly there is going to be a need for a program that monitors the learning activity and averages the results to come up with a reliable number of contacts required for establishing the Beta learning curve. That is handled in the next chapter.

The question cannot be tackled until another question is answered: How can we determine the moment when a Beta creature first establishes its habit pattern of motion? That question is really tougher to answer than the main question about the number of contacts required for learning.

One rather straightforward technique for detecting the moment full Beta learning has occurred is to count the number of *consecutive* good responses to a contact situation, and when that number reaches some predetermined level, one can say that learning has been complete. One further step finalizes the matter: Subtract the number of consecutive good responses from the current CONTACT score. The result should be a CONTACT score that represents the moment the creature entered its habit pattern of motion.

Now, the only problem is determining how many consecutive good responses to contact situations constitute full learning. It is certainly possible for the creature to be operating in the random, Alpha mode, and yet happen to score 3 or 4 consecutive good moves—pure chance allows for that. So the criterion for establishing a learned habit pattern of motion must be some number beyond that allowed by pure chance. Perhaps a criterion of 10 consecutive good responses to contact situations will do the job.

But then you might have noticed that a Beta can get into a habit pattern of motion that gradually carries it into a situation it cannot resolve. The habit pattern is maybe executed a dozen times or so without trouble; then it winds up in a corner and has to respond by setting up a slightly different habit pattern. That is an example of the Beta's adaptive quality. Thus it would not be unreasonable, in a theoretical sense, to set the criterion for full learning at 100 consecutive good responses to contact situations. But in a practical sense, it takes a long, long time to execute an experiment under those conditions.

The programs suggested in this section allow you to set your own criterion for full learning. It can be set for any integer value greater than zero. And when that criterion is met, the program displays the number of contacts that were executed the moment your definition was met, minus the number of good-response contacts. The figure thus represents the number of contacts required for entering the habit pattern of motion.

After noting the result, you can strike a key to start a new creature with the same learning criterion. If you want to run a creature with a different value for the learning criterion, you must terminate the program and start it from the beginning.

The program, as presented here, answers this question directly: How many contacts are necessary to reach full learning for a given Beta creature?

Try running the experiment a few times, using a learning criterion of 10. You will find some fast learners and some slow learners, but as established in a more formal fashion in the next chapter, the average number of contacts to full learning in a plain environment (no internal obstacles) is about 35.

Flowchart for the Program

The flowchart for this program is shown in Fig. 19-3. It begins by initializing the system in the usual way, then requesting INPUT LEARNING DEFINITION. That is where you enter your own definition, or criterion, for full learning—the number of consecutive good responses to contact situations.

From that point, the program runs pretty much like the ones for BETA WITH SCORING. Notice, however, that the loop that includes FETCH RANDOM MOTION CODE also resets a "habit counter" to zero. This is the variable that keeps track of the number of consecutive good moves, and upon entering the random motion code loop, the habit counter is reset to zero because it is clear that the creature tried a motion code that didn't work.

The program increments the habit counter each time the creature encounters a contact situation and resolves it successfully. See the INCREMENT HABIT COUNT operation in the sequence following LOAD MEMORY.

After updating the scoring display, the system compares the current habit count with the learning criterion entered in the earlier initialization phase of the experiment. That is the function of the LEARN DONE conditional. If the number of consecutive good responses is less than the criterion for full learning, the program

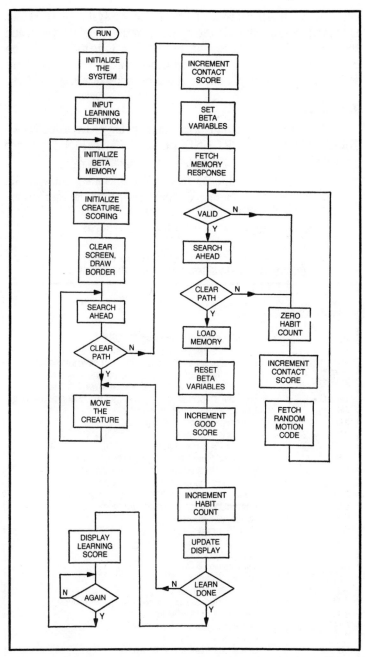

Fig. 19-3. Flowchart for FUNDAMENTAL BETA WITH SCORING AND LEARN-
ING DETECTION.

continues in its normal fashion. Otherwise the system detects that full learning—as defined in the initial operations—is complete, and the program displays the number of CONTACTs to the moment the habit pattern of motion was established. After that, the system waits for you to strike a key to run a new creature from scratch.

TRS-80 Version

The variable list and programming for FUNDAMENTAL BETA WITH SCORING AND LEARNING DEFINITION are shown in Table 19-5 and Listing 19-5, respectively.

Lines 105-135—Initialize the system, including allowing the random number generator to cycle until the user strikes the ENTER key.

Lines 140-150—Input a valid learning criterion.

**Table 19-5. TRS-80 Variable List for FUND-
MENTAL BETA WITH SCORING AND LEARNING DETECTION.**

TRS-80 VERSION	
F$	Field specifier for printing SCORE
S$	General-purpose string variable
M(m,n,k)	Beta memory variables; m is CI of current motion code, n is CJ of current motion code, k is the response motion-code selector—1 for CI, 2 for CJ
LC,LC%	Number of consecutive good moves to define learning
MI	Memory version of current CI
MJ	Memory version of current CJ
KL	Memory response select; 1 for CI, 2 for CJ
CP	Creature's current screen position
NP	Creature's next screen position
CI	Horizontal component of motion code
CJ	Vertical component of motion code
CX	Horizontal component of contact code
CY	Vertical component of contact code
CS	CONTACT score
GS	GOOD score
AS	Overall SCORE
SI	Sign value of CI
SJ	Sign value of CJ
AI	Absolute value of CI
AJ	Absolute value of CJ
GM	Current number of consecutive good moves
F0	Upper left of border figure
F1	Upper right of border figure
F2	Lower left of border figure
F3	Lower right of border figure

Lines 155-160—Initialize the Beta memory by clearing it to "invalid" motion stop codes.

Lines 165-175—Initialize the creature's screen position and motion code; zero the habit counter.

Line 180—Clear the screen and draw the border figure.

Lines 185-200—This is the main running loop. Do the SEARCH AHEAD. If the path is clear, move the creature and run this loop again.

Lines 205-215—Increment the CONTACT count, set the Beta variables, and fetch the response from Beta memory.

Line 220—Do the VALID check.

Lines 225-235—This is the basic Alpha loop. Increment the CONTACT score, zero the habit counter, fetch a randomly generated motion code, and return to the VALID check again.

Lines 240-245—Do the SEARCH AHEAD routine to test the workability of the current motion code. If it doesn't work, loop back to get a randomly selected one.

Lines 250-255—Load the current, working motion code to Beta memory and adjust the motion code for normal running.

Line 260—Increment the GOOD score, increment the habit counter, and update the score display on the screen.

Line 265—Test the current habit count against the previously entered learning criterion. If the habit count hasn't

Listing 19-5. TRS-80 Program Listing for
FUNDAMENTAL BETA WITH SCORING AND LEARNING DETECTION.

```
 10 REM   FUNDAMENTAL BETA WITH
 15 REM   SCORING AND LEARNING DETECTION
 20 REM      TRS-80
 25 REM
 30 REM
100 REM ** BETA PSYCH MAINLINE, V.3—TRS-80 **
105 CLEAR 128:F$="#.##"
110 CLS:PRINT STRING$(6,26):PRINT TAB(18);
115 PRINT "FUNDAMENTAL BETA WITH SCORING"
120 PRINT TAB(20) "AND LEARNING DETECTION"
125 PRINT:PRINT "STRIKE 'ENTER' TO START . . ."
130 S$=INKEY$:IF S$="" THEN N=RND(1000):GOTO 130
135 CLS:DIM M(4,4,2)
140 CLS:PRINT "ENTER NUMBER OF CONSECUTIVE
    GOOD MOVES"
```

```
145 PRINT "TO DEFINE FULL LEARNING":PRINT
150 INPUT LC%:LC=LC%:IF LC<=0 THEN 140
155 FOR MI=0 TO 4:FOR MJ=0 TO 4:FOR KL=1 TO 2
160 M(MI,MJ,KL)=2:NEXT KL,MJ,MI
165 CP=15773+RND(5)+64*(RND(5)-3)
170 CI=RND(5)-3:CJ=RND(5)-3:IF CI=0 AND CJ=0
    THEN 170
175 CS=0:GS=0:GM=0
180 CLS:GOSUB 1000:POKE CP,42
185 GOSUB 2000
190 IF NOT(CX=32 AND CY=32) THEN 205
195 POKE CP,32:CP=NP:POKE CP,42
200 GOTO 185
205 CS=CS+1
210 MI=CI+2:MJ=CJ+2
215 CI=M(MI,MJ,1):CJ=M(MI,MJ,2)
220 IF NOT(CI=2 AND CJ=2) THEN 240
225 CS=CS+1:GM=0
230 CI=RND(5)-1:CJ=RND(5)-1:IF CI=2 AND CJ=2
    THEN 230
235 GOTO 220
240 CI=CI-2:CJ=CJ-2:GOSUB 2000:CI=CI+2:CJ=CJ+2
245 IF NOT(CX=32 AND CY=32) THEN 225
250 M(MI,MJ,1)=CI:M(MI,MJ,2)=CJ
255 CI=CI-2:CJ=CJ-2
260 GS=GS+1:GM=GM+1:GOSUB 3000
265 IF GM <LC THEN 195
270 PRINT @ 832,STRING$(64,32);
275 PRINT @ 832,"LEARNING COMPLETE AT"CS-GM
    "CONTACTS"
280 INPUT "STRIKE 'ENTER' TO RUN A NEW
    CREATURE";S$
285 GOTO 155
290 REM
295 REM
1000 REM ** BORDER, V.1-TRS-80 **
1005 F0=15360:F1=15423:F2=16128:F3=16191
1010 FOR N=F0 TO F1:POKE N,176:NEXT N
1015 FOR N=F2 TO F3:POKE N,131:NEXT N
1020 FOR N=F0 TO F2 STEP 64:POKE N,170:NEXT N
1025 FOR N=F1 TO F3 STEP 64:POKE N,149:NEXT N
1030 POKE F0,160:POKE F1,144:POKE F2,130:POKE
```

```
      F3,129
1035  RETURN
1040  REM
1045  REM
2000  REM ** SEARCH AHEAD, V.1—TRS-80 **
2005  NP=CP:CX=32:CY=32
2010  SI=SGN(CI):SJ=SGN(CJ):AI=ABS(CI):AJ=ABS(CJ)
2015  IF AI=0 THEN 2030 ELSE AI=AI−1
2020  IF SI >0 THEN NP=NP+1 ELSE NP=NP−1
2025  CX=PEEK(NP)
2030  IF AJ=0 THEN 2045 ELSE AJ=AJ−1
2035  IF SJ >0 THEN NP=NP+64 ELSE NP=NP−64
2040  CY=PEEK(NP)
2045  IF NOT(CX=32 AND CY=32) THEN RETURN
2050  IF AI=0 AND AJ=0 THEN RETURN ELSE GOTO 2015
2055  REM
2060  REM
3000  REM ** SCORING ROUPNES, V.1—TRS-80 **
3005  AS=GS/CS
3010  PRINT @ 832,"CONTACTS","GOOD    MOVES",
      "SCORE"
3015  PRINT @ 896,STRING$(64,32);
3020  PRINT @ 896,CS,GS;:PRINT @ 928,USING F$;AS;
3025  RETURN
```

reached that definition yet, go back to the main running
loop to continue normal operations.

Lines 270-280—Do these operations only when the criterion
for full learning has been reached. Clear the scoring
portion of the screen, print the results, then wait for a
keyboard response to start a new creature from line 155.
The function CS-GM shows the total number of CON-
TACTS, less the number used for determining whether
or not the habit pattern has been established.

Lines 1000-1025—BORDER drawing subroutine.

Lines 2000-2050—SEARCH AHEAD subroutine.

Lines 3000-3025—SCORING display subroutine.

Apple II Version

The variable list and programming for FUNDAMENTAL
BETA WITH SCORING AND LEARNING DETECTION are
shown in Table 19-6 and Listing 19-6, respectively.

Table 19-6. Apple II Variable List for FUNDA-
MENTAL BETA WITH SCORING AND LEARNING DETECTION.

```
APPLESOFT VERSION

FN R(R)      Random function for motion codes, −2 to 2
N,M          General-purpose numeric variables
M(m,n,k)     Beta memory variables; m is CI of current motion
             code, n is CJ of current motion code, k is the
             response  motion-code selector—1 for CI, 2 for CJ
KL           Memory response select; 1 for CI, 2 for CJ
LC,LC%       Number of consecutive good moves to define learning
PX           Horizontal component of creature's current screen position
PY           Vertical component of creature's current screen position
NX           Horizontal component of creature's next screen position
NY           Vertical component of creature's next screen position
CI           Horizontal component of motion code
CJ           Vertical component of motion code
CX           Horizontal component of contact code
CY           Vertical component of contact code
CS           CONTACT score
GS           GOOD score
AS           Overall SCORE
GM           Current number of consecutive good moves
SI           Sign value of CI
SJ           Sign value of CJ
AI           Absolute value of CI
AJ           Absolute value of CJ
```

Listing 19-6. Apple II Program Listing for
FUNDAMENTAL BETA WITH SCORING AND LEARNING DETECTION.

```
10  REM   FUNDAMENTAL BETA WITH
15  REM   SCORING AND LEARNING DETECTION
20  REM      APPLESOFT
25  REM
30  REM
100 REM ** BETA PSYCH MAINLINE, V.3—APPLESOFT **
105 DEF FN R(R) = INT (5 * RND (1)) − 2
110 TEXT : HOME : VTAB (8): PRINT TAB(12)"BETA WITH
    SCORING"
115 PRINT TAB(10)"AND LEARNING DETECTION"
120 VTAB (15):PRINT "STRIKE 'RETURN' TO START . . ."
125 N = FN R(0):N = PEEK ( − 16384): POKE − 16368,0
130 IF N < > 141 THEN 125
135 HOME : DIM M(4,4,2)
140 PRINT : PRINT "ENTER NUMBER OF CONSECUTIVE
    GOOD MOVES"
145 PRINT "TO DEFINE LEARNING": PRINT
```

```
150 INPUT LC%:LC = LC%: IF LC < = 0 THEN 140
155 FOR M = 0 TO 4: FOR N = 0 TO 4: FOR KL = 1 TO 2
160 M(M,N,KL) = 2: NEXT KL,N,M
165 PX = 20 + FN R(0):PY = 20 + FN R(0)
170 CI = FN R(0):CJ = FN R(0): IF CI = 0 AND CJ = 0 THEN
    170
175 CS = 0:GS = 0:GM = 0
180 HOME : GR : GOSUB 1000
185 GOSUB 2000
190 IF NOT (CX = 0 AND CY = 0) THEN 215
195 COLOR= 0: PLOT PX,PY
200 PX = NX:PY = NY
205 COLOR= 9: PLOT PX,PY
210 GOTO 185
215 CS = CS + 1
220 MI = CI + 2:MJ = CJ + 2
225 CI = M(MI,MJ,1):CJ = M(MI,MJ,2)
230 IF NOT (CI=2 AND CJ=2) THEN 250
235 CS = CS + 1:GM = 0
240 CI = FN R(0) + 2:CJ = FN R(0) + 2: IF CI = 2 AND CJ = 2
    THEN 240
245 GOTO 230
250 CI = CI – 2:CJ = CJ – 2: GOSUB 2000:CI = CI + 2:CJ =
    CJ + 2
255 IF NOT (CX = 0 AND CY = 0) THEN 235
260 M(MI,MJ,1) = CI:M(MI,MJ,2) = CJ
265 CI = CI – 2:CJ = CJ – 2
270 GS = GS + 1:GM = GM + 1: GOSUB 3000
275 IF GM < LC THEN 195
280 HOME : PRINT "LEARNING IS COMPLETE AT" CS/ GM
    "CONTACTS"
285 PRINT : INPUT "STRIKE 'RETURN' TO RUN A NEW
    CREATURE";S$
290 GOTO 155
295 REM
300 REM
1000 REM ** BORDER, V.1—APPLESOFT **
1005 COLOR= 15
1010 HLIN 0,39 AT 0: HLIN 0,39 AT 36
1015 VLIN 0,36 AT 0: VLIN 0,36 AT 39
1020 RETURN
1025 REM
```

```
1030 REM
2000 REM ** SEARCH AHEAD, V.1—APPLESOFT **
2005 NX = PX:NY = PY:CX = 0:CY = 0
2010 SI = SGN (CI):SJ = SGN (CJ):AI = ABS (CI):AJ = ABS
     (CJ)
2015 IF AI = 0 THEN 2040
2020 AI = AI − 1
2025 IF SI > 0 THEN NX = NX + 1: GOTO 2035
2030 NX = NX − 1
2035 CX = SCRN(NX,NY)
2040 IF AJ = 0 THEN 2065
2045 AJ = AJ − 1
2050 IF SJ > 0 THEN NY = NY + 1: GOTO 2060
2055 NY = NY − 1
2060 CY = SCRN(NX,NY)
2065 IF NOT (CX = 0 AND CY = 0) THEN RETURN
2070 IF AI = 0 AND AJ = 0 THEN RETURN
2075 GOTO 2015
2080 REM
2085 REM
3000 REM ** SCORING ROUTINES, V.1—APPLESOFT **
3005 AS = INT ((GS / CS) * 1000) / 1000
3010 HOME : PRINT "CONTACTS","GOOD","SCORE"
3015 PRINT CS,GS,AS
3020 RETURN
3025 REM
3030 REM
```

Lines 105-135—Initialize the system, including running the
        random number generator until the user strikes the
        RETURN key.
Lines 140-150—Allow the user to enter the learning criterion.
Lines 155-160—Initialize the Beta memory by clearing its
        contents to stop codes.
Lines 165-170—Initialize the creature's screen position and
        motion code.
Line 175—Zero the CONTACT and GOOD scores; set the
        habit counter to zero.
Line 180—Clear the screen, set the graphics mode, and draw
        the conventional border figure.
Lines 185-210—This is the main running loop. Do the
        SEARCH AHEAD routine, break out of the loop if the
        path ahead is not clear, move the creature to its next

position on the screen, and jump back to continue the loop.

Lines 215-225—Increment the CONTACT score, set the Beta variables, and fetch the response from Beta memory.

Line 230—This is the VALID check.

Line 235—Increment the CONTACT score and reset the habit count to zero. The latter instruction is justified on the grounds that any ongoing succession of good moves is broken by entering this phase of the program.

Lines 240-245—Fetch a random motion code and jump back to the VALID check.

Lines 250-255—Check the workability of the current motion code by doing SEARCH AHEAD with the appropriately adjusted versions of the motion code. Take appropriate action based upon whether or not the path ahead is clear.

Lines 260-265—Load the working response to Beta memory and adjust the current motion code for normal running operations.

Line 270—Increment the GOOD score, increment the habit count, and display the current scoring on the screen.

Line 275—Check to see whether or not the habit pattern has been established. If the current habit count is less than the criterion for full learning that was established in the initialization phase, resume normal operations from line 195 in the main running loop.

Lines 280-290—Do these operations only when the criterion for full learning has been reached. Clear the scoring portion of the screen, print the actual number of CONTACTS to the beginning of the habit pattern, and wait for the user to strike RETURN to start a new creature from line 155.

Lines 1000-1020—Standard BORDER drawing subroutine.

Lines 2000-2075—SEARCH AHEAD subroutine.

Lines 3000-3020—SCORING subroutine.

A SUGGESTED EXPERIMENT WITH OBSTACLES

Question: Would the introduction of some number of fixed obstacles within the environment affect the learning curve for Beta creatures?

Hypothesis: Until there are so many obstacles that a creature can become hopelessly trapped among them, the introduction of fixed obstacles should not affect the average rate of learning.

Experiment: Devise a modified version of Listing 19-5 (TRS-80) or Listing 19-6 (Apple II) such that a desired number of fixed, randomly distributed obstacles can be introduced into the environment. Run the tests with a varying number of obstacles and a fixed number of good moves to learning.

This one, dear reader, is left to your own design. Draw your own conclusion about the validity of the hypothesis and experiment.

Appendix A
Integer Basic Versions
of the Apple II Programs

The Apple II programs and descriptive text in the main body of this book apply only to systems equipped with Applesoft BASIC. This appendix is intended for Apple users who wish to use Integer BASIC programming.

Each section refers to a chapter in the main body of the book. Included are: (1) Integer BASIC version of the *variable list*, (2) Integer BASIC version of the Apple program listings, and (3) a *line-by-line analysis* of the theory of operation as it applies to the Integer BASIC programming.

For easier identification, the listings are cited with a letter *A* preceding the listing number of the corresponding Applesoft version in the main body of the book. So if you want to write an Integer BASIC version of the Applesoft listing, Listing 6-2, look up Listing A6-2 in this appendix.

Unless stated otherwise, the instructions for loading the programs, descriptions of events taking place on the screen, and operating instructions are identical to the Applesoft versions.

SEARCH AHEAD, V.1

The following material is the Integer BASIC version of the Apple II discussion and program in Chapter 2.

Variable List

The variable list is identical to the one shown in Table 2-2.

Program Listing

```
2000 REM ** SEARCH AHEAD, V.1—APPLE INTEGER **
2005 NX=PX:NY=PY:CX=0:CY=0
2010 SI= SGN (CI):SJ= SGN (CJ):AI= ABS (CI):AJ= ABS
     (CJ)
2015 IF AI=0 THEN 2040
2020 AI=AI-1
2025 IF SI >0 THEN NX=NX+1
2030 IF SI <0 THEN NX=NX-1
2035 CX= SCRN(NX,NY)
2040 IF AJ=0 THEN 2065
2045 AJ=AJ-1
2050 IF SJ >0 THEN NY=NY+1
2055 IF SJ <0 THEN NY=NY-1
2060 CY= SCRN(NX,NY)
2065 IF NOT (CX=0 AND CY=0) THEN RETURN
2070 IF AI=0 AND AJ= 0 THEN RETURN
2075 GOTO 2015
```

Program Analysis

Line 2005—Set the horizontal and vertical components of the creature's next step equal to their present-position counterparts. Zero the horizontal and vertical components of the contact codes.

Line 2010—Set the sign and absolute values of the current motion codes.

Line 2015—If there are no more horizontal steps to search, jump down to check vertical steps.

Lines 2020-2030—Count down the number of horizontal steps to search. If the motion code is to the right, set NX to its next-higher value; otherwise, set it to the next-lower value.

Line 2035—Get the contact code for the next position.

Lines 2040-2060—Run the same routine as lines 2015-2035, but refer to vertical components of motion.

Line 2065—If SEARCH AHEAD finds somthing other than a blank space in the next position, return to the main program.

Line 2070—If all steps have been checked, return to the main program.

Line 2075—Otherwise, check the next set of steps ahead.

FUNDAMENTAL ALPHA DEMO

The following material is the Integer BASIC version of the Apple II program and discussions in Chapter 3.

Variable List

The Integer BASIC variable list is identical to the Applesoft version in Table 3-2.

Program Listing

```
  10 REM   FUNDAMENTAL ALPHA DEMO
  15 REM   APPLE INTEGER BASIC
  20 REM
  25 REM
 100 REM ** MAINLINE, V.1—APPLE INTEGER **
 105 CALL -936: GR
 110 GOSUB 1000
 115 TAB 5: PRINT "FUNDAMENTAL ALPHA DEMO"
 120 PX=18+ RND (5):PY=18+ RND (5)
 125 CI= RND (5)—2:CJ= RND (5)—2: IF CI=0 AND CJ=0
     THEN 125
 130 GOSUB 2000
 135 IF NOT (CX=0 AND CY=0) THEN 125
 140 COLOR=0: PLOT PX,PY
 145 PX=NX:PY=NY
 150 COLOR=9: PLOT PX,PY
 155 GOTO 130
 160 REM
 165 REM
1000 REM ** BORDER,V.1—APPLE INTEGER **
1005 COLOR=15
1010 HLIN 0,39 AT 0: HLIN 0,39 AT 36
1015 VLIN 0,36 AT 0: VLIN 0,36 AT 39
1020 RETURN
1025 REM
1030 REM
2000 REM ** SEARCH AHEAD, V.1—APPLE INTEGER **
2005 NX=PX:NY=PY:CX=0:CY=0
2010 SI= SGN (CI):SJ= SGN (CJ):AI= ABS (CI):AJ= ABS
     (CJ)
2015 IF AI=0 THEN 2040
2020 AI=AI—1
```

301

```
2025 IF SI >0 THEN NX=NX+1
2030 IF SI <0 THEN NX=NX-1
2035 CX= SCRN(NX,NY)
2040 IF AJ=0 THEN 2065
2045 AJ=AJ-1
2050 IF SJ >0 THEN NY=NY+1
2055 IF SJ <0 THEN NY=NY-1
2060 CY= SCRN(NX,NY)
2065 IF NOT (CX=0 AND CY=0) THEN RETURN
2070 IF AI=0 AND AJ=0 THEN RETURN
2075 GOTO 2015
```

Program Analysis

Line 105—Clear the screen; set the graphics mode.

Line 110—Call the BORDER drawing subroutine.

Line 115—Print the title at the bottom of the screen.

Line 120—Pick a random starting place for the creature.

Line 125—Select a random motion code; if it is the stop code, select another one.

Line 130—Do the SEARCH AHEAD routine to see whether or not the creature is about to run into something.

Line 135—If the path ahead is obstructed, loop back to pick a new motion code.

Lines 140-150—Move the creature to its next position on the screen. This is done by erasing the current creature figure (line 140), setting the current position equal to the just-tested new position (line 145), and drawing the creature in its new position (line 150).

Line 155—Loop back to line 130 to search the next step ahead.

Lines 1000-1020—BORDER drawing subroutine.

Lines 2000-2075—SEARCH AHEAD subroutine.

FUNDAMENTAL ALPHA WITH SELECTABLE OPTIONS

The following material is the Integer BASIC version of the Apple II discussions and program in Chapter 4.

Variable List

CT Selected creature color (0-15)
TT Selected creature trail color (0-15)
S$ General-purpose string variable
PX Horizontal component of current creature position
PY Vertical component of current creature position

302

NX   Horizontal component of next creature position
NY   Vertical component of next creature position
CI   Horizontal component of motion code
CJ   Vertical component of motion code
CX   Horizontal component of contact code
CY   Vertical component of contact code
SI   Sign value of CI
SJ   Sign value of CJ
AI   Absolute value of CI
AJ   Absolute value of CJ

Program Listing

```
 10 REM   FUNDAMENTAL ALPHA DEMO
 15 REM   WITH SELECTABLE OPTIONS
 20 REM
 25 REM
 30 REM
100 REM ** MAINLINE, V.2—APPLE INTEGER **
105 CALL -936: PRINT
110 PRINT  "SELECT  A  CREATURE  COLOR  (0-15) " :
    PRINT :  INPUT CT
115 IF CT >0 AND CT<=15 THEN 125
120 PRINT "INVALID CREATURE COLOR—TRY AGAIN":
    PRINT : GOTO 110
125 IF CT#0 THEN 145
130 PRINT "CREATURE WILL BE INVISIBLE . . ."
135 PRINT "ARE YOU SURE YOU WANT THAT (Y/N)?";:
    INPUT S$
140 IF S$="Y" THEN 145: PRINT : GOTO 110
145 CALL -936: PRINT : PRINT "YOUR CREATURE COLOR
    IS";CT
150 PRINT : PRINT : PRINT "SELECT A TRAIL COLOR
    (0-15)": INPUT TT
155 IF TT >=0 AND TT <=15 THEN 165
160 PRINT "INVALID TRAIL CODE—TRY AGAIN": PRINT :
    GOTO 150
165 IF TT#0 THEN 185
170 PRINT : PRINT "TRAIL WILL BE INVISIBLE . . ."
175 PRINT "ARE YOU SURE YOU WANT THAT (Y/N)?":
    INPUT S$
180 IF S$="Y" THEN 185: PRINT : GOTO 145
```

```
185  CALL -936: PRINT : PRINT "CREATURE COLOR IS";CT
190  PRINT "TRAIL COLOR IS";TT
195  PRINT
200  PRINT "IS THAT WHAT YOU WANT (Y/N)?";: INPUT S$
205  IF S$="Y" THEN 210: GOTO 100
210  CALL -936: GR
215  GOSUB 1000
220  PX=18+ RND (5):PY=18+ RND (5)
225  CI= RND (5)–2:CJ= RND (5)–2: IF CI=0 AND CJ=0
     THEN 225
230  GOSUB 2000
235  IF PEEK (–16384) <=127 THEN 240: TEXT : CALL
     -936: GR : GOSUB 1000
240  POKE -16368,0: IF NOT (CX=0 AND CY=0) THEN 225
245  COLOR=TT:PLOT PX,PY
250  PX=NX:PY=NY
255  COLOR=CT: PLOT PX,PY
260  GOTO 230
265  REM
270  REM
1000 REM ** BORDER,V.1—APPLE INTEGER **
1005 COLOR=15
1010 HLIN 0,39 AT 0: HLIN 0,39 AT 36
1015 VLIN 0,36 AT 0: VLIN 0,36 AT 39
1020 RETURN
1025 REM
1030 REM
2000 REM ** SEARCH AHEAD, V.1—APPLE INTEGER **
2005 NX=PX:NY=PY:CX=0:CY=0
2010 SI=SGN (CI):SJ= SGN (CJ):AI= ABS (CI):AJ= ABS (CJ)
2015 IF AI=0 THEN 2040
2020 AI=AI–1
2025 IF SI >0 THEN NX=NX+1
2030 IF SI <0 THEN NX=NX–1
2035 CX= SCRN(NX,NY)
2040 IF AJ=0 THEN 2065
2045 AJ=AJ–1
2050 IF SJ >0 THEN NY=NY+1
2055 IF SJ <0 THEN NY=NY–1
2060 CY= SCRN(NX,NY)
2065 IF NOT (CX=0 AND CY=0) THEN RETURN
2070 IF AI=0 AND AJ=0 THEN RETURN
```

304

2075 GOTO 2015

Program Analysis

Line 105—Clear the screen; skip a line.

Lines 110-140—Get a valid creature color code (0-15) from the keyboard. If it is a number outside the valid range, request a corrected version. If it is 0, make sure the user really wants to use an "invisible" creature.

Lines 145-180—Get a valid trail color for the creature (0-15). If it is a number outside the valid range, request a corrected entry. If it is 0, make sure the user really wants to use an "invisible" trail that the creature cannot sense.

Lines 185-205—Summarize the selected creature and trail colors. Ask if they are OK. If not, do again from the start.

Line 210—Clear the screen and set the graphics mode.

Line 215—Call the BORDER drawing subroutine.

Line 220—Pick a random starting place for the creature.

Line 225—Pick a random motion code. If it is the stop code (CI and CJ are both zero), then pick again.

Line 230—Do the SEARCH AHEAD routine.

Line 235—If any key is depressed, clear the screen and redraw the BORDER figure.

Line 240—If the path ahead is obstructed, jump back to pick a new motion code.

Lines 245-260—Otherwise, move the creature to its next position and jump back to search the path ahead again.

Lines 1000-1020—BORDER drawing subroutine.

Lines 2000-2075—SEARCH AHEAD subroutine.

KILLER ALPHA DEMO

The following material is the Integer BASIC version of the Apple II discussions and program in Chapter 5.

Variable List

PX Horizontal component of current creature position
PY Vertical component of current creature position
NX Horizontal component of next position
NY Vertical component of next position
TX Horizontal component of a "thing" position
TY Vertical component of a "thing" position
N   Number of "things" to be plotted

CI Horizontal component of motion code
CJ Vertical component of motion code
KC Kill code: 0 is "don't kill," 1 is "do kill"
SI Sign value of CI
SJ Sign value of CJ
AI Absolute value of CI
AJ Absolute value of CJ

Program Listing

```
  10 REM   KILLER ALPHA DEMO
  15 REM   APPLE INTEGER
  20 REM
  25 REM
  30 REM
 100 REM ** ALPHA MAINLINE, V.3—APPLE INTEGER **
 105 CALL -936: GR
 110 GOSUB 1000: TAB 16: PRINT "KILLER ALPHA"
 115 PX=18+ RND (5):PY=18+ RND (5): COLOR=9: PLOT
     PX,PY
 120 FOR N=0 TO 63
 125 TX= RND (38)+1:TY= RND (35)+1
 130 IF SCRN(TX,TY)#0 THEN 125
 135 COLOR= RND (12)+1: PLOT TX,TY
 140 NEXT N
 145 CI= RND (5)–2:CJ= RND (5)–2: IF CI=0 AND CJ=0
     THEN 145
 150 GOSUB 2000
 155 IF NOT (CX=0 AND CY=0) THEN 175
 160 COLOR=0: PLOT PX,PY
 165 PX=NX:PY=NY
 170 COLOR=9: PLOT PX,PY: GOTO 150
 175 KC= RND (2): IF KC=0 THEN 145
 180 IF SCRN(NX,NY) <14 THEN 190
 185 COLOR=14: PLOT NX,NY: GOTO 150
 190 COLOR=0: PLOT NX,NY: GOTO 150
1000 REM ** BORDER,V.1—APPLE INTEGER **
1005 COLOR=15
1010 HLIN 0,39 AT 0: HLIN 0,39 AT 36
1015 VLIN 0,36 AT 0: VLIN 0,36 AT 39
1020 RETURN
1025 REM
```

```
1030 REM
2000 REM ** SEARCH AHEAD, V.1—APPLE INTEGER **
2005 NX=PX:NY=PY:CX=0:CY=0
2010 SI= SGN (CI):SJ= SGN (CJ):AI= ABS (CI):AJ= ABS
     (CJ)
2015 IF AI=0 THEN 2040
2020 AI=AI−1
2025 IF SI >0 THEN NX=NX+1
2030 IF SI <0 THEN NX=NX−1
2035 CX=SCRN(NX,NY)
2040 IF AJ=0 THEN 2065
2045 AJ=AJ−1
2050 IF SJ >0 THEN NY=NY+1
2055 IF SJ <0 THEN NY=NY−1
2060 CY= SCRN(NX,NY)
2065 IF NOT (CX=0 AND CY=0) THEN RETURN
2070 IF AI=0 AND AJ=0 THEN RETURN
2075 GOTO 2015
```

Program Analysis

Line 105—Clear the screen and set the graphics mode.

Line 110—Draw the BORDER figure and print the title near the bottom of the screen.

Line 115—Pick a random initial position for the creature; plot it on the screen.

Lines 120-140—Plot 64 "things" on the screen. Pick a random position for one of them (line 125); but if something else is already plotted there, pick another random position (line 130). Plot the "thing" with a random color.

Line 145—Pick a random motion code for the creature. If it is the 0,0 stop code, pick another.

Line 150—Do the SEARCH AHEAD routine.

Line 155—If the path ahead is obstructed, jump down to get a kill code.

Lines 160-170—Move the creature and jump back to search the path ahead again.

Line 175—Pick a random kill code (0 or 1). If it is the "don't kill" code, jump back to line 145 to get a new random motion code. That amounts to running away from the obstacle.

Line 180—If the obstacle is one of the "things," jump down to wipe it out; kill it.

Line 185—At this point in the program, the obstacle must be a segment of the border figure. So plot a green spot there, and jump back to do the search ahead routine.

Line 190—Kill whatever is in the path ahead, and jump back to the search ahead routine to see if the destruction is complete.

Lines 1000-1020—BORDER drawing subroutine.

Lines 2000-2075—SEARCH AHEAD subroutine.

MULTIPLE ALPHA DEMO

The following material is the Integer BASIC version of the Apple II discussions and program in Chapter 6.

Variable List

CN	Current creature number (1 or 2)
AC(CN)	Operating phase for creature CN
PX(CN)	Horizontal component of current screen position for creature CN
PY(CN)	Vertical component of current screen position for creature CN
NX(CN)	Horizontal component of next screen position for creature CN
NY(CN)	Vertical component of next screen position for creature CN
CI(CN)	Horizontal component of motion code for creature CN
CJ(CN)	Vertical component of motion code for creature CN
CX(CN)	Horizontal component of contact code for creature CN
CY(CN)	Vertical component of contact code for creature CN
CT(CN)	Color code for creature CN
PX	Horizontal component of current screen position
PY	Vertical component of current screen position
NX	Horizontal component of next screen position
NY	Vertical component of next screen position
CI	Horizontal component of motion code
CJ	Vertical component of motion code
CX	Horizontal component of contact code
CY	Vertical component of contact code
SI	Sign value of CI
SJ	Sign value of CJ
AI	Absolute value of CI
AJ	Absolute value of CJ
N	General-purpose numeric variable

Program Listing

```
  10 REM   MULTIPLE ALPHA DEMO
  15 REM      APPLE INTEGER
  20 REM
  25 REM
  30 REM
 100 REM ** ALPHA MAINLINE, V.4—APPLE INTEGER **
 105 DIM AC(2),PX(2),PY(2),NX(2),NY(2),CI(2),
     CJ(2),CX(2),CY(2),CT(2)
 115 CT(1)=9:CT(2)=7
 120 FOR CN=1 TO 2
 125 PX(CN)=18+ RND (5):PY(CN)=18+ RND (5): NEXT CN
 130 IF PX(1)=PX(2) AND PY(1)=PY(2) THEN 120
 135 CALL -936: GR : GOSUB 1000
 140 AC(1)=1:AC(2)=1:CN=1
 145 IF AC(CN)=1 THEN 160: GOTO 175
 150 IF CN=1 THEN 155:CN=1: GOTO 145
 155 CN=2: GOTO 145
 160 FOR N=1 TO 2:CI(N)= RND (5)-2:CJ(N)= RND (5)-2:
     NEXT N
 165 IF CI(CN)=0 AND CJ(CN)=0 THEN 160
 170 AC(CN)=2: GOTO 150
 175 PX=PX(CN); PY=PY(CN:CI=CI(CN):CJ=CJ(CN)
 180 GOSUB 2000
 185 IF (CX=0 AND CY=0) THEN 190:AC(CN)=1: GOTO 210
 190 COLOR=0: PLOT PX,PY
 195 PX=NX:PY=NY
 200 COLOR=CT(CN): PLOT PX,PY
 205 AC(CN)=2
 210 PX(CN)=PX:PY(CN)=PY:CI(CN)=CI:CJ(CN)=CJ
 215 GOTO 150
 220 REM
 225 REM
1000 REM ** BORDER,V.1—APPLE INTEGER **
1005 COLOR=15
1010 HLIN 0,39 AT 0: HLIN 0,39 AT 36
1015 VLIN 0,36 AT 0: VLIN 0,36 AT 39
1020 RETURN
1025 REM
1030 REM
2000 REM ** SEARCH AHEAD, V.1—APPLE INTEGER **
2005 NX=PX:NY=PY:CX=0:CY=0
```

309

```
2010 SI= SGN (CI):SJ= SGN (CJ):AI= ABS (CI):AJ= ABS
     (CJ)
2015 IF AI=0 THEN 2040
2020 AI=AI-1
2025 IF SI >0 THEN NX=NX+1
2030 IF SI <0 THEN NX=NX-1
2035 CX= SCRN(NX,NY)
2040 IF AJ=0 THEN 2065
2045 AJ=AJ-1
2050 IF SJ >0 THEN NY=NY+1
2055 IF SJ <0 THEN NY=NY-1
2060 CY= SCRN(NX,NY)
2065 IF NOT (CX=0 AND CY=0) THEN RETURN
2070 IF AI=0 AND AJ=0 THEN RETURN
2075 GOTO 2015
```

Program Analysis

Line 105—Dimension the creature variables.

Line 115—Set the creature colors: creature 1 is orange, creature 2 is light blue.

Lines 120-130—Set random initial positions for the two creatures; do again if they happen to fall on top of one another.

Line 135—Clear the screen, set the graphics mode, and call subroutine 1000 to draw the BORDER.

Line 140—Set the operating phases for both creatures at 1; set the system to work with creature 1 first.

Line 145—Select the operations for the creature currently being serviced by the multiplexing cycle.

Lines 150-155—Swap the creature being serviced; repeat the multiplexing cycle.

Lines 160-165—Select random motion codes for the creature being serviced. If the codes make up a 0,0 stop code, pick another motion code.

Line 170—Set for phase-2 operations and swap creatures.

Lines 175-180—This is the beginning of phase-2 operations. Adjust the current position and motion codes to make them compatible with the SEARCH AHEAD subroutine. Call that subroutine.

Line 185—If the path ahead is clear, then jump to line 190 to move the creature being serviced; otherwise, set the creature for doing phase-operations (pick a new random motion code) again.

Lines 190-205—Move the current creature and set it up to repeat phase-2 operations when its turn comes around again.

Lines 210-215—Adjust the results of the SEARCH AHEAD routine so that the variables are compatible with those of the creature being served by the multiplexing scheme. Jump back to line 150 to service the other creature.

Lines 1000-1020—BORDER drawing subroutine.

Lines 2000-2075—SEARCH AHEAD subroutine.

SIMPLE ALPHA COMMUNITY

The following material is the Integer BASIC version of the Apple II discussions and program in Chapter 7.

Variable List

CQ	Selected number of Alpha creatures (1-10)
TQ	Selected number of fixed obstacles (0-63)
N	General-purpose numerical variable
S$	General-purpose string variable
TX	Horizontal component of an obstacle's screen position
TY	Vertical component of an obstacle's screen position
CN	Current creature number (1-CQ)
AC(CN)	Current operating phase for creature CN
PX(CN)	Horizontal component of screen position for creature CN
PY(CN)	Vertical component of screen position for creature CN
NX(CN)	Horizontal component of next screen position for creature CN
NY(CN)	Vertical component of next screen position for creature CN
CI(CN)	Horizontal component of motion code for creature CN
CJ(CN)	Vertical component of motion code for creature CN
CX(CN)	Horizontal component of contact code for creature CN

CY(CN)	Vertical component of contact code for creature CN
CT(CN)	Color code for creature CN
PY	Vertical component of current screen position
PX	Horizontal component of current screen position
NX	Horizontal component of next screen position
NY	Vertical component of next screen position
CI	Horizontal component of motion code
CJ	Vertical component of motion code
CX	Horizontal component of contact code
CY	Vertical component of contact code
SI	Sign value of CI
SJ	Sign value of CJ
AI	Absolute value of CI
AJ	Absolute value of CJ

Program Listing

```
 10 REM   SIMPLE ALPHA COMMUNITY
 15 REM   APPLE INTEGER BASIC
 20 REM
 25 REM
 30 REM
100 REM ** ALPHA MAINLINE, V.5—APPLE INTEGER
    BASIC **
105 TEXT : CALL -936
110 PRINT : PRINT "HOW MANY ALPHA CREATURES"
115 PRINT "IN THE COMMUNITY (1-10) ";
120 INPUT CQ : IF CQ >0 AND CQ <=10 THEN 135
125 PRINT : PRINT "INVALID NUMBER OF CREATURES
    ..."
130 TAB 5: PRINT "TRY AGAIN.": GOTO 110
135 CALL -936: PRINT "THERE WILL BE ";CQ
140 PRINT " CREATURES IN THE COMMUNITY."
145 PRINT : PRINT "HOW MANY OBSTACLES (0-63) ";
150 INPUT TQ: IF TQ >=0 AND TQ <=63 THEN 165
155 PRINT : PRINT "INVALID NUMBER OF OBSTACLES
    ..."
160 TAB 5: PRINT "TRY AGAIN.": GOTO 145
165 CALL -936: PRINT : PRINT "THERE WILL BE ";CQ;
    " CREATURES"
170 PRINT "AND ";TQ; " OBSTACLES ";
```

```
175  PRINT "IN THE COMMUNITY."
180  PRINT : PRINT "OK (Y/N)? ";: INPUT S$
185  IF S$="Y" THEN 190: GOTO 105
190  DIM AC(CQ),PX(CQ),PY(CQ),NX(CQ),NY(CQ)
195  DIM CI(CQ),CJ(CQ),CX(CQ),CY(CQ),CT(CQ)
200  CALL -936: GR : GOSUB 1000
205  COLOR=15: IF TQ=0 THEN 230
210  FOR N=1 TO TQ
215  TX= RND (38)+1:TY= RND (35)+1
220  IF SCRN(TX,TY)#0 THEN 215
225  PLOT TX,TY: NEXT N
230  FOR CN=1 TO CQ
235  PX(CN)= RND (38)+1
240  PY(CN)= RND (35)+1
245  IF SCRN(PX(CN),PY(CN))#0 THEN 235
250  COLOR=CN: PLOT PX(CN),PY(CN)
255  CT(CN)=CN: NEXT CN
260  FOR CN=1 TO CQ:AC(CN)=1: NEXT CN
265  FOR CN=1 TO CQ
270  IF AC(CN)=1 THEN 280: GOTO 295
275  NEXT CN: GOTO 265
280  CI(CN)= RND (5)-2:CJ(CN)= RND (5)-2
285  IF CI(CN)=0 AND CJ(CN)=0 THEN 280
290  AC(CN)=2: GOTO 275
295  REM
300  PX=PX(CN):PY=PY(CN):CI=CI(CN):CJ=CJ(CN)
305  REM
310  GOSUB 2000
315  IF CX=0 AND CY=0 THEN 320:AC(CN)=1: GOTO 335
320  COLOR=0: PLOT PX,PY
325  PX=NX:PY=NY
330  COLOR=CT(CN): PLOT PX,PY:AC(CN)=2
335  PX(CN)=PX:PY(CN)=PY
340  CI(CN)=CI:CJ(CN)=CJ
345  GOTO 275
350  REM
355  REM
1000 REM ** BORDER,V.1—APPLE INTEGER **
1005 COLOR=15
1010 HLIN 0,39 AT 0: HLIN 0,39 AT 36
1015 VLIN 0,36 AT 0: VLIN 0,36 AT 39
1020 RETURN
```

```
1025 REM
1030 REM
2000 REM ** SEARCH AHEAD, V.1—APPLE INTEGER **
2005 NX=PX:NY=PY:CX=0:CY=0
2010 SI= SGN (CI):SJ= SGN (CJ):AI= ABS (CI):AJ= ABS
     (CJ)
2015 IF AI=0 THEN 2040
2020 AI=AI−1
2025 IF SI >0 THEN NX=NX+1
2030 IF SI <0 THEN NX=NX−1
2035 CX= SCRN(NX,NY)
2040 IF AJ=0 THEN 2065
2045 AJ=AJ−1
2050 IF SJ >0 THEN NY=NY+1
2055 IF SJ <0 THEN NY=NY−1
2060 CY= SCRN(NX,NY)
2065 IF NOT (CX=0 AND CY=0) THEN RETURN
2070 IF AI=0 AND AJ=0 THEN RETURN
2075 GOTO 2015
```

Program Analysis

Line 105—Set the text mode and clear the screen.

Lines 110-140—Enter a valid number of creatures to be placed into the community. If the number is invalid, give the user another chance. Confirm the selection.

Lines 145-160—Enter a valid number of obstacles to be placed into the community. If the number is invalid, give the user another chance to get it straight.

Lines 165-185—Confirm the number of creatures and obstacles that have been selected. Give the user a chance to change things.

Lines 190-195—Dimension the variables.

Line 200—Clear the screen, set the graphics mode, and draw the BORDER figure.

Line 205—Set the obstacle color to white. But if there are to be no obstacles, jump to the creature-drawing operations.

Lines 210-225—Plot the designated number of obstacles at random, non-overlapping places on the screen.

Lines 230-255—Plot the designated number of creatures in non-overlapping initial positions. Use a different color (CN) for each creature.

Line 260—Initialize all creatures for phase-1 operations.

Lines 265-275—Cycle the creatures, one at a time, through their operating phases. Jump to line 280 for phase-1 operations, and to line 295 for phase-2 operations.

Lines 280-290—Phase-1 operations: select a random motion code, and select again if it's the stop code. Set the creature being serviced for phase-2 operations and return to the multiplexing routine to work with the next creature.

Lines 295-310—Adjust the current creature variables to make them compatible with the SEARCH AHEAD subroutine. Run the SEARCH AHEAD subroutine.

Line 315—If there is no contact with an obstacle, then move the current creature. Otherwise, set the current creature for phase-1 operations and return to the multiplexing routine.

Lines 320-330—Move the current creature.

Lines 335-345—Adjust the SEARCH AHEAD variables to make them compatible with the creature currently being serviced. Return to the multiplexing routine.

Lines 1000-1020—BORDER drawing subroutine.

Lines 2000-2075—SEARCH AHEAD subroutine.

DUAL KILLER DEMO

The following material is the Integer BASIC version of the Apple II discussions and programming in Chapter 8.

Variable List

CN	Creature being serviced by the multiplexing system (1 or 2)
AC(CN)	Operating phase for creature CN
PX(CN)	Horizontal component of current screen position for creature CN
PY(CN)	Vertical component of current screen position for creature CN
NX(CN)	Horizontal component of next screen position for creature CN
NY(CN)	Vertical component of next screen position for creature CN
CI(CN)	Horizontal component of motion code for creature CN
CJ(CN)	Vertical component of motion code for creature CN

CX(CN)	Horizontal component of contact code for creature CN
CY(CN)	Vertical component of contact code for creature CN
CT(CN)	Color code for creature CN
PX	Horizontal component of current screen position
PY	Vertical component of current screen position
NX	Horizontal component of next screen position
NY	Vertical component of next screen position
CI	Horizontal component of motion code
CJ	Vertical component of motion code
CX	Horizontal component of contact code
CY	Vertical component of contact code
SI	Sign value of CI
SJ	Sign value of CJ
AI	Absolute value of CI
AJ	Absolute value of CJ
TX	Horizontal component of a killable thing position
TY	Vertical component of a killable thing position
N	General-purpose numerical variable
S$,T$	General-purpose string variables
KC	Kill code (0 for "no-kill," 1 for "kill")
PP	Color code of object about to be killed

Program Listing

```
 10 REM   DUAL KILLER DEMO
 15 REM   APPLE INTEGER BASIC
 20 REM
 25 REM
 30 REM
100 REM ** ALPHA MAINLINE, V.6—APPLE INTEGER **
105 DIM AC(2),PX(2),PY(2),NX(2),NY(2)
110 DIM CI(2),CJ(2),CX(2),CY(2),CT(2)
115 DIM S$(6),T$(6)
120 CT(1)=9:CT(2)=7
125 CALL -936: GR : GOSUB 1000
130 FOR CN=1 TO 2
135 PX(CN)= RND (38)+1:PY(CN)= RND (35)+1
140 IF SCRN(PX(CN),PY(CN))#0 THEN 135
145 COLOR=CT(CN)
150 PLOT PX(CN),PY(CN)
155 AC(CN)=1: NEXT CN
```

```
160 COLOR=13: FOR N=0 TO 63
165 TX= RND (38)+1:TY= RND (35)+1
170 IF SCRN(TX,TY)#0 THEN 165
175 PLOT TX,TY: NEXT N
180 FOR CN=1 TO 2
185 IF AC(CN)=1 THEN 195: IF AC(CN)=2 THEN 215:
    GOTO 270
190 NEXT CN: GOTO 180
195 CI(CN)= RND (5)-2
200 CJ(CN)= RND (5)-2
205 IF CI(CN)=0 AND CJ(CN)=0 THEN 195
210 AC(CN)=2: GOTO 190
215 PX=PX(CN):PY=PY(CN)
220 CI=CI(CN):CJ=CJ(CN)
225 GOSUB 2000
230 IF CX=0 AND CY=0 THEN 235:AC(CN)=3: GOTO 255
235 COLOR=0: PLOT PX,PY
240 PX=NX:PY=NY
245 COLOR=CT(CN): PLOT PX,PY
250 AC(CN)=2
255 PX(CN)=PX:PY(CN)=PY
260 NX(CN)=NX:NY(CN)=NY
265 GOTO 190
270 KC= RND (2)
275 IF KC=1 THEN 280:AC(CN)=1: GOTO 190
280 PP= SCRN(NX(CN),NY(CN))
285 IF PP <14 THEN 300
290 COLOR=14: PLOT NX(CN),NY(CN)
295 GOTO 330
300 COLOR=0: PLOT NX(CN),NY(CN)
305 IF NOT (PP=CT(1) OR PP=CT(2)) THEN 330
310 IF PP#9 THEN 315:S$="ORANGE":T$="BLUE":
    GOTO 320
315 S$="BLUE":T$="ORANGE"
320 CALL -936:PRINT T$;"HAS JUST KILLED ";S$
325 INPUT S$: CALL -936
330 AC(CN)=2: GOTO 190
335 REM
340 REM
```

```
1000 REM ** BORDER,V.1—APPLE INTEGER **
1005 COLOR=15
1010 HLIN 0,39 AT 0: HLIN 0,39 AT 36
1015 VLIN 0,36 AT 0: VLIN 0,36 AT 39
1020 RETURN
1025 REM
1030 REM
2000 REM ** SEARCH AHEAD, V.1—APPLE INTEGER **
2005 NX=PX:NY=PY:CX=0:CY=0
2010 SI= SGN (CI):SJ= SGN (CJ):AI= ABS (CI):AJ= ABS
     (CJ)
2015 IF AI=0 THEN 2040
2020 AI=AI−1
2025 IF SI >0 THEN NX=NX+1
2030 IF SI <0 THEN NX=NX−1
2035 CX= SCRN(NX,NY)
2040 IF AJ=0 THEN 2065
2045 AJ=AJ−1
2050 IF SJ >0 THEN NY=NY+1
2055 IF SJ >0 THEN NY=NY−1
2060 CY=SCRN(NX,NY)
2065 IF NOT (CX=0 AND CY=0) THEN RETURN
2070 IF AI=0 AND AJ=0 THEN RETURN
2075 GOTO 2015
```

Program Analysis

Lines 105-115—Dimension the program variables.

Line 120—Set the creatures' colors; orange for creature number 1, light blue for creature number 2.

Line 125—Clear the screen, set the graphics mode, and call the BORDER drawing subroutine.

Lines 130-155—Initialize the killer creatures. Pick a random initial position (line 135). If the spot is not clear, pick another position; otherwise, plot the creature and set its operating phase for phase 1.

Lines 160-175—Plot 64 killable things. Pick a random screen position (line 165). If the spot is not clear, pick another position; otherwise, plot the thing.

Lines 180-190—Select a creature to be serviced by the multiplexing scheme (line 180). Select the phase of operation for that creature (line 185), and set things up for working with the other creature (line 190).

Lines 195-210—Phase-1 operations. Select random motion codes. If it is the stop code, select again. Then set for phase-2 operations and return to service the next creature.

Lines 215-220—Beginning of phase-2 operations. Adjust the creature variables to make them compatible with the SEARCH AHEAD subroutine.

Line 225—Do the SEARCH AHEAD routine.

Line 230—If the path ahead is clear, then jump to line 235 to move the creature; otherwise, set it for phase-3 operations and get out of the current phase of operation.

Lines 235-250—Move the creature and set it for phase-2 operations.

Lines 255-265—Adjust the SEARCH AHEAD variables to make them compatible with those of the current creature. Return to service the next creature in the system.

Lines 270-275—Beginning of phase-3 operations. Select a random kill code. If it is the kill code, jump down to the kill operations; otherwise, set for phase-1 operations and return to service the other creature.

Line 280—Get the color code of the obstacle in the path ahead.

Lines 285-295—If it isn't a portion of the BORDER figure, jump down to line 300. Otherwise, "take a bite at the BORDER figure" and jump down to get out of the routine.

Line 300—Kill the obstacle in the path ahead.

Lines 305-325—If the obstacle isn't the other creature, jump down to line 300 to get out of the routine. But if it is the other creature, determine its color and print the kill message. Hold up the experiment until the user acknowledges the kill by striking the RETURN key.

Line 330—Set the current creature for phase-2 operations and return to the multiplexing routine to service the next creature.

Lines 1000-1020—BORDER drawing subroutine.

Lines 2000-2075—SEARCH AHEAD subroutine.

ALPHA COMBO DEMO

The following material is the Integer BASIC version of the Apple II discussions and programming in Chapter 8.

Variable List

CN	Creature being serviced by the multiplexing scheme (1 through 5)
AC(CN)	Operating phase for creature CN
PX(CN)	Horizontal component of current screen position for creature CN
PY(CN)	Vertical component of current screen position for creature CN
NX(CN)	Horizontal component of next screen position for creature CN
NY(CN)	Vertical component of next screen position for creature CN
CI(CN)	Horizontal component of motion code for creature CN
CJ(CN)	Vertical component of motion code for creature CN
DA(CN)	"Dead-or-alive" code for creature CN (0 for "dead," and 1 for "alive")
CY(CN)	Vertical component of contact code for creature CN
CT(CN)	Color code for creature CN
PX	Horizontal component of creature position
PY	Vertical component of creature position
NX	Horizontal component of creature's next position
NY	Vertical component of creature's next position
CI	Horizontal component of motion code
CJ	Vertical component of motion code
CX	Horizontal component of contact code
CY	Vertical component of contact code
SI	Sign value of CI
SJ	Sign value of CJ
AI	Absolute value of CI

AJ	Absolute value of CJ
TX	Horizontal component of obstacle position
TY	Vertical component of obstacle position
N	General-purpose numerical variable
KC	Kill code (0 for "no-kill," 1 for "kill")

Program Listing

```
 10 REM   ALPHA COMBO DEMO
 15 REM   APPLE INTEGER BASIC
 20 REM
 25 REM
 30 REM
100 REM ** ALPHA MAINLINE, V.7—APPLE INTEGER
105 DIM AC(5),PX(5),PY(5),NX(5),NY(5)
110 DIM CI(5),CJ(5),DA(5),CY(5),CT(5)
115 CT(1)=9
120 FOR N=2 TO 5:CT(N)=7: NEXT N
125 CALL -936: GR : GOSUB 1000
130 FOR CN=1 TO 5
135 PX(CN)= RND (38)+1:PY(CN)= RND (35)+1
140 IF SCRN (PX(CN),PY(CN))#0 THEN 135
145 COLOR=CT(CN)
150 PLOT PX(CN),PY(CN)
155 AC(CN)=1:DA(CN)=1: NEXT CN
160 COLOR=13: FOR N=0 TO 15
165 TX= RND (38)+1:TY= RND (35)+1
170 IF SCRN(TX,TY)#0 THEN 165
175 PLOT TX,TY: NEXT N
180 FOR CN=1 TO 5
185 IF DA(CN)=0 THEN 195
190 IF AC(CN)=1 THEN 200: IF AC(CN)=2 THEN 215:
    GOTO 275
195 NEXT CN: GOTO 180
200 CI(CN)= RND (5)−2:CJ(CN)= RND (5)−2
205 IF CI(CN)=0 AND CJ(CN)=0 THEN 200
210 AC(CN)=2: GOTO 195
215 PX=PX(CN):PY=PY(CN)
```

321

```
220 CI=CI(CN):CJ=CJ(CN)
225 GOSUB 2000
230 IF NOT (CX=0 AND CY=0) THEN 235:AC(CN)=2:
    GOTO 245
235 IF CN#1 THEN 240:AC(CN)=3: GOTO 260
240 AC(CN)=1: GOTO 260
245 COLOR=0: PLOT PX,PY
250 PX=NX:PY=NY
255 COLOR=CT(CN): PLOT PX,PY
260 PX(CN)=PX:PY(CN)=PY
265 NX(CN)=NX:NY(CN)=NY
270 GOTO 195
275 KC= RND (2)
280 IF KC#0 THEN 285:AC(CN)=1: GOTO 195
285 IF SCRN(NX(CN),NY(CN)) <14 THEN 295
290 COLOR=14: PLOT NX(CN),NY(CN): GOTO 315
295 FOR N=2 TO 5
300 IF NX(CN)=PX(N) AND NY(CN)=PY(N) THEN DA(N)=0
305 NEXT N
310 COLOR=0: PLOT NX(CN),NY(CN)
315 AC(CN)=2: GOTO 195
320 REM
325 REM
1000 REM ** BORDER,V.1—APPLE INTEGER **
1005 COLOR=15
1010 HLIN 0,39 AT 0: HLIN 0,39 AT 36
1015 VLIN 0,36 AT 0: VLIN 0,36 AT 39
1020 RETURN
1025 REM
1030 REM
2000 REM ** SEARCH AHEAD, V.1—APPLE INTEGER **
2005 NX=PX:NY=PY:CX=0:CY=0
2010 SI= SGN (CI):SJ= SGN (CJ):AI= ABS (CI):AJ= ABS
     (CJ)
2015 IF AI=0 THEN 2040
2020 AI=AI−1
2025 IF SI >0 THEN NX=NX+1
2030 IF SI <0 THEN NX=NX−1
2035 CX= SCRN(NX,NY)
2040 IF AJ=0 THEN 2065
2045 AJ=AJ−1
```

322

```
2050  IF SJ >0 THEN NY=NY+1
2055  IF SJ <0 THEN NY=NY−1
2060  CY= SCRN(NX,NY)
2065  IF NOT (CX=0 AND CY=0) THEN RETURN
2070  IF AI=0 AND AJ=0 THEN RETURN
2075  GOTO 2015
```

Program Analysis

Lines 105-110—Dimension the creature variables.

Line 115—Set killer creature color to orange.

Line 120—Set non-killer creatures' color to light blue.

Line 125—Clear the screen, set the graphics mode and draw the BORDER figure.

Lines 130-150—Select random, non-overlapping initial screen positions for all the creatures. Plot them on the screen.

Line 155—Set each creature for phase-1 operations and give them the "alive" code.

Lines 160-175—Select random, non-overlapping screen positions for the 16 yellow obstacles. Plot them on the screen as those positions are located.

Lines 180-195—This is the multiplexting routine. If the creature being serviced is dead, then skip to service the next creature (line 185). Go to the appropriate operating phase for the creature being serviced (line 200 for phase 1, line 215 for phase 2, and line 275 for phase 3). Repeat the entire routine for the next creature to be serviced.

Lines 200-210—This is the phase-1 operation. Select a random motion code. If it is the stop code, select another one. Set for phase-2 operations and return to service the next creature.

Lines 215-225—Adjust the creature variables to make them compatible with the SEARCH AHEAD routine; do the SEARCH AHEAD.

Line 230—This is the beginning of phase-2 operations. If the path ahead is not clear, do the operations line lines 235-240. Otherwise, set the creature to repeat phase 2, and move it by jumping down to line 245.

Line 235—If the creature being serviced is not the killer creature, then skip to line 240; otherwise, set it for phase-3 operations and jump down to line 260.

Line 240—Set the creature for phase-1 operations (flight response), and jump down to line 260.

Lines 245-255—Move the creature to its next position on the screen.

Lines 260-270—Adjust the SEARCH AHEAD variables to make the compatible with the creature that has just been serviced. Conclude the phase-2 operations by returning to the multiplexing operations.

Line 275—This is the beginning of the phase-3 operations. Select a random kill code.

Line 280—If it is the kill code, jump down to line 285; otherwise set for phase-1 operations (flight response) and return to the multiplexing operations to service the next creature.

Line 285—Is the obstacle something other than the BORDER figure? If so, jump down to line 295.

Line 290—"Take a bite" at the BORDER figure and jump down to line 315.

Lines 295-305—Determine which passive creature is in the path ahead, and set its "dead-or-alive" status to "dead."

Line 310—Wipe out whatever obstacle remains in the path ahead.

Line 315—Set the creature for phase-2 operations, then return to the multiplexing operations to service the next creature.

Lines 1000-1020—BORDER drawing subroutine.

Lines 2000-2075—SEARCH AHEAD subroutine.

FUNDAMENTAL BETA DEMO

The following material represents the Integer BASIC version of the Apple II discussions and program in Chapter 10.

Variable List

MI	Value of stimulus CI (adjusted to 0-4)
MJ	Value of stimulus CJ (adjusted to 0-4)
M(MI+5*MJ)	Memory value of response CI (adjusted 0-4)
M(MI+5*MJ+24)	Memory value of response CJ (adjusted to 0-4)
TC	Creature's trail color code
CI	Horizontal component of motion code
CJ	Vertical component of motion code
CX	Horizontal component of contact code

CY	Vertical component of contact code
NX	Horizontal component of next screen position
NY	Vertical component of next screen position
SI	Sign value of CI
SJ	Sign value of CJ
AI	Absolute value of CI
AJ	Absolute value of CJ
PX	Horizontal component of current screen position
PY	Vertical component of current screen position
N	General-purpose numerical variable

Program Listing

```
 10 REM   FUNDAMENTAL BETA DEMO
 15 REM   APPLE INTEGER BASIC
 20 REM
 25 REM
 30 REM
100 REM ** BETA MAINLINE, V.1—APPLE INTEGER
105 DIM M(49)
110 FOR N=0 TO 49:M(N)=2: NEXT N
115 REM
120 TC=13
125 PX=20+ RND (5)−2:PY=20+ RND (5)−2
130 CI=RND (5)−2:CJ=RND (5)−2: IF CI=0 AND CJ=0
    THEN 130
135 CALL -936: GR : GOSUB 1000
140 COLOR=9: PLOT PX,PY
145 GOSUB 2000
150 IF (CX=0 OR CX=TC) AND (CY=0 OR CY=TC) THEN
    195
155 MI=CI+2:MJ=CJ+2
160 CI=M(MI+5*MJ): CJ=M(MI+5*MJ+24)
165 IF NOT (CI=2 AND CJ=2) THEN 175
170 CI= RND (5):CJ= RND (5): GOTO 165
175 CI=CI−2:CJ=CJ−2: GOSUB 2000:CI=CI+2:CJ=CJ+2
180 IF NOT ((CX=0 OR CX=TC) AND (CY=0 OR CY=TC))
    THEN 170
185 M(MI+5*MJ)=CI:M(MI+5*MJ+24)=CJ
190 CI=CI−2:CJ=CJ−2
```

```
195 COLOR=TC: PLOT PX,PY
200 PX=NX:PY=NY
205 COLOR=9: PLOT PX,PY
210 N= PEEK(-16384): POKE -16368,0
215 IF N >127 THEN 135
220 GOTO 145
225 REM
230 REM
1000 REM ** BORDER,V.1—APPLE INTEGER **
1005 COLOR=15
1010 HLIN 0,39 AT 0: HLIN 0,39 AT 36
1015 VLIN 0,36 AT 0: VLIN 0,36 AT 39
1020 RETURN
1025 REM
1030 REM
2000 REM ** SEARCH AHEAD, V.2—APPLE INTEGER
     BASIC **
2005 NX=PX:NY=PY:CY=0
2010 SI= SGN (CI):SJ= SGN (CJ):AI= ABS (CI):AJ= ABS
     (CJ)
2015 IF AI=0 THEN 2040
2020 AI=AI-1
2025 IF SI <=0 THEN 2030:NX=NX+1: GOTO 2035
2030 NX=NX-1
2035 CX= SCRN(NX,NY)
2040 IF AJ=0 THEN 2065
2045 AJ=AJ-1
2050 IF SJ <=0 THEN 2055:NY=NY+1: GOTO 2060
2055 NY=NY-1
2060 CY= SCRN(NX,NY)
2065 IF NOT ((CX=0 OR CX=TX) AND (CY=0 OR CY=TC))
     THEN RETURN
2070 IF AI=0 AND AJ=0 THEN RETURN
2075 GOTO 2015
```

Program Analysis

Line 105—Dimension the memory variables.
Line 110—Initialize the BETA memory to stop codes.
Lines 120—Set the trail color to yellow.
Line 125—Initialize the creature's initial screen position.'

Line 130—Get the creature's initial motion code. If it is the
         stop code, get another one.

Line 135—Clear the screen, set the graphics mode, and draw
         the BORDER figure.

Line 140—Plot the creature in its initial position.

Line 145—Do the SEARCH AHEAD routine.

Line 150—If the path ahead is clear or made up of some section
         of previously drawn trail, jump down to move the creature
         at line 195.

Line 155—Adjust memory version of motion code to the range
         of 0-4.

Line 160—Fetch remembered response.

Line 165—If the remembered response is not the stop code (an
         event never experienced), then jump down to line 175 to
         try it.

Line 170—Fetch a random motion code, and jump back to test
         its workability.

Line 175—Adjust motion code to make it compatible with the
         SEARCH AHEAD routine; do the SEARCH AHEAD
         routine; readjust the motion code to make it compatible
         with the memory operations.

Line 180—If the path ahead is obstructed by something other
         than previously drawn trail, jump back to line 170 to get
         another random motion code.

Line 185—Save the workable motion code in memory.

Line 190—Adjust the motion codes to the range of −2 to 2.

Lines 195-205—Move the creature to its next position on the
         screen.

Lines 210-220—If any key is depressed, clear the screen;
         otherwise, jump back to line 145 to search the path
         ahead again.

FUNDAMENTAL BETA DEMO WITH OBSTACLE OPTIONS

The following material is the Integer BASIC version of the
Apple II discussions and program in Chapter 11.

Variable List

NT	Number of obstacles in the environment
TX	Horizontal component of an obstacle's screen position
TY	Vertical component of an obstacle's screen position

TX(N)	Horizontal component of obstacle N's position
TY(N)	Vertical component of obstacle N's position
MI	Memory value of stimulus CI (adjusted to 0-4)
MJ	Memory value of stimulus CJ (adjusted to 0-4)
M(MI+5*MJ)	Memory version of CI response
M(MI+5*MJ+24)	Memory version of CJ response
TC	Creature's trail color code
TT	Obstacle color code
CI	Horizontal component of motion code
CJ	Vertical component of motion code
PX	Horizontal component of current screen position
PY	Vertical component of current screen position
NX	Horizontal component of next screen position
NY	Vertical component of next screen position
SI	Sign value of CI
SJ	Sign value of CJ
AI	Absolute value of CI
AJ	Absolute value of CJ
N,S	General-purpose numerical variables

Program Listing

```
10 REM   FUNDAMENTAL BETA DEMO
15 REM   WITH OBSTACLE OPTIONS
20 REM   (APPLE INTEGER BASIC VERSION)
25 REM
30 REM
100 REM ** BETA MAINLINE, V.2—APPLE INTEGER **
105 NT=64
110 TC=13:TT=15
115 DIM M(49)
120 DIM TX(NT),TY(NT)
125 FOR N=0 TO 49:M(N)=2: NEXT N
130 CALL -936: GR : GOSUB 1000
135 COLOR=TT
140 FOR N=1 TO NT
145 TX= RND (38)+1:TY= RND (35)+1
150 IF SCRN(TX,TY)#0 THEN 145
155 PLOT TX,TY:TX(N)=TX:TY(N)=TY
160 NEXT N
165 PX= RND (38)+1:PY= RND (35)+1
170 IF SCRN(PX,PY)#0 THEN 165
```

```
175 COLOR=9: PLOT PX,PY
180 CI=RND (5)-2:CJ= RND (5)-2: IF CI=0 AND CJ=0
    THEN 180
185 GOSUB 2000
190 IF (CX=0 OR CX=TC) AND (CY=0 OR CY=TC) THEN
    235
195 MI=CI+2:MJ=CJ+2
200 CI=M(MI+5*MJ):CJ=M(MI+5*MJ+24)
205 IF NOT (CI=2 AND CJ=2) THEN 215
210 CI= RND (5):CJ= RND (5): GOTO 205
215 CI=CI-2:CJ=CJ-2: GOSUB 2000:CI=CI+2:CJ=CJ+2
220 IF NOT ((CX=0 OR CX=TC) AND (CY=0 OR CY=TC))
    THEN 210
225 M(MI+5*MJ)=CI:M(MI+5*MJ+24)=CJ
230 CI=CI-2:CJ=CJ-2
235 COLOR=TC: PLOT PX,PY
240 PX=NX:PY=NY
245 COLOR=9: PLOT PX,PY
250 S= PEEK (-16385): POKE -16368,0
255 IF S <=127 THEN 185
260 IF S#193 THEN 275
265 FOR N=0 TO 49
270 M(N)=2: NEXT N: GOTO 185
275 IF S=203 THEN 180
280 IF S#196 THEN 300
285 COLOR=0: PLOT PX,PY
290 PX=   RND   (38)+1:PY=   RND   (35)+1:  IF
    SCRN(PX,PY)#0 THEN 290
295 COLOR=9: PLOT PX,PY: GOTO 185
300 TEXT : CALL -936: GR : GOSUB 1000
305 IF S#197 THEN 335
310 COLOR=9: PLOT PX,PY
315 FOR N=1 TO NT
320 TX= RND (38)+1:TY= RND (35)+1: IF SCRN(TX,TY)#0
    THEN 320
325 COLOR=TT: PLOT TX,TY:TX(N)=TX:TY(N)=TY
330 NEXT N: GOTO 185
335 COLOR= TT
340 FOR N=1 TO NT: PLOT TX(N),TY(N): NEXT N
345 GOTO 185
```

```
 350 REM
 355 REM
1000 REM ** BORDER,V.1—APPLE INTEGER **
1005 COLOR=15
1010 HLIN 0,39 AT 0: HLIN 0,39 AT 36
1015 VLIN 0,36 AT 0: VLIN 0,36 AT 39
1020 RETURN
1025 REM
1030 REM
2000 REM ** SEARCH AHEAD, V.2—APPLE INTEGER
     BASIC **
2005 NX=PX:NY=PY:CY=0
2010 SI=SGN (CI):SJ= SGN (CJ):AI= ABS (CI):AJ= ABS (CJ)
2015 IF AI=0 THEN 2040
2020 AI=AI—1
2025 IF SI <=0 THEN 2030:NX=NX+1: GOTO 2035
2030 NX=NX—1
2035 CX= SCRN(NX,NY)
2040 IF AJ=0 THEN 2065
2045 AJ=AJ—1
2050 IF SJ <=0 THEN 2055:NY=NY+1: GOTO 2060
2055 NY=NY—1
2060 CY= SCRN(NX,NY)
2065 IF NOT ((CX=0 OR CX=TX) AND (CY=0 OR CY=TC))
     THEN RETURN
2070 IF AI=0 AND AJ=0 THEN RETURN
2075 GOTO 2015
2080 REM
2085 REM
```

Program Analysis

Lines 105-110—Set values for number of obstacles, obstacle
  color and creature's trail color.

Line 115-120—Dimension subscripted variables.

Line 125—Initialize memory contents to stop code.

Line 130—Clear the screen, set the graphics mode, and draw
  the BORDER figure.

Lines 135-160—Plot the obstacles at random, non-overlapping
  positions on the screen.

Lines 165-175—Plot the creature at a random position that
  does not overlap anything else on the screen.

Lines 180—Pick a random motion code. If it is the stop code, pick another one.

Line 185—Search the path ahead via the SEARCH AHEAD routine.

Line 190—If the path ahead is clear or is the trail, jump to line 235 to move the creature to its next position on the screen.

Line 195—Adjust motion code to make it compatible with the BETA memory scheme.

Line 200—Fetch the remembered response.

Lines 205-210—If it is not the stop code (if the response has been tried before), jump down to line 215 to try it. Otherwise, pick a new random motion code and test it out.

Line 215—Adjust variables for SEARCH AHEAD; do SEARCH AHEAD; readjust variables.

Line 220—If the path ahead isn't clear or part of a trail, loop back to line 210 to get another motion code.

Line 225—Remember the workable response.

Line 230—Adjust the motion code to make it compatible with non-memory operations.

Lines 235-245—Move the creature to its next position on the screen.

Lines 250-255—Scan the keyboard. If no key is depressed, loop back to line 185 to continue normal BETA operations.

Lines 260-270—If A key is depressed, reinitialize the BETA memory; loop back to line 185 to resume SEARCH-and-move operations.

Line 275—If the K key is depressed, loop back to line 180 to get a new random motion code.

Lines 280-300—If the D key is depressed, get a new random screen position for the creature.

Lines 305-330—If the E key is depressed, plot a whole new environment of obstacles.

Lines 335-345—Plot the old obstacles in their original positions.

Lines 1000-1020—BORDER drawing subroutine.

Lines 2000-2075—SEARCH AHEAD subroutine.

Index

Index